D0876345

Dean of the Birdwatchers

Dean of the
Birdwatchers

A Biography of LUDLOW GRISCOM

William E. Davis, Jr.

Smithsonian Institution Press

Washington and London

Editor: Jack Kirshbaum
Designer: Alan Carter

Library of Congress Cataloging-in-Publication Data

Davis, William E. (William Edwin), 1936–
    Dean of the birdwatchers : a biography of Ludlow Griscom /
    William E. Davis, Jr.
        p. cm.
    Includes bibliographical references and index.
    ISBN 1-56098-310-8
    1. Griscom, Ludlow, 1890–1959.   2. Ornithologists—United
States—Biography.   3. Ornithology—United States—History.
4. Bird watching—United States—History.   5. Wildlife conservation—
United States—History.   I. Title.
QL31.G737D38   1994
598'.092—dc20
[B]   93-38095

British Library Cataloging-in-Publication data available

00 99 98 97 96 95 94 5 4 3 2 1

∞ The paper used in this publication meets the minimum
requirements of the American National Standard for Permanence of
Paper for Printed Library Materials Z39.48-1984.

Jacket illustration: Ludlow Griscom on honeymoon in Montana, 1926.
Photograph by Edith Griscom. Courtesy Andrew Griscom.

To my wife, Betsy, and my daughters, Susan and Lisa, who put up with me during the years of preparation of this book

Contents

PART THREE. IN THE FIELD

PART FOUR. CONSERVATION

PART FIVE. THE FINAL YEARS

Foreword by Roger Tory Peterson

As a lad of seventeen, I attended my first meeting of the American Ornitholo-gist's Union (AOU), held at the American Museum of Natural History in New York City. That was in 1925. I needed a signature so as to become an associate of the AOU and took the museum's elevator to the bird department on the fifth floor. There, I got the confirming signature from Ludlow Griscom.

That was our first meeting, but it was not until I returned to New York to take up my art education that I got to know Ludlow Griscom well. At the bi-monthly meetings of the Linnaean Society of New York, he dominated discus-sions and kept in line a group of young upstarts, seven teenagers who called themselves the BCBC (Bronx County Bird Club). Those kids were talented loners of various ethnic origin who somehow found each other in the sprawling Bronx. I became the only non-Bronx member. Ludlow was our guru and we could quote chapter and verse almost everything he had said or written. Among academics, Griscom was a rebel who broke with tradition and proved that one need not shoot a bird to know what it was. In fact, he could identify birds correctly almost at the limit of his vision.

When Griscom transferred his residence from New York City to Cambridge, he soon had his devotees in the Nuttall Ornithological Club, the oldest ornitho-logical club in the country. Although a few staid old-timers may have resented

Ludlow's aggressive approach, most of his New England friends were proud to acclaim him as their own.

Through Ludlow and his young disciples, I learned the tricks of field recognition and, being trained as an artist, was able to pull things together and give them form. In 1934 my first field guide was published. William Vogt had taken it in unfinished form to four publishers who turned it down. Inasmuch as I was an unknown author, it seemed too much of a gamble. However, Francis Allen, the top editor at Houghton Mifflin, was himself a member of the Nuttall Club. He saw the validity of my unorthodox approach—patternistic drawings with arrows pointing to the key field marks. He brought in Ludlow Griscom, then at the Museum of Comparative Zoology at Harvard, and seated him at the far end of the long table in the Houghton Mifflin board room in Boston. He then held up one plate after another. Without hesitation, Ludlow identified every bird. Having passed the test, Houghton Mifflin decided to gamble— 2,000 copies in the first printing; I was to get no royalty on the first 1,000. These were gone overnight and now, nearly 60 years later, Houghton Mifflin seldom prints fewer than 100,000 at a time. The field guides have gone into the hands of millions and are regarded as of primary importance to the public's knowledge of biodiversity. Had it not been for Griscom and his disciples in the BCBC, I would not have been able to prepare the field guide. Inasmuch as it was Ludlow who sparked all this, we might regard Ludlow as the grandparent of the environmental movement.

Because of his extraordinary field skills, we started to call him "Dean of the Birdwatchers." The origins of this title are obscure—I may have coined it myself—but certainly it arose during those exciting days of activity with the Linnaean Society and the BCBC. Ludlow, however, was far more than a "lister," as he was labeled by some. He was deeply interested in population dynamics, the ups and downs, the wheres and whys. No one of his generation spent more time giving counsel and direction to state and federal wildlife agencies as well as to the sometimes divisive Audubon movement.

This book, so meticulously researched, tells us not only about Griscom but also about the network of birders, biologists, conservationists, and movers and shakers with whom he shared his life. It is an extraordinary book about a complicated, sometimes controversial but always influential man. I was one of those lucky enough to be literally embraced by him, probably because, like him, I simply couldn't do anything about my fascination with birds; it was just there.

Preface

I was never formally introduced to Ludlow Griscom, but I have several vivid recollections of the man. When I was a boy back in the 1940s, my father frequently took me birdwatching to Plum Island, Newburyport, and Cape Ann, and it was not uncommon for us to encounter Ludlow Griscom and his entourage, as they swept through the area on one of the typical Griscom birding expeditions. He also took me on a number of the bus trips around the north shore that were sponsored by the Massachusetts Audubon Society, and from time to time we would again cross paths with Griscom. I recall the whispers that circulated among the birders about the "great man." I remember one trip in particular, where the busload of birders stood looking down from the cliffs at Cape Ann at a large alcid that no one was able, with certainty, to identify. Eventually Griscom appeared on the scene—whether by chance or by phone call I do not know—and proceeded to sit down on the ground and peer through his enormous telescope at the bird that bobbed about on the water. Everyone awaited the final pronouncement, which no one would dispute. Finally it came, "Immature Atlantic Murre." It was a life bird for many of us, and still the only Common Murre that I have seen in Massachusetts. On another occasion, probably in December 1953, I had been with my father on the Newburyport Christmas Count, and at the end of the day we had gone to the tally session. Griscom, partially paralyzed, confined to a wheel chair, and accompanied by a nurse who fed him bottled liquid through a straw, made his appearance. Illness and all, he managed to dominate the gathering with his presence and the sheer strength of his personality. I was curious to know more about this forceful man, and it was these recollections that a decade ago prompted me to make inquiries at the Nuttall Ornithological Club about whether anyone was planning to do a biography of Ludlow Griscom. It appeared that no one was seriously considering it, and so I decided to contact the Griscom family and determine the feasibility of undertaking such a task. After a tough round of inquiry from Edith Griscom, Ludlow's wife, and receiving encouragement from other family members as well as a number of Griscom's friends and birding companions, I decided to attempt it.

I was most fortunate in that many of Griscom's contemporaries, birding and professional acquaintances and friends, were still alive and willing to be interviewed. The willingness of Edith to allow me extensive interviews and the support of two of their children, Andrew and Joan, were of particular importance. Of significance, as well, was the fact that Ludlow Griscom was a faithful correspondent and for nearly fifty years kept careful files of his correspondence. At the Museum of Comparative Zoology at Harvard University, where Griscom was a research curator for nearly thirty years, he had the habit of answering the letters he received and doing his business correspondence every Friday, providing, of course, that he was not in the field. These files were acquired by the Cornell University Library, Rare and Manuscripts Collections, and thus organized and kept intact. In addition, all of the carefully written field journals that detail Griscom's thousands of field trips were preserved at the Peabody Museum of Salem, Massachusetts.

This enormous written record has had a marked effect on the ultimate structure of this biography. I had intended originally to make the book largely the story of the man as related by his family and friends, concentrating primarily on Griscom's personality, character, and his birding adventures. But a careful review of the voluminous correspondence revealed a man whose aspirations and accomplishments went far beyond the "Dean of the Birdwatchers" character that is probably his major claim to fame. Then there was the darker side of the Griscom personality, an arrogance and class consciousness that offended his children and many associates as well.

As my research progressed, it became clear that Griscom's correspondence reflected the "true" Griscom far better than I could portray him. Griscom spoke and wrote his mind with great insight and clarity. Thus what had originally been planned as a simple biographical sketch of Ludlow Griscom, evolved into an essay incorporating numerous excerpts from Griscom's own writings. I have selected these excerpts from letters and other documents from the thousands available and woven a storyline through them. The written record for some periods of Griscom's life is more complete than for others. Thus the chapters describing Griscom's early years are not nearly as well supported by documentation as are later chapters.

The structure of the book was also influenced by the complexities revealed by my research. I decided that a straight chronological presentation of the material was not feasible. At many critical points in Griscom's life, he was involved in so many seemingly unrelated activities that a totally chronological presentation would have produced a topically cluttered and confused picture. Hence the book begins and ends chronologically, but contains a number of topical chapters in between. Part 1 traces Griscom's development from childhood in a wealthy New York City setting through graduate school at Cornell University. By this time Griscom had developed the nucleus of his method of rapid identification of birds in the field, was an avid birdwatcher, and had received the professional academic training in ornithology. Part 2 deals with professional ornithological pursuits, and Part 3 emphasizes Griscom's field exploits and his influence on the development of birdwatching as a national pastime. Part 4 examines Griscom's deep concerns with the conservation movement, and Part 5 returns to a chronological sequence for Griscom's final years.

I found Ludlow Griscom to be a fascinating character. Forceful, brusque, and dogmatic, beloved by his birding companions, yet disdained by many of his professional colleagues, he crossed the stage of life with a flourish, and left his mark on American ornithology, conservation, and the sport of bird-watching.

Acknowledgments

Many people have contributed to the formulation of this book. Some graciously allowed me to talk with them about their recollections of Ludlow Griscom; others provided me with written accounts of anecdotes, copies of their journals, and other pertinent information. Hence I wish to thank the following people who have contributed in a substantial way to the information base from which this book was written: Donald and Ruth Alexander, Arthur and Margaret Argue, Oliver L. Austin, Jr., W. Wallace Bailey, James Baird, Carl Buchheister, Roland C. Clement, G. William and Annette Cottrell, Theodore L. Eliot, Jr., Kimball Elkins, David Garrison, Garrett Eddy, David Emerson, Ruth Emery, Juliet Richardson Kellogg French, Herbert Friedmann, James Greenway, Joseph A. Hagar, Joseph Hickey, Sibley and Ruth Higginbotham, Norman Hill, Richard Hinchman, Thomas R. Howell, C. Russell Mason, Harold Mayfield, Ernst Mayr, Allen Morgan, Nathaniel Nash, Henry Parker, Raymond A. Paynter, Jr., Wayne Petersen, Roger Tory Peterson, Hustace Poor, Tudor Richards, S. Dillon Ripley, Chandler S. Robbins, Douglas Sands, Dorothy Snyder, Ruth Turner, Charles Walcott, and Bradford Washburn.

I wish also to acknowledge the help of staff members, librarians, and archivists at a number of institutions, including the Peabody Museum in Salem, the Museum of Comparative Zoology Library at Harvard University, and the Olin Library at Cornell University. Of particular help were Julia Parker of the Division of Rare and Manuscript Collections, University Library, at Cornell; Mary LeCroy at the American Museum of Natural History; Doris Ann Sweet at Mugar Library, Boston University; and William Deiss at the Smithsonian Institution.

Jean Allaway, P. A. Buckley, Brian E. Cassie, Annette and William Cottrell, Andrew Griscom, Joan Griscom, John C. Kricher, and Roger Tory Peterson read earlier drafts of the manuscript, made many helpful suggestions, and corrected errors in fact and interpretation. Robb Reavill made important editorial contributions to the reorganization and rewriting of the original manuscript. Thanks also go to my wife, Betsy, who was enormously helpful when the vagaries of the word processor overwhelmed me.

My editor at the Smithsonian Institution Press, Peter Cannell, has been of invaluable assistance throughout the publication process. His enthusiasm and editorial expertise have kept me going through the tedious periods of manuscript rewrite and reorganization. Jack Kirshbaum did a marvelous job of putting the final version into acceptable English.

I wish to offer a very special thanks to Ludlow's wife, Edith Griscom, for whom I developed an enormous affection—an indomitable woman, who was willing to share her many recollections, some pleasant but some sad, of her many years with Ludlow. I am sorry that she did not live to see the completed work. The Griscoms' children, Andrew and Joan, were very supportive of the project and shared their recollections as well. Andrew Griscom graciously provided nearly two dozen Griscom family photographs. The rather speculative psychological suggestions about the influence of Griscom's parents on the development of his personality and interest in birds are adapted from the comments of his wife and children.

The errors in fact, emphasis, and interpretation that remain in this book, despite the efforts of all of these individuals, are my own.

Part One

THE EARLY YEARS

Background and Family   1

With wealth and station on both sides of the family, it appears at first glance that Ludlow Griscom was born lucky. He was educated by private tutors and at the best private schools. He learned piano, visited Europe every summer, and was in every way advantaged. A closer look, however, indicates troubling elements in his upbringing. The skeletons in the Griscom closet were formidable. The combination of advantages and disadvantages in his early life no doubt helped develop strength of character, but they induced some blemishes as well.

Griscom's forebears exuded importance, position, and wealth.[1] The Griscoms trace their antecedents in North America back to Thomas Lloyd, who twice served as president of the Provincial Council, Philadelphia (1684–88, 1690–91). John Denn Griscom, Ludlow's great grandfather, was a well-known physician of Philadelphia.

Ludlow's grandfather Clement Acton Griscom was a successful merchant and capitalist. President of the International Navigation Company, he purchased the Inman Line and the majority of stock in the Red Star Line, and he also established the American Line. In 1902 the firm was consolidated and its name was changed to the International Mercantile Marine Company. Clement Acton remained as president until 1904, when he retired to become chairman of the board. For the maiden voyage of one of his most famous ships, *The City*

of New York, President Benjamin Harrison came from Washington to raise the
ship's flag. Clement Acton also served on the boards of the Pennsylvania Railroad, the United States Steel Corporation, five major banks, and several other
railroads. Ludlow, the oldest grandchild, would often be invited out on his
grandfather's yacht. "The ocean was a priceless opportunity in summer for a
young man whose main interest in life was birds! Ludlow always accepted."[2]

Ludlow's maternal side also carried prestige and accomplishment. His maternal grandfather, General William Ludlow, achieved a distinguished military
record. Chief engineer with Generals Hooker and Slocum in the Atlanta campaign of 1864, he served in the same capacity with the left wing of Sherman's
army in the Savannah and Carolinas campaign in 1864 to 1865. He saw action
in the Spanish-American War, rising to the rank of major general of the United
States Volunteers. He acted as military governor of Havana, and became president of the War College.

Ludlow's father, Clement Acton Griscom, Jr., was the director of a number
of financial and industrial organizations, mostly in the New York City area.
Ludlow's mother, Genevieve Ludlow Griscom, also had great wealth. Aunt
Frances Canby Griscom, who never married, was feisty, independent, and eccentric; she was one of the first woman golf champions and a crack shot. It is
reported that in her late eighties, after a cataract operation had restored her
eyesight to some degree, she would be pushed in her wheelchair, shotgun
across her lap, down to the pond on her Florida plantation. From across the
pond she would have her staff flush stocked gamebirds, which she would shoot
for dinner. Uncle Lloyd Griscom had a brilliant diplomatic career, holding the
positions of *charge d'affaires* in Constantinople from 1899 to 1901, and minister plenipotentiary first to Persia from 1901 to 1902 and then to Japan from
1902 to 1906. In addition, he served as ambassador to Brazil and Italy. Young
Ludlow's many trips to Europe often involved Uncle Lloyd. An array of wealthy,
important, and powerful people were part of Griscom's early life.

The only written account of Griscom's early years are the opening pages of
his ornithological diary. Although only a rough chronology of major events,
such as important trips or household moves, it reveals how early in his life
birds began to play an important role. The diary also shows how his youth was
a series of glittering events, the expected scenario for "a person of means" at
the turn of the century.

1890—Born June 17 in an apartment in New York City on East 59th St.,
just off Fifth Ave.
1891–1899—Move to Flushing, Long Island, when it was a village in the
country, long before Greater New York was thought of. . . . I can remember

the arrival of the Robins on the lawn the spring of 1894. In 1896 I received for my birthday John B. Grant's "Our Common Birds and how to know them," and a pair of 3x field glasses. In 1897 "Bird Neighbors" and a subscription to the magazine "Birds and All Nature." I remember quite a few common birds around Flushing, & a pair of Red-headed Woodpeckers nested in an old willow tree in front of our house in 1896 & 1897.
1896—Brief trip to London, visiting my grandfather, Military Attaché to Great Britain.
1898–1899—Winter trip to Arizona, staying at Hot Springs, Castle Creek, about midway between Phoenix & Prescott, a 24 mile drive from the R.R. My father was ill, & we went out in a private car, stopping a day at Louisville, Kentucky & another in New Orleans, where we drove out to Lake Pontchartrain. We also stayed at Phoenix some days, met Gov. Murphy of the Territory & visited the famous Tombstone Gold Mine. In Arizona we were in the Navajo Indian country, from whom we bought baskets, blankets & venison. Pumas occasionally screamed and caterwauled near the inn. The only birds I can remember, were the Cardinals, the Roadrunners & the coveys of Gambel's Partridge.[3]

Certainly, on the face of things, young Griscom had a full and active childhood. But all may not have been quite so wonderful as it would seem. Griscom rarely talked about his childhood or adolescence, even to his wife and children. Perhaps there were things that he would rather have forgotten.

Although Griscom's parents led the life of wealthy cosmopolitans, they developed an eccentric life-style. Nominally connected with the Episcopal Church, they fell under the influence of Madame Blavatsky, leader of the Theosophical Society in England. The organization's beliefs and philosophy incorporated a strange mixture of Christianity, various Indian religions, and the occult. From this time on his parents lived a secret, isolated existence, gathered around them a small cluster of devotees, and virtually excluded the rest of the world. Eventually the Griscoms formed a splinter group, and became even more mysterious and secretive, with an "inner circle" of seven or eight rich and important people. These included Henry B. Mitchell, a mathematics professor at Columbia University who lived for years in his own little house on the Griscom estate.

Genevieve Griscom, an austere Victorian, presided over the group at the Chapel Farm estate. Their faith included a strong belief in reincarnation. Their immense library on Joan of Arc and Napoleon gives some indication of their thoughts about their earlier lives. Mitchell is rumored to have considered himself a reincarnated Charles II of England. Genevieve Griscom is reported to have talked to "her angels," and when she died in 1959, her ashes were mixed together in the ground with those of other deceased inner circle members.

Into this rather bizarre early 1890s setting appeared the three Griscom children. Ludlow, the oldest, survived this environment the most successfully. Joyce, born in 1898, burned to death at the age of three when her white flair skirt caught on fire from the stove while her nursemaid was out of the room. When referring to the tragedy, Ludlow's mother is quoted as mentioning her instructions to the child to stay away from the stove, and ending, "She was always a very willful child."[4]

Acton Griscom, born a year after Ludlow, was unable to escape the effects of religious fanaticism. He attended divinity school but could never achieve stability, and he became something of a black sheep in the family. Ludlow rarely mentioned his brother, but in a 1952 letter he described Acton's plight: "My brother's life has been a tragic and unfortunate one, and in recent years has been mostly spent in New Mexico and Venezuela. I know that he has had serious financial reverses and I would be surprised if he had not been forced to sell his library and his manuscripts for whatever sum of money he could obtain."[5]

Ludlow seemingly had few playfellows or friends of his own age, and, together with Acton, was virtually isolated from the outside world for substantial periods of time. Love and affection were apparently sparingly bestowed upon him during a large part of his early years in these isolated surroundings. A rather harsh Victorianism dominated his upbringing.

Griscom lived at home and was educated by private tutors until the age of eleven, after which he was enrolled in a private school. His education included extensive language studies, which, combined with long periods abroad, produced amazing competency in foreign languages that served him well during both world wars. He developed great skill on the piano, practicing a reported four hours a day and fueling his mother's ambitions for a professional musical career for her son. About his youthful instruction, he later wrote, "I went to Europe 15 times before I was 28. I never could speak but 5 languages fluently, I could read 10 easily, and with the aid of a grammar and a dictionary, could translate up to a total of about 18. I had a great deal of musical training in my youth and at 18 my teacher tried his darndest to make me become a professional concert pianist. I was especially accomplished in playing Chopin."[6] His aristocratic, wealthy parents were educating him for a cultured role in the upper echelons of the world of diplomacy or law "because that is what people of our class do."

Ludlow's passion for birds, however, led him in other directions. We begin to see glimpses of this developing interest in the appendix to his ornithological diary, which covers the years 1894 through 1907.[7] A list of 90 species has a few annotations including: "Robin—Flushing 1894," "Red-headed Woodpecker—Flushing, 1896 & 1897," and "Scarlet Tanager— Flushing 1897." That this was something of a lonely, although satisfying outlet for his energy, is attested to in a 1934 letter: "I am old enough to go back to the days when an interest in birds was so unusual and extraordinary that I was studying birds for eleven years before I ever met anyone who thought I wasn't half crazy in being interested in them, and I have tried ever since never to go birding alone."[8] By the time he was seventeen years old, his interest in birds had matured, and indications that he might pursue a career in ornithology were beginning to emerge.

The Linnaean Society and a Career Chosen

2

The year 1907 held several watershed events for seventeen-year-old Ludlow Griscom. First, he "graduated" from the Reed *Bird Guide*[1] to a bird calendar, which described what birds one could expect each month on the Ramble in Central Park. It included a list of the 140 species that had been seen there. His ornithological diary for 1907 begins: "Inspired by Parkhurst, 'Bird Calendar,' begin serious steady birding in Central Park, May 11 & never stop!"[2]

Ludlow's study in Central Park led to his first contact with someone else interested in birds, Reverend Walter E. Clifton Smith, the minister of a church on Fifth Avenue. He not only encouraged young Griscom in his ornithological pursuits but proposed him for membership in the august Linnaean Society of New York. Decades later Ludlow recounted the importance of this event:

> I started learning local birds back in 1898. In New York City unlike Boston an interest in birds was not respectable. It just wasn't done. You could hunt and shoot birds, but you couldn't ogle birds with a glass. Many is the time a derisive and unfriendly crowd has run me out of Central Park! . . .
>
> Finally the heavens opened and the sun began to shine when I joined the Linnaean Society in 1907. Then I finally met someone else interested in birds; and I had some blessed companionship for the first time in 15 years![3]

The Linnaean Society was one of the oldest and most prominent natural history societies in North America. It had been founded in 1878 by ornithologist C. Hart Merriam,[4] natural history writer John Burroughs, and others, and although the scope of the organization encompassed all of natural history, the focus was usually on birds. The roll glittered with such prominent names as Vanderbilt and Roosevelt. William Dutcher, a prominent bird protectionist, and Frank M. Chapman, guiding light of the ornithology department at the American Museum of Natural History, were frequent attendees. The society met at the American Museum, and gossip, bird notes, and bird lists were frequent topics of discussion. The Linnaean Society was progressive for the time, allowing Mrs. F. E. B. Latham to become the first woman member in 1890. In the next few years Florence Merriam, Olive Thorne Miller, and Mabel Osgood Wright, all influential writers on birds, joined the ranks of the organization.

It was a heady time for someone interested in birds. Between the Civil War and the turn of the century, America's fascination with natural history in general, and with birds in particular, had grown tremendously.[5] The roots of this cultural trend may be found in the upper-class emulation of a similar, earlier trend in Europe and in an expanded middle class, which grew with the general economic expansion following the war. Those decades also witnessed the development of major museums of natural history and the pressure to collect specimens that they exerted. The U.S. National Museum, under the direction of Spencer Fullerton Baird, became functional about 1850. Thereafter followed the Museum of Comparative Zoology at Harvard University in the late 1850s, under the leadership of Louis Agassiz; the American Museum of Natural History in 1869; the Field Museum of Chicago in 1893; and the Carnegie Museum in 1895. The handful of professional ornithologists had extensive networks among the amateurs who provided a large share of their growing collections. The "shotgun school" of ornithology, wherein birds were shot rather than studied alive in the field, was widely practiced. Commercial supply establishments facilitated the exchange of stuffed birds and "study skins"—unmounted, flat-prepared, stuffed specimens that became the currency of museums. Private collections were commonplace as well, and the result of this widespread collecting focus has been called the "culture of collecting."[6]

A crosscurrent developed within the bird protectionist movement, which after an aborted start in the 1880s, rapidly expanded at the turn of the century. There was growing alarm among many bird enthusiasts and professional ornithologists at the population crashes of mammals such as the American bison and birds like egrets, which were slaughtered for the millinery trade.[7] The wholesale slaughter of shorebirds, doves, and waterfowl for urban food markets was also stimulating concern. The Massachusetts Audubon Society, the first of many local Audubon societies, was founded in 1896 with prominent ornithologist William Brewster as its president. These organizations, aided initially by the premier society of scientific ornithologists, the American Ornithologists' Union, lobbied for protective legislation and released polemical pamphlets in staggering numbers. Their often radical stance brought them into increasing conflict with the collectors, who felt threatened by the perceived extremism and feared their bird collecting might be curtailed.

A growing number of bird enthusiasts were becoming birdwatchers rather than bird shooters. Opera glasses had been used for several decades to aid in watching birds, and bird books to aid in identification were available, but it was the advent of German prism binoculars about the turn of the century that presented new possibilities for the identification and study of living birds in the field. The "Big Day," when birdwatchers would attempt to see as many species of birds as possible in one day, came into practice at the turn of the century. The challenge of bird listing, much later referred to as "ornithological golf" by ornithologist James Lee Peters, was appealing to growing numbers of bird enthusiasts.

The membership of the Linnaean Society was a mixture of the older, shotgun ornithologists and a newer breed—watchers of live birds. It also included many professional ornithologists, who were often not only tossed about in the cross-currents of these competing groups but also ambivalent because they saw the need both to collect specimens for their scientific ornithology and to have constraints on hunting. It was an invigorating atmosphere for young Ludlow.

In 1907 Griscom compiled his first "year list" of birds seen, a somewhat meager 84 species. He was not yet the sure and instant identifier of birds that he was to become. His journal states, for example, "a large flock of birds was seen flying rapidly overhead. They were either Red-winged Blackbirds or Cowbirds, most probably the latter."[8] He kept a daily checklist of the birds seen but had not yet begun to list the numbers of each species.

A major family crisis had begun to brew a few years earlier concerning future directions for Ludlow. He presumably had done well in school, for he had been accepted at Harvard University when he was only fifteen years old. His brother, Acton, was too young for college and the family felt that they should remain together. It was decided that Ludlow should stay home, and so he attended Columbia University instead of Harvard (the story goes that he read the *Iliad* in Greek on the subway for pleasure). In New York, Griscom continued his growing involvement with the Linnaean Society, and he became a respected and influential member of the New York City and Riverdale ornithological communities. It was nearly six years later that Griscom received his A.B.

degree from Columbia with a major in pre-law—a rather long time, but he made three trips to Europe during this period, including one in the winter, and was continually busy exploring new localities and ferreting out birds. For example, his ornithological diary in 1908 reads, "Sept.—26. first visit to Van Cortlandt Park. . . . Dec. 23. first trip to Bronx Park,"[9] and in 1909, "May 12. first trip to Staten Island, N.Y. . . . June 12 first trip to Long Beach, L.I."[10] As these years passed, Griscom's level of ornithological sophistication increased. By October of 1908 he was listing the numbers of individuals of each species seen and by November the weather conditions as well. Even on his European trips, he carefully documented each ornithological event. A 1909 entry states, "July 8th. London to Cambridge with a good deal of time at Cambridge. Was not able to pay much attention to birds. No glasses. Temp. 65°."[11] Then followed a list of 22 species with exact numbers of individuals recorded.

In October 1909 Anne M. Crolius shows up in his notes, the first mention of a birding companion. Also, the sequentially numbered list of species seen are listed in taxonomic order. The thrill of the chase and the challenge of the list was apparent in Ludlow at this time, but he was fast developing a sophisticated scientific interest in birds that went well beyond a fascination for bird listing. Detailed behavioral notes begin to appear along with the species lists by 1911. "Mr. Miller found a Mourning Dove's nest with two eggs *on the ground* last Sunday."[12] Griscom recorded extensive notes on the location, habitat, and song of Mourning Warblers in the Slide Mountain region of the Catskills. By early 1912 Griscom regularly identified his birding companions and recorded in detail bird identification notes. Included with these notes are long lists of the plants observed. Ludlow rapidly became a broadly based naturalist. In fact, botany came to be as important to him in his youth as birds.

In his journals there are frequent references to the Linnaean Society meetings, including names of people and their field note reports. These meetings provided Ludlow with a source of birding companions and intellectual stimulation, as he later stated in the preface to *Birds of the New York City Region* (1923).

The writer must, however, go further and state that such local knowledge as he possesses is in a large measure due to the Linnaean Society and its members. The meetings have stimulated him since boyhood; there he has gained new information, new ideas, and a broader viewpoint. How can one over-evaluate the priceless companionship of years afield with one's fellow-members, the sympathy, the bond of a great interest shared in common. Every wood and field, every marsh and beach near New York City, is laden with memories of most of them; few discoveries, few sights of rarities, but were shared with one or more of them; we have been hot, cold, hungry or wet together; we have been storm-bound on islands, bogged in swamps, carried out to sea in rowboats together.[13]

During the six years that he was at Columbia University, an impending family crisis became more and more apparent. "My family were thoroughly down on me, and I was not allowed to mention ornithology at home."[14] He worked for at least a summer on Wall Street and spent some time with Macmillan in the publishing business, but Griscom was determined to become an ornithologist, despite his parents' strong objections. He refused to go to law school and instead made plans to do graduate work at Cornell University.

The decision to become an ornithologist against the explicit wishes of his strong-willed parents must have been tough. It would have been in keeping with his parents' personalities if they tightened up the purse strings when he disobeyed their wishes. Griscom's reflections on his academic training give some insight into how difficult his situation was.

> Years ago Frank M. Chapman formulated a most sound and excellent test by which a young man could decide whether he should or should not become a professional ornithologist, and consequently asked him the following questions: Have you so burning and overwhelming a love and interest in this subject that you are prepared to make any immediate financial sacrifice necessary to gain your end? and are you prepared to face the lack of normal financial rewards, no matter how successful and distinguished an ornithologist you might become? If the answers to these questions were both "yes" the young man began work in the Department of Birds at $50 a month. It was entirely his business as to whether he could support himself in New York City on this sum. Or he was sent to some university to get a Ph.D. degree, presumably on the basis on which I personally was, that he worked his way through the graduate school by some hook or crook.[15]

Griscom entered Cornell in summer school, July 1914. He was the first graduate student in ornithology of Arthur A. Allen, the first professor of ornithology in the United States. Allen had received his doctorate in 1911, and he soon became a member of the Graduate School faculty, "so that he could direct the advanced work of several students, including Ludlow Griscom, who were knocking at Cornell's door with ornithology in mind."[16] In 1915 Allen became an assistant professor of ornithology in the Department of Entomology, and the name Laboratory of Ornithology was provided to justify an allocation of space for him. Allen's long and successful career witnessed the development of the Laboratory into a major research and educational facility. More than one hundred students received graduate degrees from Cornell before Allen's retirement in 1953.

In less than a year, Ludlow completed his master's thesis, *The Identification of the Commoner Anatidae of the Eastern United States in the Field,* which illustrated in subject and method his growing commitment to the study of live birds. He received his M.A. degree in June 1915. Presumably as part of his "working his way through school," Ludlow taught a course in ornithology at the University of Virginia summer school in Charlottesville, in July and August 1915. During the 1915–1916 academic year, he returned to Cornell and took courses toward a doctorate. He gained further teaching experience through an assistantship in the College of Agriculture at Cornell and repeated his summer teaching at the University of Virginia. He apparently did quite well, since he was asked to teach there again several years later. His financial status had much to do with his polite refusal. "There is nothing I should like better than to revisit the scene of two happy and profitable summers but I very much regret that a permanent position on the staff here [American Museum of Natural History] makes it impossible to leave as you can readily understand. Even should I obtain a leave of absence without pay, which would be doubtful, attendance [teaching] in the summer school would inevitably involve considerable financial sacrifice and ornithologists are poor men."[17]

As in New York, Griscom was active in the field during his Cornell years. He became secretary of the Cayuga Bird Club, in which capacity he wrote a series of four articles in the spring of 1916 for the local newspaper, the *Ithaca Daily Star,* reporting the progress of the spring migration around Ithaca.

At this time, Griscom became good friends with Louis Agassiz Fuertes, the premier bird painter of the day, who lived near Cornell. He shared with Griscom keen powers of observation, and it is probable that Griscom and Fuertes learned something about field identification from each other. Their warm relationship and mutual interests are illustrated by a cordial letter from Fuertes, which began "My dear Griscom," and concluded with the following remarks about identification and a drawing of a Ring-necked Duck. "Incidentally female ringnecks often have the white patch on the side of the fore-face almost if not quite as prominent as female scaups. a.a.a. [Allen] has two, one of wh. shows it plainly. . . . in the male the pointed pate and white △ before the wing gives this species a "look" that is entirely unlike the scaup."[18]

Griscom did not go on to earn a Ph.D., and this may eventually have limited his professional aspirations. For example, many years later, he did not succeed Thomas Barbour as director of the Museum of Comparative Zoology at Harvard University, even though he had virtually run the day-to-day functions of the museum for years. His failure to do so may have been due, in part, to his lack of a doctoral degree. Ludlow had intended to pursue a doctorate, and he outlined his plans in a letter to Frank Chapman at the American Museum of Natural History asking for his counsel. "Dr. Allen and the other members of the Zoological Staff up here have strongly advised me to continue here and take a Ph.D. degree. My father has given his consent, provided it seems the best thing to do, and I should be grateful for your opinion and advice. Should this plan be put in operation I should work my way through by teaching, holding a fellowship and money made during the summer, one or the other of these methods."[19]

In a subsequent letter to Chapman, Griscom indicates that he took Chapman's advice and applied for summer work with a survey. He was turned down for that position, as well as for another job that involved collecting birds, on the grounds of inexperience. This second letter requested a recommendation for a fellowship at Cornell.[20] He had no reason to count on his parents' support; in fact after his Cornell days, he paid rent whenever he was living at home, until his father's death in 1918. But whether he ultimately found himself in a financial crunch, or whether he was not pleased with Allen (about whom he later expressed reservations), is not known. Certainly he was a good student, extremely bright and interested in his subject matter. Perhaps he simply felt that it was time to get on with his career.

Marriage and Private Life 3

One of the most important events in Griscom's life occurred in July 1925, when on a trip to Newfoundland he met Edith Sumner Sloan. Edith came from wealth and station. Her grandfathers were Samuel Sloan, of the Delaware Lackawanna Railroad and the Farmers Loan and Trust Company, and Antonio Rapallo, chief justice of the New York State Supreme Court. She was born in New York City on 19 June 1895, the youngest of six children. She grew up in New York and attended Miss Spence's School, graduating in 1914. She did not attend college because "before World War II proper women didn't go to college—the only women who went to college had big feet and wore their hair in a bun on the back of their head."[1] During World War I she worked six days a week for the Trade Board.

When the war was over she looked around for something civic to do and located a job teaching school year-round for the Grenfell Mission in Eddy's Cove, a remote area on the northwest coast of Newfoundland. She lived with a fisherman's family, a rugged existence in which she became the first Grenfell Mission woman volunteer to spend a winter in an outpost village. During the second winter she became an emergency nurse, moving about by dogsled, treating patients during a diphtheria epidemic, because the nurse for the area was incapacitated by the disease. Edith was made of tough fiber and had just as strong a personality as Ludlow. Her description of the courtship is quite remarkable and provides some insights into her character as well as Ludlow's.[2]

Edith reported that it was a strange and funny courtship because she disliked him at first. Ludlow "being a confirmed chauvinist and hating women, could hardly bring himself to speak to her." When they met, Griscom was on a botanical expedition with M. L. Fernald of the Gray Herbarium at Harvard University. Edith and Ludlow happened to be on the same boat crossing from North Sydney, New Brunswick, to Port aux Basques, Newfoundland. According to Edith, Ludlow fell in love with her at first sight. Certainly he showed an interest; that first evening on shipboard a drunk was pestering Edith on deck, and Ludlow kept a close watch, ready to interfere if necessary. It turned out that the drunk was a Grenfell worker, so that Edith had to be courteous. "I'd have bitten Ludlow's head off if he had interfered, I didn't need a stranger butting in. Ludlow's courtship was really comical—Ludlow had decided as he watched me and the drunk that he was going to marry me—he told me that."

They arrived in Newfoundland and boarded a train. Edith irritated Ludlow by passing on to Fernald information she had received that in order to make their next boat connection they would have to get off the train a stop earlier than planned. "Ludlow was very annoyed at this girl telling the head of the expedition to get off the train." They all boarded the boat, and Edith became upset with Griscom and the other men because they had commandeered the cabins, so she stayed on deck gossiping with her landlady. According to Edith, the next morning Griscom said:

> "You had to stand outside our cabin and talk so loud, you kept us up after six o'clock." I said, "Good enough for you." I was beginning to really not care for him. Also a bunch of the "flower pickers" [a derogatory term used by Newfoundlanders to describe the members of the botanical expedition] were up on deck doing a crossword puzzle. I kept a little on my guard where Ludlow was concerned, and Ludlow said, in the sweetest tone of voice, "to use a needle in three letters, I think that Miss Sloan can tell us what that is." I glared at him.

After their arrival Ludlow asked to take Edith for a walk, "which we did—a gorgeous sunset—we sat there and had our first sensible conversation and I enjoyed him and he enjoyed me. . . . He said goodby and walked down the path. He didn't know we were watching him. When he got to the picket fence he put one hand on it and vaulted over it, obviously in good spirit."

The courtship continued, as Edith reported:

> I had decided to visit a friend of mine, Mrs. Wayland, and there were Arthur Pease and Ludlow. Ludlow was fretting because a button was off the back

of his pants, and his suspenders weren't holding them up, so Mrs. Wayland came over to me with a button and a threaded needle and told Ludlow to turn around, and that I would put the button on, which I proceeded to do. Then Ludlow said would I like to play bridge, he would set up a table that evening, and I said sure—I was beginning to like him—you can't sew a button on a man's pants and not be friendly.

Griscom obtained Fernald's permission to take some time off in order to continue his pursuit of Edith. "Meanwhile I was teaching school, and Aunt Rose came over and said 'The flower picker's here,' and I said 'damn it,' and dismissed school. . . . I went to the door and said hello, he came in, and we were talking when one of the younger children came rushing in to ask me something, and was terrified to see a stranger there. I knew my name was mud—alone in the schoolhouse with a man—a flower picker at that."

Griscom eventually returned to New York and made arrangements for correspondence with Edith. Meanwhile, Edith had written to one of her close friends and asked her to find out what she could about Ludlow. "Was he a gentleman? He was rough and in Khaki clothes, and you couldn't tell." The friend had a cousin that had been a classmate of Griscom's at Columbia and told of Ludlow reading Greek for pleasure on the subway on the way to class. Ludlow's letters "began to get a little warmer," and they went for long walks in the evenings.

When Edith went on a tour of Europe in March 1926, Ludlow responded gallantly in a letter to the Farmers Loan & Trust Company, in Paris. "I also understand that from time to time she gives you directions for the forwarding of mail or cables. What I am asking you to be so good as to do is to see that flowers are telegraphed her on every occasion that she gives you a definite address. The flowers will, of course, be sent in my name and will, of course, be of a respectable quantity and quality on each occasion."[3]

Soon after Edith's return, Ludlow asked her to marry him, to which she replied that she didn't know. Griscom's mother opposed the marriage, which certainly was pouring gasoline on the flames as far as Ludlow and Edith were concerned. Ludlow had recently received a modest inheritance from his grandmother, had thus gained a certain degree of financial independence from his mother, and apparently felt he could afford to propose to Edith. Ludlow told Edith that he was to leave for Colorado in ten days and wanted her answer by then. Edith played it to the hilt and said nothing for the ten days, although Ludlow visited her daily. At the end of ten days, with his customary tact Ludlow said, "Well, what is it?" at which point Edith said yes. After they were married Edith asked Ludlow if he would really have gone to Colorado with Maunsell

Crosby, to which she says he replied, "Of course not, I wanted you and I wouldn't have budged until I got you." Two enormously strong personalities were about to join forces.

In a July letter, Griscom thanked Fernald for his help. "Edith and I are getting married in September. Thank you most warmly again for those days at Eddy's Cove. They helped enormously, & gave me a head start. I hope, now, that you won't think they were entirely wasted!"[4]

They were married on 14 September 1926. There were no entries in Griscom's bird journal after 4 September, but on the fifteenth he recorded two species, Laughing Gull and Common Tern, and on the following day a single species, a Caspian Tern.[5] On 17 September they left on their "wedding trip" to Arizona, and he recorded 47 life birds (some were subspecies) during the next ten days.

Ludlow and Edith, whom he affectionately called Mouse, maintained a very warm and positive relationship. Their marriage was a very successful one, strongly influenced by Ludlow's need for love and affection and Edith's ability and willingness to provide them. But Edith brooked no nonsense from Ludlow, and he gave in to her in a number of important matters. Edith was Ludlow's match, and hence the relationship developed into, and remained, a partnership.

Edith made it her duty to accompany Ludlow on his birding trips, even though she never became a birder (she described herself as "just the driver of the car"). She also accompanied him on many botanizing trips and appears to have influenced his decision to turn his attention strictly to birds.

The botanizing trips could be quite noteworthy, largely because of Griscom's devil-may-care attitude when there was a plant that he wanted and something stood in his way. On one occasion the Griscoms and Mary and Robert Walcott, a distinguished judge and president of the Massachusetts Audubon Society, drove up to Vermont to locate a pond where a particularly rare aquatic plant might be found. Instead of being in the middle of an isolated field as they had supposed, the pond was in the center of a small town, they were dressed in their fancy clothes, and there were people around. Edith described the situation and events that followed.

It was a beautiful pond, like a small lake, big trees, grass cut, in the center of a park, early Sunday afternoon in June, people were walking out there, maybe forty people, and there were no boats available. Bob had a suit on, Mary and I dresses, and Ludlow had a suit on that he would wear for business to the museum. We stopped the car and got out and Ludlow said, "I'm going to get it." Ludlow wore a fedora hat. So he took off his shoes and took off his coat and handed it to Bob. Mary and I sat on the grass, acting as though everything is perfectly natural. Ludlow took off his necktie, left his shirt on, and with his fedora on quietly walked into the lake, and did the breast stroke, perfectly indifferent—he had looked through his field glasses to make sure the plant he wanted was there. When he got to the middle, here was this thing streaming, very fine seaweed-like. Nobody was near us, everybody was keeping clear of us, all standing still in fascination, in tiny groups. I said to Bob, "How on earth can he bring it in?" Ludlow put it across in his mouth, turns around with his fedora on his head, completely dressed, and swims back with this solemn, slow, breast stroke, this thing streaming from his mouth. He came ashore, perfectly quietly, no excitement from any of us, and said to Bob, 'Here it is.' Ludlow put on his shoes, coat, not his tie, and then as though this was a perfectly normal performance we got into the car and drove away.[6]

The Griscoms moved to Massachusetts in 1927, and in a period of a little more than four years, Edith Rapallo, Andrew, and Joan Ludlow were born. This string of births had a rather jolting effect on Griscom. He apparently needed Edith's love and attention and was not psychologically prepared to share them with anyone, even his children. This trait, when combined with Griscom's Victorian morality and aristocratic ways, produced an almost constant friction with his children, and he never learned to cope fully with the situation.

Griscom was apparently quite jealous of the children for drawing Edith's attention away from him. The children were not invited to the dinner table, which was formally set with linen table cloths and candelabra. Edith stated that the only time they quarreled was when she got between Ludlow and the children. Andrew Griscom made the rather stark revelation that his father was not a person to live close to, that he was just too "thorny," and that jealousy was an important factor in his life.

He didn't get along well with his contemporaries, and he certainly didn't get along with his children. He was a man who probably shouldn't have had children because he didn't know how to relate to them, or what to do about them. He was a very Victorian sort of father who needed to have his children at a substantial distance from him, and just sort of tidied up and brought in to see him for a short while, and then taken away again. His mother and father were very Victorian, and very isolated. They isolated themselves substantially from the world, and they provided him, very clearly, with absolutely no love, no affection as a child or as an adult, and I think that it was a standard psychological problem that children who have received no love are unable to give any, because they don't know what it is. I always thought my father didn't have the slightest idea what it was—he knew that he was getting something from my mother that he really liked and he valued it very much, because he said so, and talked about how generous and giving my mother was—but it still puzzled him. . . . He needed and wanted her entire attention, and his children deprived him of that.[7]

Andrew is of the opinion that his older sister, Edith, took the brunt of his frustrations. Joan, the youngest daughter, feels that she received little attention from her father as a person. "He just didn't think in those terms. We were trained, in fact, to stay out of his way and he would be in the study with the glass doors closed, and you don't interrupt your father! . . . I was constantly told that I must be lady-like. When I was bad I was told I wasn't being lady-like. When he was mad at my sister and me he reverted to archaic language and called us things like 'sluts and hussies.'"[8]

But the familial picture was not entirely bleak. Griscom was encouraging of the children's music, taking them to the various concerts at Symphony Hall and providing sound musical educations. The Cottrells, close family friends, remember Ludlow and Edith bringing the children on picnics and being patient and particularly proud of the two little girls and their musical accomplishments. Ludlow showed a certain pride when describing them in a letter to his aunt. "My oldest daughter, Edith, now twelve, is doing well at the fashionable but excellent Winsor School in Brookline, my son Andrew, aged eleven, will be going to boarding school at Milton next year. And my youngest daughter, Joan, an attractive handful aged nine, is trying to remain a baby as long as possible."[9]

Andrew frequently went birding with Ludlow. "He would always tap me if he ran out of people to go with. We got along very well on those birding trips. It was always fun. We got along terribly in the house, but as angry as he got at me and his other children, I don't recall him ever getting annoyed at me during a day's birding."[10]

Andrew also recalled some fine family moments with Ludlow playing soccer in the field behind the house at Chatham, occasionally rowing the skiff, or amazing Andrew by holding his breath under water, doing handstands on the bottom with his feet sticking out of the water.

In both his private and professional lives, Ludlow Griscom was a controversial figure, whose personality struck different people in very different ways. He had his strengths and weaknesses of character, moments of great vision and spots of blindness, and people's overall assessment of him as a human being depended largely on to which of these polar attributes they were most exposed, or on which they wished to place the greater emphasis.

He was perhaps five feet seven or eight inches tall and stocky, or, as Annette Cottrell, a long-time friend and birding companion of Griscom's, put it, "square rather than tall or short."[11] He was somewhat barrel-chested, and when he walked he held his elbows away from his body, giving him the appearance of strutting. He walked with an erect posture, rather military in bearing, which added to his "pouter pigeon" image. Yet his step was light and graceful, almost catlike, as Cottrell described: "I can remember him coming onto our porch on Lake View Ave., and you could hardly hear his footsteps—a very delicate way of moving."[12] He had fine, almost silky hands, and he had a habit of drumming his fingers on the table, an extension, perhaps, of his piano playing. He was extraordinarily energetic and proud of his physique, commenting that he could have a man stand on his chest and throw him off by just taking a deep breath. He was proud, as well, of his stamina and the distances he could walk. Accordingly, people remember him as a physically larger man that he actually was.

It appears that Ludlow received, in his early family years, a set of conventions that muted his emotional life to a significant degree. Griscom lived in his somewhat paradoxical world, constricted by Victorian mores, yet conducting a productive professional career in a thoroughly non-Victorian environment. The circle of friends around whom his "social" world revolved was largely peopled by "men of parts" from old families of wealth and proper station. His active world of birding included a wider variety of people, many of whom would be considered "lower class" by Victorian standards. He developed close friendships with women and men from both circles, but he seemed able to separate these different worlds with surprising success, and completely ignored the inconsistencies and contradictions that this circumstance produced. He was an "old-fashioned gentleman, with a nineteenth-century quality to him. He always dressed up in his suit and hat, and vest usually, when he went birding [but he did wear sneakers]."[13] Carl Buchheister, a friend of Griscom and a president of the National Audubon Society, remembered that "another attitude of Griscom's was courtesy. He disliked the lack of it in others. A gentleman himself, he wanted his associates to be. If they were not, they were not close associates."[14]

Griscom did a number of things that typified his assumed high position in society. For example, he put his son, Andrew, up for three schools shortly after he was born. He routinely bought his suits from Davies & Son, in London, England, and his cigarettes from the Union Club in New York, which he had delivered weekly. He worked for the proper charities, including the Community Fund Campaign, and to avoid paying "profit tax" when he sold securities, he donated securities to the Children's Museum of Boston, the Massachusetts

Audubon Society, and the Boston Museum of Science. Griscom clearly considered himself aristocratic, and played that role whenever possible. It has been suggested that Griscom's nearly complete lack of mechanical aptitude was a rather Athenian outgrowth of his aristocratic background, whereby mechanical interests would be too plebeian for him.

A darker side of Griscom's personality was his tendency toward racial prejudice. This was apparent in his early writings when he disdained the "low class" southern European immigrants who ate birds around New York City, and when he stated that "in the nineties a horde of low-grade Italian immigrants began swarming over the countryside."[15] It showed up in his World War II "Dago-dazzlers," official documents that helped him in tight situations with police and various military personnel, and in his comments about the Armenians as a "natural race of bastards."[16] His daughter, Joan, remembers an undertone of anti-Semitism, which appeared regularly in his conversation, and anti-black bias as well. Joan was upset by her father's snobbery and arrogance, and his bigotry helped move Joan toward work in race relations and a career in multi-cultural studies. His attitudes are not defensible from a late-twentieth-century standpoint, but such views were not atypical of the aristocratic, late-nineteenth-century framework from which, much of the time, he viewed the world.

Prejudices aside, Griscom lived by a strict code of conduct. Andrew Griscom summed this up in a discussion about Ludlow and his mother.

> Neither he nor his mother could possibly understand the Golden Rule, and they didn't know how to relate to other people. They both had a very strong code of ethics, but then, the Victorian world did. Dad had a clear-cut code of ethics which he followed really very carefully. He was very consistent, a very ethical man, absolutely unforgiving of people who violated the code. People in his world were pretty much black and white. If you violated it in any significant way you went over to the black side and there was no way you could recover. Forgiveness was not something my father understood. Not letting anyone into the house who had been at fault in a divorce was an adoption of the Victorian code that he brought right into the middle of the twentieth century."[17]

Under the rather tough outer appearance was a more vulnerable and sensitive man. This is seen in an incident related by Allen Morgan, one of Griscom's protégés, which suggests that Griscom was genuinely mystified by the mistreatment he occasionally received from others. At an American Ornithologists' Union meeting in Boston, he had invited Alexander Wetmore, an important ornithologist and a secretary of the Smithsonian Institution, out for dinner, but Wetmore declined, citing a previous engagement. Ludlow then invited Morgan to have dinner at the Chez Dreyfus Restaurant before going to the evening session of the meeting. When they sat down, Griscom spotted Wetmore sitting together with Wendell Taber, Jim Peters, Jim Greenway, and Joseph Hagar—all ornithologists who harbored anti-Griscom feelings. Wetmore had been invited to join the group, but Ludlow hadn't, and it was a clear insult to him. Morgan said that "Ludlow was absolutely stricken—he wept several tears, and said 'Allen, I just do not understand why these people treat me so.' He got his composure back, and we had a delightful meal. But it was terribly sad."[18]

Griscom was a great theater, music, and opera buff. The family had season tickets to the Theater Guild performances, and Ludlow particularly enjoyed piano concerts. Griscom cut a dashing figure in his tuxedo at his box seats at the Metropolitan Opera. His own piano playing was a great pleasure for him throughout his life. He could play several hundred pieces from memory, mostly Chopin, his favorite, and romantic pieces by Liszt. The tremendous auditory memory that served him so well in his bird work also was expressed in his musical talents. When the Griscoms would have friends over for dinner parties, as they did almost weekly for some years, upon request Ludlow would frequently give a concert for a half hour or forty-five minutes. At the house at Chatham, Massachusetts, after a day of birding with Roger Ernst, Norman Hill, or Richard Eaton, for example, he would play Chopin after dinner, much to the delight of everyone.

Griscom greatly enjoyed reading. He and Edith belonged to a local, private book club in which they bought books and swapped them with other people in the group every two weeks or so. He particularly loved murder mysteries, reading many works by Agatha Christie and Erle Stanley Gardner. Griscom was also a member of the Scientific Book Club, and the area of keenest interest to him is no surprise: "A special hobby of mine is collecting rare and handsomely illustrated books on birds, primarily those outside the United States."[19]

Griscom had no use for movies or radio programs; he thought of them as "opiates for the masses." There were exceptions for both, however. He had reserved seats for *Fantasia,* the Walt Disney cartoon feature that incorporated some natural history and had classical music as background; he commented that it was "all right," but he went to no further Hollywood movies. Later in life he praised the photographer-naturalists who did the filming for Disney nature films. The only radio shows that were acceptable were news shows, especially those broadcast during World War II, and "Information Please," which featured his friend from New York, John Kieran, and often dealt with bird-related topics.

If the radio was on when he came home, Griscom would roar, and the children had better hop to turn it off. Legitimate theater was distinctly separated from vaudeville and "related horrors," and he considered jazz an abomination.

Of course, Griscom's favorite hobbies were botany and birding. He loved to walk along railroad tracks identifying all the exotic plants, brought in from all over the world as seeds on wool shipments and such. He and Richard Eaton, a neighbor and friend, would work late into the night over their plants in the barn behind the Griscom house, heated on cold evenings by an antiquated wood stove. Eaton recalled, "We went on many collecting expeditions, much to my edification, particularly in respect to the genus *Carex!* At that time, he later told me, it was a toss-up as to whether to concentrate on Botany or Ornithology!"[20] But birds were his true love. Andrew, his son, recalled that birds were, "his own personal thing." He remembers that as a boy he saw twenty or more crude tracings and drawings of birds that his father had made at perhaps the age of seven or eight. Ludlow's fascination and interest never diminished.

Part Two

ORNITHOLOGY

American Museum of Natural History 4

Griscom was eager to obtain a position with Frank Chapman, curator of birds at the American Museum of Natural History in New York City. The museum housed one of the finest research collections of birds in the world, and under Chapman's active leadership it had become not only a fine research institution but also a major instrument for the popularization of birds and conservation. There were no openings in the Department of Mammalogy and Ornithology, but there was one in the Department of Fishes, which Griscom took, presumably with the understanding that he would transfer at the first opportunity. He began his duties at the museum in the fall of 1916, where he collaborated with the ichthyologist John T. Nichols in the preparation of *Fresh Water Fishes of the Congo Obtained by the American Museum Congo Expedition, 1909–1915.*[1] The switch to the ornithology department occurred early the following year.

In February 1917 Griscom sailed for Cuba, Panama, Costa Rica, and Nicaragua on a collecting trip that focused on birds. This was the first of many expeditions to Central America, and he would become an authority on the birds of this region. The trip lasted until mid-June. His career was interrupted by the entrance of the United States into of World War I, and on 24 August 1917 he reported to the Second Plattsburg Training Camp, a military training facility in New York. His wartime service was to cost him two years at the museum, but he nonetheless maintained his interest in birds.

Griscom's enormous facility with language equipped him well for the military duties he was to assume, as his service was to be primarily as a linguist. He came out of the training camp a second lieutenant and was ordered to Camp Stanley, Texas, where he remained from mid-December through mid-March 1918. At the Plattsburg Camp he managed to keep his eyes open for birds. His journal includes many entries such as, "Arctic Three-toed Wood-pecker 1 male Nov. 4. in pine trees on Parade Ground. Very tame."[2] At Camp Stanley he managed to wangle a number of passes: "Dec 23rd. Corpus Christi, Texas, by boat to Port Aransas & Aransas Pass. all day. . . . "Dec. 30. Medina Dam. Dawn-dark."[3] Ludlow's year list would exceed 300 in 1918, surpassing the 240 for 1916 (his lists at this time included subspecies that were easily identifiable in the field).

In March he was transferred to Military Intelligence Headquarters in Washington, D.C., where he became the executive officer of the newly formed Propaganda Section. Things began to happen rapidly at this point, but he managed to sneak in a "Big Day" of birding: "4 a.m.—10:30 p. m. fair & mild. H.C. Oberholser [an avian taxonomist] & B.H. Swales (part of the time). Birds very abundant."[4] (His list for that day totaled 118.) He was soon sent overseas, where he was active on the American front in France. His primary responsibility was sending up hydrogen balloons with attached propaganda leaflets.

Griscom had left from Hoboken, New Jersey, 14 July 1918, and arrived in Brest, France, where he spent a few days before going to Paris and then to London for a conference on 4 August. From 29 August to 13 January 1919, he was on active duty out of general headquarters at Chaumont, France. All the while, Griscom never forgot about birds:

> Now for what I shall term military ornithology. On Oct. 2nd. left Chaumont for the Vosges front and reached St. Die, headquarters, 1 1/2 kilometers from the front line, Oct. 3. this town is under direct observation from Germany, is constantly shelled, and has the reputation of being the most gassed place in the American sector. In spite of this fact, Swallows and House Sparrows were common. At dusk during heavy firing at the front, and while two Hun aeroplanes were flying over the town, saw three Bullfinches feeding peacefully in a mountain ash tree near the office window. . . .
>
> About 10 A.M. the village was shelled by 14-inch high explosive. I was standing in the street when the first shell fell 200 yards away. A cloud of House Sparrows and Tree Sparrows flew away. Shells fell every five minutes for over an hour, and birds and man took to dug-outs or the equivalent. One shell burst almost in front of my dug-out, 75 ft. away, and I can posi-

tively affirm that a Redbreast was singing 50 ft. from where it burst five minutes after the shelling was over.[5]

By the end of 1918 he had seen 127 species in Europe, and his year list was 324. Ludlow was not easily distracted from his ornithological pursuits.

The war now over, Ludlow had no intention of remaining in the military, and in a letter had discussed his hope of getting a discharge in Europe so that he could take a trip to Egypt.[6] Unfortunately, Griscom's military service was instead cut short by the death of his father from influenza. The death was a great blow to Ludlow. According to Edith, Ludlow had been very fond of his father, and she suggested that at this point in his life, his father was the only person whom Ludlow really cared for. Apparently, the senior Griscom doted on his son a bit during the war, once even writing to his commanding officer. On Ludlow's return from the war, his mother's brutal statement that his father had died without receiving a letter from him hurt him deeply.

Ludlow returned to his post in the ornithology department in 1919 and continued with that museum as an assistant curator until 1927. He succinctly reported on his activities there:

During the ten years I was connected with the American Museum my ornithological activities developed into two sharply distinct lines, (1) my first and greatest love, field ornithology and the identification of birds in the field, and as such was the member of the staff who was supposed to be a leader and guide for all the local interest in birds in New York City region. This culminated in my Handbook to the Birds of the New York City Region, which seems to have had a steady and successful sale. On the more technical side (2), I became a specialist in the birds of the American tropics, particularly Central America, and went on a long series of exploring expeditions to various parts of Central America in the next ten years. This, of course, led to a steady stream of technical and more scientific papers, the longest of which was my book on the distribution of bird life in Guatemala, published in 1932.[7]

Griscom was as proficient in botany as he was in ornithology, and he included in his peregrinations botanical expeditions to Newfoundland in 1920, 1921, 1922, and 1925, and to the mountains of Quebec, mostly under the direction of M. L. Fernald. In 1924 he visited Haiti and collected birds in Panama. In 1926 he went on an expedition to British Honduras (Belize), Yucatan, and Cozumel Island, Mexico. (For a detailed account of these expeditions, see chapter 6).

His years at the American Museum were years of growth, bringing to him a scientific and professional maturity. He had become an elective member of the American Ornithologists' Union in 1917 and joined the inner circle of that organization when he was elected a fellow in 1923, at the age of 33. His expertise in botany became firmly established, and he was elected a nonresident member of the New England Botanical Club, which publishes the journal *Rhodora*. Locally he became a fellow of the Linnaean Society, and by 1927 its president. He collaborated with many of the other outstanding ornithologists of the first half of the twentieth century while at the American Museum, including Jonathan Dwight, a doctor who became an authority on avian molt; W. DeW. Miller, an associate curator of birds at the American Museum of Natural History; and Frank Chapman.

His early publications largely concerned bird distribution, dealing with sight and collecting records, often of vagrants. By the time he left the American Museum in 1927, he had published more than fifty articles, mostly notes, in the *Auk,* but gradually gave up the practice of publishing sight records of vagrants in this journal, the last appearing in 1941. After he moved to Massachusetts in 1927, he began publishing many of his sightings in the *Bulletins* of the Essex County Ornithological Club and Massachusetts Audubon Society. In addition to the *Auk,* he published many records in the *Abstracts* of the *Proceedings of the Linnaean Society of New York* and in *Bird-Lore.* These distributional notes were important to him and one of the ways in which he was able to publicize his emphasis on rapid field identification of birds.

His first major local bird distribution publication was *Birds of the New York City Region* in 1923. The reviews were uniformly excellent. In the species accounts Griscom emphasized the critical characters for identification and drew the following comment in an unsigned review in *Ibis:* "This [species status account] is accompanied by a few lines on the more conspicuous characters by which each bird can be recognized in the field—a most valuable portion of the work and one on which Mr. Griscom is eminently qualified to write."[8]

Witmer Stone, for many years editor of the *Auk,* wrote perhaps the most laudatory review, wherein he assesses Griscom's influence on new directions for ornithology:

> As is well known Mr. Ludlow Griscom has for some years been studying the possibilities of sight identification with the idea of eliminating so far as possible errors in field observations. He is not alone in this work as its importance is at once recognized by all students of living birds, but he has taken a leading part in it, and the results are beginning to show in the mention in our books of field marks by which a bird at some distance may be recog-

nized, in addition to the older type of description based upon specimens which can only be used satisfactorily when the bird is in the hand. . . .

Mr. Griscom's method of treatment is admirable. . . .

All of this, however [reviewing the large number of sight records], Mr. Griscom has done with admirable judgement and the result is the most satisfactory local treatise that we have seen. In cutting away from many of the traditional requirements of the last generation and considering primarily the needs of the host of present day field students it sets a standard and example for what, as we have said elsewhere, might be termed the "new ornithology."

While neither Mr. Griscom nor the writer oppose the collecting of birds when science requires it, we realize that the necessity for collecting in the eastern states at least, has been greatly lessened. . . . Powerful binocular glasses now bring the birds reasonably close and constitute the instrument for the work and it remains to teach the observer what characters to look for under these conditions and how to use his collected data for the best interests of ornithology. Towards these ends Mr. Griscom's little book points the way and we congratulate him upon an important piece of work well done.[9]

During his years at the American Museum of Natural History, he published more than a dozen systematic works as American Museum *Novitates* and several papers in *Natural History,* another, more popular American Museum publication. By the end of 1927 he had described and published (often with other workers) more than 90 new subspecies and 11 species. Peters' Checklist reduces five of the species to subspecies status, and places one new species in synonymy with an existing species. Five retained their species status. His one new genus, *Xenotriccus,* published with Dwight, still stands.

Early reviews of his work often suggest that Griscom was a careful worker, at least in his earlier years. An unsigned 1927 review in *Ibis,* for example, states that his paper on summer birds of the west coast of Newfoundland is "an excellent historical review of the literature, and a discussion of the nature of the country and its avifauna."[10]

His professional services and advice were more and more in demand. For example, he was invited to review *Française d'Ornithologique* for *Biological Abstracts,* and Outram Bangs, an ornithologist at the Museum of Comparative Zoology (MCZ) at Harvard, asked him if a subspecies identification Bangs had made was correct. Yet his growing authority did not exempt him from the intense competition of scientific inquiry. The story is widely circulated that

Thomas Barbour, MCZ director and later a mentor of Griscom, happened to be down from Boston visiting the American Museum and noticed among some bird skins that Griscom had out on a table, an example of a new subspecies that Barbour and Bangs had been working on. Barbour discreetly asked Griscom about the bird and Ludlow told him that he thought that he had a new subspecies. Barbour said nothing, but on leaving the museum sent a telegram to Bangs telling him to drop everything and describe the new subspecies immediately. He wanted the description in print by the following morning. Barbour took the train back to Boston. He and Bangs had an arrangement with a printer in Cambridge who printed the *Proceedings of the New England Zoölogical Club,* which they apparently often treated as their personal publication. Barbour arrived at midnight, gave his approval to the paper, and they carried it to the printer at 2 A.M. The following morning the freshly printed paper was in the mail and they had established priority, scooping the unknowing Griscom. This story may contain some apocryphal elements, but it does give some flavor of the rivalry among the museum people and the kind of chase that Griscom loved.

While at the museum, Griscom had lost neither his brusque personality nor his assertive manner, and in a pattern that was to characterize his interpersonal dealings throughout life, he tended to polarize people into pro- and anti-Griscom factions. On one side, Griscom's relationship with Robert Cushman Murphy, an expert on oceanic birds, was always warm and friendly, and James P. Chapin, a leading authority on African birds, ended letters to Griscom with "most cordially yours." A letter from Jonathan Dwight the year after Griscom left the Museum also suggests an amiable collegiality: "I hope you are enjoying your new environment much as I regret your leaving us here. I find I am plodding along when I used to gallop with your assistance & I have so many paths to follow that I don't get to the end of any."[11]

On the other side, the blustery, self-assured aspect of Griscom's character may have contributed to some friction with W. deW. Miller and others on the staff. Griscom was blocked for promotion by an unusually talented and ambitious group of ornithologists at the American Museum. He felt frustrated by this and gradually developed interpersonal difficulties with Frank Chapman. We can see glimpses of this in a letter Griscom later wrote to James Bond, an ornithologist at the Academy of Natural Sciences in Philadelphia: "My own observation over a long period of years is that Dr. Chapman's opinion on critical matters is absolutely worthless unless he himself is personally interested in the problem. Whenever the members of his staff wished his opinion or assistance in some problem of their own he was always bored, always hasty and superficial, and could not for one moment be relied upon. I am consequently not surprised to hear that you had exactly the same experience with him."[12]

It is clear that relations between these two men deteriorated, and even Edith thought that Griscom was at least somewhat to blame. Whatever the causes, Griscom was pleased to accept a position at the Museum of Comparative Zoology in 1927, when it was offered by none other than Thomas Barbour. It meant leaving New York, which had been for so long his home, and his many birding friends, whose companionship he cherished. But it would put some distance between him and his mother, the dominant negative force in his life.

Personality conflicts and professional frustration notwithstanding, Griscom's decade of service to the American Museum did not go unappreciated. In November 1927 he received a letter from museum president Henry Fairfield Osborn that said in part:

> I can hardly express my feeling of regret in learning that you have gradually gotten out of sympathy with Head Curator Chapman of the Department of Birds and feel that you have not been generously treated in the American Museum. This is even more regrettable than your resignation from the Department because Curator Chapman has always represented your service in terms of warmest and highest appreciation and certainly the American Museum, through its President and Officers, has invariably valued and recognized your services both in the field and in the Museum.[13]

In his response, Ludlow explained his position.

> I regret that any rumors should have reached you regarding my being out of sympathy with Dr. Chapman and my supposed feeling that I had not been generously treated by the American Museum. Who ever gave you this impression, was either incorrectly informed or misrepresented the facts. My differences with Dr. Chapman were purely personal, never official, and consequently I never confused him with the Museum treatment as a whole. My letter of resignation to Mr. Sherwood gave exactly my reasons for resigning. The conditions alluded to were facts, but were not facts for which any one was to blame. I can consequently assure you most warmly that I shall do everything in my power to promote the spirit of mutual cooperation which has always existed between the two institutions, particularly because I have loved the American Museum for many years, have always admired its President and am grateful to him for the many opportunities which he afforded his young assistant curator.[14]

Decades later, Griscom suggested that there were a number of crosscurrents at the museum that may have influenced his falling out with Frank Chapman.

Your letter inadvertently opens up some old wounds and difficulties. Miller, a man whom I know very well indeed, was a curious fellow in many respects, and could not or did not write up the results of his ornithological research and his wide and thorough knowledge of birds in many districts. Back in the fall of 1916, he became outraged that he had never been sent on any kind of museum expedition and demanded and insisted that he be given the chance. As the American Museum had at some previous time purchased a Nicaraguan collection from Richardson, it occurred to Chapman that the working up of this collection could be assigned to Miller, and he found the money to send Miller to Nicaragua where he was to join Richardson and I was sent along as an assistant.

Miller worked hard, did very well, and acquitted himself remarkably in view of his total lack of travel or collecting experience of any kind. Upon return from Nicaragua, Miller behaved in a quite remarkable fashion. His interest extended solely to working up and identifying birds collected in the field that he did not know, and all of Chapman's efforts to persuade Miller to work on a report on the birds of Nicaragua completely failed. Finally, very much annoyed, Chapman handed over to me the problem of getting the report done as Miller's assistant. This not only strained the relationship between Miller and Chapman, but also completely spoiled the relations between Miller and me, as he deeply resented my being wished on him as it was.

The net result was that things in the bird department became so unpleasant that I resolved to leave the moment I could secure a decent position elsewhere, which I, in fact did. At that time, I became involved in the Dwight Guatemalan collection of birds. As you probably know, Miller was soon killed in an automobile accident, and somewhat later Chapman died himself, all of which period of time I have never received the slightest work [sic] from anybody in the bird department of the American Museum asking about or expressing any interest in the Nicaraguan report.[15]

Griscom's resignation was effective 1 November 1927. On the same date he became research curator of zoology in the Museum of Comparative Zoology at Harvard University.

Pattern of Change: Museum of Comparative Zoology

5

When Ludlow Griscom moved to Massachusetts in 1927 to join the staff of Harvard University's Museum of Comparative Zoology (MCZ), the entire pattern of his professional life began to change. It is difficult to separate completely his involvement in the work of the museum from the other aspects of his professional life, such as his work with professional and conservation organizations. His involvements intermesh, and, for example, what he did for the American Ornithologists' Union (AOU) was considered part of his responsibilities at the museum.

There were undoubtedly a number of reasons that Thomas Barbour chose Ludlow for Research Curator of Zoology (a title that he held until 1948, when he became Research Ornithologist). One consideration was that Griscom was the only member of the staff who had a wide knowledge of North American botany and could therefore answer questions relating to this subject. A more compelling reason for Barbour's choice was recalled by Bradford Washburn, who knew both men well:

[Griscom] had had a very distinguished career at the American Museum of Natural History and came up here, as I understand it, to be a sort of administrative assistant to Tom Barbour, who was then the Director of the MCZ. Tom was very wealthy and very generous, one of the last of the generation of professional scientists who knew a great deal about a lot of things—was into everything, was all over the place. I have the feeling that Ludlow was brought up here to give some structure to that office, see to it that commitments were carried out, and above all things, that the budget was adhered to. Ludlow was very precise, very orderly, maybe too orderly, too precise. He was great at pulling the confused, informal, pleasant MCZ, at least at the top level, into a good sharp, operating machine. . . . I think Tom Barbour would have been lost without Ludlow, because Tom was not a person who liked structure and order, he just liked to get things done. He kept making all sorts of commitments and Ludlow had to keep running after him trying to make sure everything was worked out properly and to the satisfaction of the staff.[1]

This general thesis is supported by a number of comments in Griscom's correspondence of the time. There are numerous references to new directions, reorganization, retirement of personnel, and the like.

Ludlow dug into his varied administrative responsibilities, at an annual salary of $3,000. He also assumed the editorship of the museum's scientific series, which brought him an additional stipend of $2,000. This was, apparently, the top salary paid to MCZ staff (as director, Barbour received $1 per year), and Ludlow was still making $3,000 when he retired in 1956 (he lost the editorial stipend when he retired as editor in the early 1950s).

Among Ludlow's responsibilities were selling off duplicate books, handling job inquiries, and library loan and specimen loan requests. He oversaw the affairs of the Australian expedition, advised Barbour on buying a collection of birds and mammals from Brazil, and even handled the purchase of a leopard skin. In 1927 he described one of his duties: "Ever since your letter arrived I have been moving camels, whales, sharks, mice, etc. from nine until five, in the exhibition halls of the museum."[2] This letter is corroborated by one to Ludlow from Jonathan Dwight. "Mathews gave me an amusing account of how you were all carrying stuffed hippos & such things out on the lawn to be dusted off."[3]

As the administrative responsibilities mounted, his time for other professional activities became severely eroded. How could Griscom handle all of this administrative detail and still have time for carrying on his ornithological and botanical research and publication? We get some hint of the energy that he was able to muster from an excerpt from the 1935 journal of David Garrison, a Griscom birding protégé, who faithfully recorded Ludlow's comments.

Mr. Griscom this afternoon, when I called to see him, expatiated a little on the dangerous but stimulating doctrine of long working hours. After spending his days in orni. research and editorial and administrative duties at the museum, he regularly joins Fernald three times a week at the Herbarium, and works till around one o'clock over his private collection in the barn behind his house. This schedule allows him to publish many, various papers covering a wider biological field than he could ever cope with in a regulation working day. . . . He maintained today that *anybody* could do as much work as he does—assuming "normal" physical & mental health. He spoke of people's being happier when driven & pressed a bit. He said that most people not only were happier but turned out their best production under such adverse circumstances; and he distinguished the real leaders as those who, between periods of outside pressure, instead of slumping kept up their effort and production to *capacity* levels.[4]

Among the charges Griscom assumed at the MCZ, the one that was perhaps most demanding of his time was his editorial duties. He not only had to edit the two scientific series of the museum, the *Memoirs* and *Bulletin,* but also undertook the peripheral activities involving acquisition and sales of publications for the museum. His Annual Reports suggest that these duties consumed nearly half of his time.

His ancillary work involving sales produced a substantial number of hassles with customers. Griscom was remarkably blunt with customers whose claims he thought unfounded. An excerpt from a 1932 letter to the Philadelphia Book Company serves to illustrate his belligerent style.

I acknowledge receipt of your letter of July 12th, with the comment that it was high time we heard from you, and note that on June 2nd you claim to have ordered one copy in cloth binding of Brues & Melander's Classification of Insects to be sent to the Philadelphia College of Pharmacy and Science. It is further alleged that they received a copy bound in paper which you are returning to us.

We wish to register the strongest protest at the improper manner in which this small transaction has been handled. In the first place your original order, which is before me as I write, did not specify that a copy in cloth binding be sent, and as this is more expensive than the paper bound copy it is quite properly our invariable custom to forward a paper bound copy unless the order specifically mentions the cloth binding. . . . As a matter of fact, after waiting two weeks for some explanation from you of the [damage to the book], I wrote a letter of complaint to the Bursar of Harvard University, entrusted with the sending out of the bill and the collection of the money, and he replied suggesting that you be put on the University blacklist upon a final word from me. Under the circumstances I most certainly will not forward a cloth bound copy of this book to your customer until the preceding matters are adjusted.[5]

The customer's reply demonstrates that Ludlow didn't always intimidate those whom he attacked and suggests that life would have been easier for him if he had taken a more relaxed approach to his business dealings.

Dear Sir:
We have been in business for the past 36 years and we have never received such a discourteous letter as yours of August 10th, but then our business contacts have been with publishers of books and not with research curators of zoology. . . .

We would advise you to develop a sense of humor and to learn to distinguish between the sublime and the ridiculous and not to take yourself too seriously. We should also thank you to place our name in nomination to the Bursar of Harvard University, who we imagine is waiting breathlessly for final word from you to put us on the blacklist, which we take it, is an old Harvard custom.[6]

The editing of the *Bulletins* and *Memoirs,* which averaged about a thousand pages per year, took a great deal of time. In fact he did at least some of this work at home in the evening. Andrew remembered that "Dad would put piles of proof on the table, proof reading these damn MCZ *Bulletins,* which were difficult to read unless you knew a great deal about natural history. But he did it and I was always impressed by him. He would be reading something on fishes and he would start correcting the Latin names of the fish, and I couldn't see how in the world he knew that some of these things were misspelled. He had a good background in Latin and Greek."[7]

Ludlow had his problems from time to time with the authors whose work he was editing. In 1931 he wrote to Robert Payne Bigelow:

I am naturally sorry to hear that there was an error in fig. 4, but do not understand your statement that you were "not allowed to see the inked drawings." It is my impression that I employed the Museum artist, Mr. Edward A. Schmitts, to make inked drawings from your pencil sketches and that when these drawings were complete I sent him down to your office at the Massachusetts Institute of Technology to show them to you. At the same time there was one drawing which he was unable to complete as he was not sure of just what parts of your pencil sketch were to be included. I certainly told him to go down to see you and he certainly told me he had.

I have just been over the page proof of your article, with what I hope was a fine tooth comb. There were so many corrections necessary and so many citations of literature which had to be corrected that I have been forced to demand a revised page proof, so that the publication of your paper will suffer a little delay.[8]

Griscom's expertise in publishing matters is evident in a 1940 letter to Josselyn Van Tyne, an ornithologist at the Museum of Zoology, Ann Arbor, Michigan.

I know nothing, of course, about printing costs in your section of the Central States, but I do know that our printing costs here are the envy of all other local scientific publications. Various editors have called upon me in this matter and the Harvard University Press has been trying for ten years to bring their costs down so as to get our business. What it actually boils down to is this: The average editor knows nothing about the printing business and printing costs and the prices charged him by any given printer are in part based on a guess by the printer as to how much he can get away with with the ignorance of that particular editor. Fortunately for me, I spent a year and a half in my youth in Macmillan & Company, and when I took charge of the publications here demanded a brand new and very itemized contract on printing costs with our printer and told him flatly that his charge for press work would have to be reduced 20% and that his composition costs for ten point type would also have to be reduced. I was also well aware of the value of a steady sum per annum in the way of business and was equally aware of the importance of keeping their press staff busy during the lean summer months, all factors which were duly reflected in specially reduced rates to us. It is my experience that the average scientist who becomes an editor knows absolutely nothing about these things and is to a certain extent at the mercy of the printer.[9]

Ludlow could turn on the smooth language when he was trying to get something from someone. In a letter to Samuel Henshaw, he tested the waters to find out if he might be able to acquire responsibility for finishing up William Brewster's *Birds of the Lake Umbagog Region*.[10]

As the editor of the Museum publications, I am venturing to ask you for some information with regard to the manuscript of the final part of Brewster's Birds of the Lake Umbagog Region. As an ornithologist I have always valued the two beautifully edited parts of this work which have already appeared, and am naturally hoping to see it concluded. Some time ago, I believe, the diaries were turned over to you with the natural hope that you might feel able to complete the editing of this final part, though I do not pretend to know what arrangements were made.

Almost every week now I receive letters of inquiry from various libraries and amateur ornithologists in this country asking me when they may expect the appearance of this final part and I don't know just how to answer these inquiries. Would you therefore be so good as to drop me a line at your convenience telling me the present state of this manuscript? I can easily imagine, on the other hand, that your time may be fully occupied with more pressing interests, and if this should prove to be the case would you not feel perfectly free to return these diaries and I would endeavor to substitute for you to the best of my poor ability.[11]

Griscom eventually edited part three of this series and authored part four.

Ludlow's spectrum of administrative duties ranged from writing thank-you notes for museum contributions to preparing the budget. One of his obligations was to oversee the expansion of museum collections. He was constantly negotiating with collectors, and in this area, too, there were numerous difficulties. In correspondence with H. Wedel over the course of two years, we see Ludlow first patient and supportive of this collector, then turn harsh and impatient, and finally sever connections with him. If you lived up to Griscom's expectations you were well treated. If not, you tended to be treated rather sternly.

> No museum or other institution . . . with painfully limited resources, can possibly afford to maintain a collector in a given region until the list of possible species is absolutely exhausted. . . .
>
> If you could make a good collection of birds along the Boquete Trail or anywhere else in the mountains of western Panama on the Caribbean side of the divide *above 3,000 feet,* it would be a very desirable collection. . . .
>
> You will, of course, go under museum auspices and with the great advantage of your arrangements being made by us direct with the officials of the fruit company concerned and your transportation will be paid. For a man who has collected birds for so short a time as you, you make a surprisingly good skin and you have shown unusual aptitude in your ability to find the rarer and more desirable species. . . . There is also no doubt but what you can make a better living as a collector than you have recently in Almirante if you move to a new and more desirable locality.[12]

The financial side of collecting and whether or not it is satisfactory, depends entirely upon the point of view of the collector. There is, of course, "no money" in collecting, but there is a living. . . . Like any form of scientific work, the interest and pleasure in performing the work has got to be sufficient to compensate for the financial disadvantages of not being a successful banker. On the side of interest I can be of great assistance to you in helping you to learn the Panama birds. . . . I can send you a check list of all the birds recorded from Panama and with each collection, I can send you a report of what you have sent in and you can check them off on this list and see at a moment's glance just what you have been able to accomplish. . . .

Museums do not usually take this much trouble with collectors, but I have always done so with mine and I have found it to work to our mutual advantage. . . .

You are limited to a maximum of 10 of all common birds in any one general locality. . . .

If there is anything in this letter which is not clear or which sounds unsatisfactory, do not hesitate to ask and defer judgment until these doubts can be answered. For many years I have been connected with two great museum[s]. We have been buying specimens from collectors in many parts of the world. Not one of these men has ever been cheated or has ever gone on the rocks and you, in your turn, will never be left really in the lurch.[13]

We have on several occasions advanced you money for a trip into the mountains at an altitude of 3,000 ft. or greater and you have never gotten there. The director has consequently forbidden me to advance you any further sums for this or any other reason.[14]

Shortly thereafter, in a letter to Herbert Friedmann, an ornithologist at the U.S. National Museum, we see Griscom tarnishing Wedel's reputation.

Nevertheless we are more than glad for you to take him over if you wish. Wedel is more or less of a beach comber, well over fifty years old, and inspires every white man with whom he comes in contact with strong contempt in about two months time. He makes very good skins, is not really able to remember one bird from another, but succeeds in the course of time in getting quite a variety of interesting material, largely on a hit or miss basis. He is very slow and does not average a thousand specimens a year. He is also lazy and entirely lacking in initiative, and cannot be persuaded to go more than a mile or two back into the woods from a settlement. . . .

We have about all the birds from the tropical lowlands that we want, and if you wish to take him over we will fire Wedel with pleasure.[15]

Finally, Griscom sums up his exasperation at this matter in a letter to the Harvard bursar: "Most unfortunately, Wedel proves to be still alive."[16] Wedel was only one of the collectors with whom he had difficulty.

Griscom also had to deal with a wide variety of requests for information from the general public, and his files contain hundreds of examples of his patient and thoughtful responses. The following replies suggest the range of questions and expertise of the letter writers.

> The second question [about Starlings] I cannot answer so definitely, as it has not yet been tried and I can only fall back on supposition. I am exceedingly doubtful of the success of any proposed radio gadgets unless they make enough noise often enough to run the risk of disturbing the neighborhood. General evidence among birds is that their capacity to put up with disturbances which are exceedingly nerve shattering to human brings is positively extraordinary once they learn that the disturbance causes them no real harm. Probably a much less expensive and difficult device which would be well worth trying first would be Big Ben alarm clocks at $1 each. If several of these are hung in the trees of the roost and are timed to go off every hour during the night it might easily cause the starlings to desert. I should be inclined to try it first.[17]

> Acknowledging your letter of January 8th, you have obviously been seriously misled by such literature as you have seen on the Passenger Pigeon. This bird has been extinct for over three decades and at no time ever occurred west of the Great Plains. The birds you know about in your country in Oregon are the Band-tailed Pigeon.[18]

In addition to serving the general public, Griscom had extensive correspondence with other professionals. Much of it was related to the more mundane aspects of a research curator's job such as filling requests for specimen loans, giving or receiving information on museum materials, or making comparisons among materials. But the tone of his letters often went far beyond businesslike collegiality. His correspondence tended to be rather personal and largely cordial. But whether he was writing to a private collector of bird skins, an overseas counterpart in Berlin, or a longtime colleague, he couldn't resist an occasional snide comment about the American Museum of Natural History or a cutting remark to one of his friends about one of his enemies:

> About all that I have done to date is to examine the alleged new species of partridge from Costa Rica which Oberholser has described, and Bangs, Peters, and I have studied this bird very carefully. Needless to say, I am very much obliged to you indeed for your kind thought in sending it on, but I am sorry to have to advise you that it is a typical piece of stupidity on Oberholser's part. Far from being a new species, the bird is a mere melanism of

the well known *O. leucolaemus,* and its description as a new species was preposterous.[19]

I have your very kind and informative note of January 2nd and I am much obliged to you indeed for your trouble in making the necessary comparisons of the orioles I sent you with the type in your museum. I shall look forward with interest to your review of Austin's Birds of Newfoundland-Labrador in Ornithologische Monatsberichte. The German ornithologists are now almost the only ones who write real reviews. Most of the so-called reviews in the Auk and the Ibis today are mere notices of a very stereotyped kind.[20]

It was nice to hear from you [Alexander Wetmore] again and I take pleasure in telling you what little I used to know about the Newfoundland caribou. . . .

Greenway and I have finished the identification of the Olalla collection from the Lower Amazon and are now half way through with a report. . . . We, of course, were not allowed to see any of the unworked Amazon collections in the American Museum, and with the exception of a few particular groups, Todd [W. E. Todd, curator of birds at the Carnegie Museum of Natural History], of course, has not the remotest idea of what he's got, and will probably never live long enough to find out, so that those collections have got to go to sleep for awhile.[21]

Despite the critical commentary, it is evident that Griscom developed deep and lasting friendships with a number of his colleagues. He would help a young man get a job—or not, if he thought it was the wrong job—and would, without conceit, offer assistance in a wide variety of circumstances:

I certainly hope that all your questions will not be as difficult and unsatisfactory as the one about the natal down of the king vulture. I didn't know of either specimens or descriptions of the natal down and I spent one solid day in this library without succeeding in finding the slightest reference to the natal down of the king vulture. . . .

I send along a few notes about the immature plumages on the chance that they might save you a little trouble. Spix in his "New Birds of Brazil" has a plate of the first immature plumage which is, I believe, the only one there is and might be worth citing in this connection.[22]

I shall be more than willing to look over your manuscript and will certainly enjoy reading it very much, but I do not promise to do very much criticizing, so many matters in systematic ornithology are matters of opinion rather than fact, and I have always tried to maintain that the other fellow had just as good a right to his opinion as I had to mine. However, send it along if you really want me to look it over, and you can count upon me for any possible assistance, no matter how trivial."[23]

In 1939 he wrote to Joseph J. Hickey at the Linnaean Society on the subject of Carl Buchheister's leaving the directorship of the Massachusetts Audubon Society for the National Audubon Society:

I have, of course, known about Carl's prospective move to New York for some months and have been consulted to a most surprising extent with regard to a possible successor. Carl was inclined to think of you as one, but the group of people running the outfit have a background which would prejudice them strongly against you to start with, a very bad start for all concerned. However, everybody asked what I thought of you as a possibility, and I have played straight with absolutely everybody all round. I told them that I thought you were much too high class a man for the job, that your interests were much more along scientific and research lines, and that if they approached you and you were so good as to ask me my advice I would tell you not to take the job.

You simply can't imagine how disappointed I was not to be able to have a real good talk with you alone when I was last in New York. I want one with you darn soon.[24]

Allan Cruickshank of the National Association of Audubon Societies had been asked by the American Museum to prepare a new handbook on birds of the New York City region—a work that would replace one by Griscom, whom he consulted.

I, of course, have been well aware that my handbook has been out of date for many years past and have been prodding one friend after another in the Linnaean Society as to when they were going to get on the job.

I shall certainly be delighted to give you and the Linnaean Society any help and advice in my power, and I should indeed be disappointed in my friends if after twenty years or more they could not devise a better system than the one used in my own work.[25]

Ludlow conducted a warm correspondence with George Miksch Sutton. It was typical of Griscom that if he liked something he said so, and he had written a positive review of Sutton's book *Mexican Birds: First Impressions*,[26] which had received a negative review from R. C. Murphy. He also wrote Sutton to express his strong favorable response and to praise him for his editorship of the *Wilson*

Bulletin. Griscom's extra effort in writing a personal note made a big difference, as is evident in Sutton's response, in which he really lets down his hair.

> Among the embarrassingly many things I do not know is one which I do—namely, that your letter of January 28, just received, is one of the nicest ever written me by a "higher up"— if you know what I mean. I swear I believe you like the book, and since you do, I wonder why Murphy didn't. In any event, were I to write objectively all the time, I'd never write at all. My feelings are just as important to my life as my thoughts, so far as I can see. Lord knows I'm no mental giant, so I can't depend on said giant to carry all my weight.[27]

One of the ways in which Ludlow Griscom was to have a marked effect on a generation of young ornithologists was in his role as a freshman advisor at Harvard. At first he acted in an informal capacity, but he was subsequently appointed to the Board of Freshman Advisors for the 1934–1935 academic year and continued in this capacity for more than a decade. It is probably through his role as Advisor that he became involved with the Harvard Ornithological Club. The "H.O.C. Boys," as they were generally called, solicited Griscom's advice and frequently recruited him as a speaker at their meetings. In 1934 Griscom formally became an associate of Kirkland House, one of the seven Harvard houses, after he had been affiliated with it for several years. A letter initialed E.A.W. in 1935 suggests that Ludlow's efforts at Kirkland House were well received.

Dear Ludlow:

I can't possibly thank you for all the interest you have taken in Kirkland House, or for all the help you have given to me during the past four years, so I won't even try. But you know, I hope, what I feel, and also how much you have meant to the House. My own feelings about you as an Associate are shared by all the members of the House, and I can only hope that your interest and enthusiasm will continue. You were one of my really inspired appointments, and I trust that you have received some rewards in return for all you have given to us.[28]

When the museum needed a representative on a university committee, it often fell to Ludlow to make the appointment. In addition, Ludlow himself was often appointed to committees. For example, in 1942 he was appointed by President Conant to the University Committee on Pan American Relations. In 1944 he was appointed to the Publishing Committee, in part at least, to increase editorial contact between Harvard University and the Harvard University Press and to keep the press knowledgeable about new faculty manuscripts. In a more informal capacity, Ludlow compiled in 1946 a long list of sixteenth- and seventeenth-century quotes for Conant on early bird migration theories. A curator at the MCZ had a multitude of regular and ad hoc duties.

Ludlow's showmanship rubbed a number of his museum colleagues the wrong way. The dogmatic pronouncements and sharp tongue that made him such a hit in the field with the birders, made for cool relations with many of his museum colleagues. This was particularly so for James L. Peters, curator of birds, and an associate curator, James L. Greenway. Peters was in many ways the antithesis of Ludlow. He was primarily a "museum man," rather than a field-oriented ornithologist. He did significant collecting for the museum, and at times did quite a bit of birdwatching, but rapid field identification of birds was neither his forte nor his inclination. He was rather quiet and precise, whereas Griscom was flamboyant and often at least gave the impression that he was not as careful as he might have been. Certainly the latter opinion was shared by Peters, Greenway, and such notables as Ernst Mayr, who felt that Griscom was something of a dilettante, who didn't spend enough time, effort, and care on his museum studies. How much of this was actually justified is difficult to ascertain, since Ludlow, as part of his gallery playing, undoubtedly enhanced this image. The idea that he could get all the necessary information out of a tray of specimens in an hour when others might take a week, was one that Ludlow cultivated. His critics called it sloppy work. Herbert Friedmann, who worked with Griscom for years on various Central American projects, considered Griscom's museum work acceptable and professional but not imaginative or inspired.[29] His close friend Richard J. Eaton in retrospect provided a general statement of the situation: "Griscom, who rubbed some of his professional colleagues the wrong way (to put it mildly) was a good friend of mine. He had rather irritating faults, to be sure, but on the balance I was very fond of him."[30]

Roger Tory Peterson suggested that Peters was not a field man at all but was strictly a museum person. Further, at public meetings, such as the annual meetings of the Massachusetts Audubon Society, Ludlow's showmanship placed him constantly in the limelight while Peters received little attention, "In a room full of people Griscom would dominate, while Peters would be off in the corner somewhere."[31] Ludlow was getting the attention from the people around Boston, and it could be that a little bit of jealousy was involved.

Ludlow's relations with his colleagues at the museum and elsewhere were a mixed bag, and personality interactions must be factored into any attempt to analyze the quality of his work. In a letter to Witmer Stone, Griscom gave one example of the faultfinding that his work often engendered.

I have been much amused at one reaction I have already received about my Panama Check List. It is curious how people completely fail to read explanations in one's introduction, and several people seem to have failed to notice that I specifically included in my bibliography only those papers which recorded new birds from Panama and omitted all earlier and briefer papers if there was a subsequent one, like yours on the birds of the Canal Zone, that compiled all previous records. My colleague Peters came in in a great huff with quite a pile of his separates dealing with birds of Panama, with which of course I am familiar, annoyed that they had been left out of my bibliography, whereas I, of course, was able to show that they were all summed up and included in his own complete paper on the birds of the Almirante region. And Chapman wrote in great annoyance to Barbour, complaining that I had omitted mention of the list of birds of Barro Colorado Island, in spite of the fact that it doesn't add one single new bird to Panama. Goodness knows I suppose that your expert eye will find enough mistakes in this paper without my being saddled with imaginary ones.[32]

The general pattern of accepting ever-expanding administrative responsibilities at the MCZ, was compounded by the financial deprivations of the Great Depression and by the manpower, material, and financial difficulties accompanying World War II. Ludlow became badly overextended. He spread his time and talents too thin, and this led to his virtual abandonment of serious museum research.

These problems are a consistent theme in Griscom's correspondence. In 1932 Griscom already found himself overburdened and resigned from his editorial position with *Biological Abstracts.* "The situation here at Harvard has developed for me to a certain extent, and I consequently have far more things to do, more varied interests and responsibilities than I did at the time I undertook the section editorship. My real thought in this matter, therefore, is that I have undertaken to do more than I can adequately perform, and the result inevitably is that one or more activities are inadequately covered."[33] The same year he described how the effects of the Great Depression were beginning to be felt: "You are entirely correct in believing that the apple-selling profession is overcrowded here in the East. We are all busted cold and stony broke, and the Museum's endowment fund has been cut 20% and the outside gifts have been reduced to zero for the coming year. I am afraid that we are going to have another hard year in front of us."[34]

Griscom's annual report further underscores the financial difficulties at the museum.

Another indispensable support was the granting by the Corporation of enough money from the Wyeth Fund to take over the salaries of such of our curatorial staff as have hitherto been paid by private gift. The financial security of these men had become almost desperate.[35]

World War II cost the museum dearly in personnel. By 1943 Thomas Barbour had abandoned efforts to replace any of the curatorial staff that had left for military service.[36] In a letter Ludlow expresses how thinly spread his own efforts had become at that time and how difficult it was for him to carry out his responsibilities both inside and outside the museum.

The war has practically eliminated any reasonable possibility of research work that involves long continued writing. My administrative and editorial duties have enormously increased due to the disappearance of all the younger men and in addition to the Museum here at Harvard I now have a great deal to do with the New England Museum in Boston, the Children's Museum in Brookline and the National Audubon Society. In addition to that I have two different war jobs, I'm supposed to be giving a course of Lowell Lectures next winter and am also supposed to be collaborating with Moore and Friedmann on a distributional check-list of the birds of Mexico. I have not fifty percent of adequate time for a single one of these activities.[37]

Despite increased responsibilities, Ludlow managed to publish significant research. His work in systematic ornithology was largely restricted to the twenty-year period 1917–1937, though his collaboration with A. H. Miller, H. Friedmann, and R. T. Moore on the *Distributional Checklist of the Birds of Mexico* was not completed until 1957. After moving to the Boston area, he often published in Boston Society of Natural History and New England Zoological Club publications. Much of his systematic research was done in collaboration with other scientists, but he published a number of substantial monographs under his name alone. Reviews of Griscom's systematic works are generally laudatory and lack the harsh criticism that some of his faunistic work drew. He named a large number of new subspecies, and a few new genera and species, but he also relegated a number of subspecies to synonymy, producing the impression that he was neither an avid "lumper" nor "splitter." Most of his shorter papers and notes were never reviewed in the literature, but some of the more important papers and monographs were, including all of his books.

The Distribution of Bird-Life in Guatemala, dedicated to the memory of Jonathan Dwight, Jr., was published in 1932. It was welcomed by reviewers. The *Wilson Bulletin* review stated that "the work shows all the evidence of being an accurate and authoritative treatise, and will be of great value to all who are concerned with the bird life of Central America."[38] *Ibis* declared, "This will be a standard work for many years on Guatemalan birds, and Mr. Griscom, whose former experience in Central America has fitted him so eminently for the task, has produced a work which is not only of value to the systematist, but which provides much food for reflection for zoogeographers in general."[39] And the reviewer for the *Auk* said that Griscom had "produced a most satisfactory volume, following the model established by Dr. Frank M. Chapman in his reports on the birds of Colombia and Ecuador. . . . While others may not agree with all of his deductions, we congratulate him upon an excellent piece of faunistic work."[40]

The Birds of Dutchess County, New York, from the Records Compiled by Maunsell S. Crosby was brought out the following year to equally favorable reviews. The *Wilson Bulletin* reviewer commented, "Mr. Griscom has done another very creditable piece of work in the compilation of this local list."[41] In *Auk*, Witmer Stone concludes that "Mr. Griscom in his careful preparation of this report, has evidently considered it a labor of love and a tribute to a dear friend, and it will be a satisfaction to Mr. Crosby's many associates to see this work which he had always had in mind, completed in such an admirable manner."[42]

In *The Ornithology of the Republic of Panama* (1935), Griscom returned to his Central American research. *Ibis* noted that "Mr. Griscom has done most useful work in bringing together the bibliography of this region, in giving us a reliable list, and pointing out future work for ecologists."[43]

In 1936 Stone applauded Griscom's work on field identification, and he used two full pages of text in the *Auk* to review a seven-page paper by Griscom on problems of field identification which had appeared that year in *Bird-Lore*.[44] Stone's reviews were in part responsible for Ludlow's growing reputation as a preeminent figure in sight recognition and field ornithology.

Griscom's *Monographic Study of the Red Crossbill* (1937) garnered uniformly positive reviews, receiving criticism only for his choice of the name *anglica* rather than *scotia* for the Scottish crossbill. The *Wilson Bulletin* review concluded that "this paper seems an admirable example of the detailed study of abundant material, and the keen comprehension and admirable restraint through which, alone, the difficult problems of taxonomy seem likely to be solved."[45] Though not without disagreement with some of Griscom's conclusions, the review in *Ibis* is also laudatory:

A revision of the crossbills has been needed for a long time; race after race has been described as new without any attempt to revise the genus, and this has left the ordinary worker in a cloud of doubts. These doubts Mr. Griscom has attempted to settle in what is evidently a very thorough and painstaking work. . . .

This is an excellent systematic study of this difficult group, the proper understanding of which it will go far to elucidate, and it has been very clearly presented.[46]

In 1937 Griscom completed his work on the fourth volume of William Brewster's *Birds of the Lake Umbagog Region*.[47] In his review in the *Auk,* Glover Allen asserted that "the compiler's work has been done carefully, with the advantage of a long perspective, so that he has been enabled to bring out many important contrasts and comparisons."[48]

Birds of Lower Amazonia, written by Griscom and J. C. Greenway, appeared in 1941. "There is much comment with useful critical observations, which render this a valuable and suggestive paper," declared one reviewer. "At the same time the treatment is conservative and the authors point out how little is really known of the habitat preferences of literally hundreds of species."[49]

In all Griscom published descriptions of 174 subspecies and five new species after he arrived at the MCZ. Two of the species still stand in Peters' Checklist; three were relegated to subspecies status.

When he published *Modern Bird Study* in 1945, he received substantial criticism in several reviews. His friends and associates Thomas Barbour, in the *Wilson Bulletin,*[50] and Francis H. Allen, in the *Bulletin of the Massachusetts Audubon Society,*[51] gave the book favorable reviews, as did J. T. Zimmer in the *Auk.*[52] The critiques by Herbert Friedmann in *Bird-Banding*[53] and Frank Pitelka in *Condor,*[54] however, expressed some serious reservations. Both men challenged Griscom's interpretations of adaptability and adaptation. In addition, Friedmann pointed out that the areas of ornithology that Griscom chose to omit—including anatomy, physiology, banding, and experimental behavioristic studies—were some of the areas of greatest advance in modern bird study. The general sense of several reviews suggested that the book was mistitled. All acknowledged, however, that the book was aimed at a lay or amateur audience, and that the faunistic chapters were the strongest in the book.

The Birds of Nantucket (1948) received noncritical reviews from Winsor Tyler in the *Bulletin of the Massachusetts Audubon Society,*[55] and John W. Aldrich in *Bird-Banding,*[56] as well as a rather positive review by Frederick C. Lincoln in the *Wilson Bulletin,* which concludes: "The book is admirably written and may well serve as a model for future reports on insular avifaunas."[57] But his *Birds of Concord,* published the following year, was met by mixed notices. In general, the reviewers thought that in this work Griscom was not as careful as he should have been, oversimplified situations, and tended to be dogmatic. Some found

the book sloppy in places. The following excerpts, arranged in increasing critical tone, give some of the strengths and shortcomings that the reviewers
saw.

To this reviewer this book has three outstanding values: (1) there is a valuable discussion (100 pages) of population changes and their actual or pre-
sumed causes in many instances, appropriate for the book's subtitle, "A
study in population trends." (2) these same pages would be a good reading
assignment for students in ornithology at the college level; and (3) the record of nearly a century of field work in the Concord area lays the foundation for important studies in the future there. . . .
The experienced student soon will realize that the author presents many
of his data in a rather dogmatic fashion, making the picture seem clearer,
and often simpler, than actually it may turn out to be. . . . No bibliographic
citations are given for any of the population figures. . . .
A familiarity with two preceding works authored or co-authored by Griscom [*Modern Bird Study* and *The Birds of Nantucket*] . . . does not prepare
one to expect the wealth of useful data contained in the present volume.
It should be stimulating to both amateur and advanced students of North
American birds.[58]

Nobody can have read thus far in this very inadequate review without realiz-
ing something of the reviewer's admiration for the book, as well as the hope-
lessness of his attempting to condense its value into the few pages available.
It is not, however, without faults in details. . . . " [Then follows a listing of
errors on eighteen different pages.][59]

This is by no means an ordinary book of the birds of a restricted area; it
differs from the "usual treatment" in that trends in populations and the ecological factors behind them are stressed continually. . . .
Throughout the book an attempt has been made to apply general biological principles to birds. Many applications are admirably done in straightforward and simple fashion. However, in many instances the author seems to
rely on broad, sweeping statements; in others, there is confusion and misuse
of various terms. . . .
Although I take exception to various other such generalizations [con-
cerning population trends], the book represents one of the first attempts to
deal quantitatively with localized populations of birds over long periods of
time. It is well written and is worthwhile, pleasant, and thought-provoking
reading."[60]

In this book, the most expert field ornithologist of our generation compares his notes with those of William Brewster, the most expert of the preceding generation. . . .

While these histories of populations are fascinating, the critical ornithologist will be concerned at the superficiality of the discussion of results. Terms such as Gaussian curve, periodicity, capacity, etc. are loosely used. Furthermore, the author, who is also an expert botanist, could have given a more specific description of the vegetation, citing the numbers and kinds of plants. The discussion of cycles (p. 123) shows an amazing lack of understanding of cyclic phenomena. The words density (birds per unit) and population (total birds) are frequently confused. . . .

While the Concord ornithologists will find this book of immense value, its numerous deficiencies will tantalize the serious ornithologist.[61]

The book is in two parts, the first dealing in a rather general manner with population trends and their causes, while the second is a systematic list of the species occurring in the district, with notes on their status since the latter half of the last century. It must be said at once that the first part, although purporting to take the modern biological standpoint, is a quite inadequate treatment of the subject. On almost every page examples of loose writing, inconsequential reasoning, and unwarranted generalizations may be found. No supporting data are given. . . .

It is a pity that the tremendous body of quantitative data collected (so we are told) by Brewster has not been more adequately presented.[62]

In *The Birds of Concord,* Griscom had tried to make significant ecological correlations and establish causal relationship in the changes in bird distribution with time. His supporters found the attempt challenging and provocative; his detractors found it superficial and careless. Certainly a more thorough peer review before publication could have spared Ludlow much of the more biting criticism.

On 8 January 1946 Thomas Barbour died unexpectedly, leaving the MCZ without a leader. Henry Bigelow became the acting director, not Ludlow, and the search began for a successor to Barbour. Griscom's lack of a doctorate would probably have prevented him from becoming the director in any case, but political forces made this a moot point. According to Edith Griscom, Bigelow disliked Barbour and was an avowed enemy of Ludlow. He not only blocked any chance that Ludlow might have had for the directorship but from time to time subjected him to minor humiliations, such as requesting Ludlow to punch in on a time clock. She added that Barbour had promised the directorship to Ludlow, but he clearly lacked the authority to do so. There is nothing in the written record to suggest that Ludlow even wanted the job. Surely he must have seen the handwriting on the wall.

A July 1946 letter to his good friend Guy Emerson suggests that Ludlow was sincerely pleased with the man finally selected to head the MCZ and that he fully understood the changing directions for the museum and other factors that would not have made his own candidacy feasible.

> I am delighted with the new Director selected and he is personally my private preference and hope, but Dr. Bigelow and I were afraid that he would decline. He is Alfred S. Romer, one of the brilliant paleontologists of the country and already a member of the National Academy of Sciences. He is consequently most qualified to act as the scientific leader of a research institution. There has been some talk that this Museum should be tied in more closely to the primary educational functions of the University. Should any such trend develop, Romer has been a full Professor of Zoology for years, Chairman of the Division, and has served as Director of the Biological Laboratories. He has, therefore, a perfect liaison between the research and the teaching staffs. Moreover, he is only about 45, so that he has a good 20 years to go before any question of retirement could arise.[63]

Although Griscom developed a warm relationship with Alfred Romer, it would not be of the same depth he had enjoyed with the previous director. His position as an associate of Thomas Barbour had been professionally a desirable and profitable one. Ludlow summed this up nicely in his condolence letter to Mrs. Barbour. "I consider that I had a most fortunate life in being in almost daily contact with so forceful, energetic, and stimulating a spirit and personality as Thomas Barbour. No matter what fate may have in store for me in the future, I will never again be as really well off and fortunately circumstanced as when I had the privilege of being his assistant."[64]

Five years later Ludlow would suffer his first major stroke, and his full participation in the affairs of the MCZ would be at an end.

Ornithological and Birding Expeditions   6

Ludlow Griscom loved to travel. At the age of seventeen, he discovered birds in a serious way, and thereafter his trips were busman's holidays, with birding the prime focus, or at least a dominant one. Griscom did not keep an extensive diary of his early adventures in Central America or Europe. Usually all that was recorded, or now remains, are bird lists. On several trips, however, either Edith or other companions did keep more detailed records, and sometimes people wrote down stories that Griscom would relate about his adventures.

In September 1908 Griscom, with his newfound obsession with birds, camped out for nearly three weeks in the wilderness north of Lake Temiacouata, in Quebec. The following June he was off to Europe, where he visited England, France, and Switzerland. This was his first journey since joining the Linnaean Society, and it sharpened his focus on birds. He sailed to Europe again the same year, taking the northern route, crossing the Grand Banks of Newfoundland on 25 November, and again on the return on 9 December. In 1911 and 1912, he again made European junkets.

By 1910 he had begun making local forays into ornithologically interesting areas. In June he visited North Pownal, Vermont, and climbed to the summit of Mt. Greylock, in Massachusetts. That December, he took a sea trip to the fishing banks off Seabright, New Jersey, looking for pelagic birds. He spent Christmas at his grandfather's Horseshoe Plantation in Tallahassee, Florida. He was to make winter and spring visits to the plantation on a fairly regular basis for decades, often inviting guests to birdwatch with him. The following year he visited Cobb's Island, Virginia, an important waterfowl hunting area, and reached the summits of Slide Mountain in the Catskills of New York and Killington Peak in Vermont.

In 1915 Griscom made a winter trip to Currituck Sound, in North Carolina, and while teaching a summer course in Charlottesville, Virginia, he managed a trip through the Blue Ridge country.

Griscom's more professionally oriented expeditions were mostly to Central America. To understand their ornithological significance, including his naming dozens of new subspecies, it is important to understand the background and context for his work in avian systematics.

In North America observations on geographic variation in physical characteristics within bird species date back to the last half of the nineteenth century to Spencer F. Baird, second secretary of the Smithsonian Institution, and Joel A. Allen, who became editor of the *Auk,* the most prestigious journal of American ornithology, and a president of the American Ornithologists' Union (AOU).[1] Thinking about variation was stimulated by Darwin's theory of evolution and eventually led to the idea that geographical differences were manifested as varieties, which intergraded in characters, and species, which did not. Elliott Coues, an aggressive nineteenth-century ornithologist, argued strongly for a trinomial nomenclature in which a third Latin name designated the variety, or what we would now call subspecies, and incorporated their use into his publications. J. A. Allen threw his considerable influence behind the case for trinomials, as did other prominent ornithologists such as Robert Ridgway. This school of thought was primarily American; strong resistance to trinomials developed in England and in much of the rest of Europe.

The controversies over bird names (different ornithologists sometimes used different names for the same bird) was one of the issues that led to the formation of the American ornithologists' Union (AOU) in 1883. It was hoped that an authoritative body of ornithologists could produce a standardized set of bird names. In the first AOU checklist trinomials were incorporated. Hence the subspecies concept became important to American ornithologists and taxonomists. However, subspecies meant different things to different ornithologists. Some, like J. A. Allen, viewed subspecies as a means of describing geographical variation within species; others became preoccupied with naming things, enumerating finer and finer morphological differences, causing a proliferation of described subspecies and clogging the literature with Latin names.

Opposition to trinomials developed both among some professionals and particularly among amateur ornithologists, who found subspecies confusing.

Nonetheless, the subspecies concept became an important part of American ornithological thinking by the end of the nineteenth century. Large numbers of specimens were required in order to identify small, persistent differences in morphological characters, and as museum collections swelled, ornithologists named large numbers of new subspecies. This was particularly true for regions of the world where little or nothing was known of the avifauna.

It was into this setting that Ludlow Griscom entered the American Museum of Natural History (AMNH), as an assistant curator of birds, in 1917. Systematics, at least as practiced in the early twentieth century, was largely learned through apprenticeship, which Griscom served with Frank Chapman and other experts on the museum staff. Although we have little record of his early years at the museum, Griscom states in a letter to Frank Chapman, "It is a pleasure to add that should this paper have any real merit it is largely due to the training that I received in this field at your own hands."[2]

Griscom would become an internationally acknowledged authority on Central and South American birds, naming more than 250 new subspecies and 14 new species of birds, although only a small part of these would be birds collected on his own expeditions. Griscom made it quite clear what he thought about naming subspecies:

The recognition of the finely drawn subspecies of the day is another question entirely. I wish clearly to distinguish between the bearing which systematic ornithology has upon geographical distribution and evolution (in which I am very much interested), and the purely taxonomic problem as to what degree of difference is worth recognizing as a subspecies (in which I am not at all interested). It will be apparent in the latter case that we are dealing with a matter of opinion, subject to a wide degree of individual or personal variation based in part at least on the particular interests of each one. What is more to the point, any such criterion is an artificial one, a mere rule of thumb, and the variations of animals will not conform to any as yet proposed, nor will they even approach conformity.[3]

Why Griscom chose Latin America as an area of concentration is unknown, but a letter by Chapman about Griscom states, "there have been absolutely no restrictions on the extent or nature of his researches in the field in which he was given essentially complete freedom of action. This field (Mexico, Central America, the West Indies and Galapagos) contains more interesting problems than the remainder of the Western Hemisphere."[4] Perhaps it was simply that he opportunistically chose to accompany W. DeW. Miller on a collecting trip to Nicaragua in 1917.

Griscom went on this extended collecting trip when most of Central America was still wild and little known. He sold a small piece of property near Tallahassee to provide some of the funds for the expedition. He sailed from New Orleans with Miller on 21 February, for Havana, Cuba, and from there to Guanajay on the twenty-fourth. They made two-day stops in the Canal Zone, taking the train from Colón to Panama City, and then by boat up the east coast of Costa Rica to Port Limón. They crossed Costa Rica by train, stopping in San José overnight before embarking on the Nicaragua expedition, which was to last from 6 March through 22 May, when by previous arrangement Griscom left the expedition and returned to the United States. Griscom recorded little of his adventures on this expedition besides the usual bird lists. However, Miller, the leader of the expedition, kept both a field notebook and a diary, and so we can piece together some of the expedition's adventures.

On 6 March their ship was anchored at San Juan del Sur, Nicaragua. By the next day they were in Corinto, where William B. Richardson, a collector with considerable Nicaraguan experience, joined the party. They went by train (there were only five or six automobiles in the entire country at that time)[5] to León and then to Managua. On 11 March they traveled to Savanna Grande, about twelve miles south of Managua, where they picked up their mules and prepared to leave for Matagalpa, over 100 miles to the north. They began to collect birds; Griscom shot a trogon (*Trogon melanocephela*). On 14 March the field journal reads, "Left . . . 2.30 AM on mules . . . rode 37 miles."[6] Matagalpa became their base of operations, with short trips made by mule into the surrounding countryside. They often traveled by moonlight to escape the heat and dust. They collected at San Rafael del Norte among the mountains of northern Nicaragua, where they recorded fourteen birds new for Nicaragua before there return to Matagalpa.[7]

On 28 March the journal reads, "At house in S. Rafael all day to abt 3.30 when we started on mules for the high cold mtn-forest where is Quetzel etc." Three days later they encountered "wonderful birds today, the Swallow-tailed Kite, the Scarlet Macaw, the Quetzal and the Grey Solitaire. . . . We were all sitting in our camp beside the little house on the bare hill after 'cafe' when Griscom exclaimed something about Quetzals and looking down the steep hillside I saw a couple of brilliant green birds flying by along the brook at the foot of the hill. . . . [He] handed me my gun and I brought down the female with a #10, not without compunction at killing so wonderful a bird."[8] The journal mostly lists birds collected, but occasionally includes asides such as, "The sd [second] bird Griscom shot at such close range that it was too greatly mutilated to preserve,"[9] or "Griscom photograph[ed] tree with bird at or near nest."[10]

In early May they returned to Managua, took a train to Granada, and after a few days collecting at the extinct volcano Mombacho, they took the steamship *Victoria* across Lake Nicaragua to San Carlos. Then they went by motor boat to Los Sabalos, which they had decided to make their local headquarters for a nine-day stay. On the return trip they stayed for three days of collecting at San Francisco. They returned by steamship to Granada, where Griscom left the expedition to catch an early steamer home.

The bulk of the scientific aspects of the expedition were published in three American Museum *Novitates* in 1925. Miller and Griscom described 36 new subspecies and a new species of poorwill (*Nyctiphrynus lautus*), which was reduced to a subspecies of *N. ocellatus* in the 1940 Checklist of J. L.Peters.[11] Miller apparently was not interested in publishing a general avifauna for Nicaragua and was frequently chastised by Frank Chapman at the AMNH for his tardiness in working up the Nicaraguan material. Finally, Chapman handed over the publication of the Nicaraguan material to Griscom.[12] Because Griscom left the AMNH in 1927, the report on the entire collection was never published.

World War I produced a hiatus in Griscom's museum work. After his discharge from the army in February 1919, Griscom went to Florida for a month, grieving with his family over the death of his father. It is clear from his bird lists that he managed to slip away for a trip to Miami, the Everglades, and Long Key. Before the year was out, he also took several short trips to Cape May, New Jersey, made his first trip to the Kittatinny Mountains, and returned for a visit to Florida.

The year 1920 was a fairly quiet one for Ludlow, with only a brief trip to Hatley, Quebec, and the first of his trips to Newfoundland, botanizing and birding. The latter trip lasted three weeks in August, and he traveled to Blanc Sablon, Labrador, stopping at North Sidney, Cape Breton Island, and Curling, and Frenchman's Cove in Bay of Islands, Newfoundland.

The following year Griscom made his first and second trips to Rhinebeck, Dutchess County, New York, where his best friend Maunsell Crosby lived. These trips were to become frequent, until Crosby's untimely death in 1931. Most of the month of July and early August was spent on the west coast of Newfoundland, as would be the case the following summer. In his ornithological diary for 1923, Griscom mentions a swing south through New Orleans and on to Brownsville, Texas. On 6 January he visited the famed King Ranch. Most of July was spent in the Shickshock Mountains of Gaspe County, Quebec, where he climbed Mount Logan and Mount Albert.

In February 1924, Griscom set sail from New York on a collecting expedition to Panama, which was to last through March and on which he had some significant adventures. The expedition sailed through the Bahamas and spent a day on Haiti before steaming on to the Canal Zone. They left Panama City, steamed west along the Pacific coast until disembarking near Aguadulce, and headed inland to the mountains. Griscom detailed his adventures in a 1924 *Natural History* article that also hints at their ornithological importance.

> Between the Volcan de Chiriqui and the Pico Calovevora in Veraguas lies a mountainous country unexplored and unvisited by white men, inhabited only by wild Indians. No knowledge exists regarding its topography. The courses of the rivers of the interior and their tributaries are pure guesswork, the location of the higher peaks varies from map to map as much as twenty miles, and their altitude as much as 2000 feet! . . .
>
> I left New York February 5, 1924, accompanied by three assistants, to make a preliminary reconnaissance of the region. . . .
>
> Nor had anybody ever been in the interior, and two years before a couple of Panamanians who had gone there to take a census of the Indians had been killed. Unless the Indians themselves, therefore, would guide us into their own country, there was not the remotest prospect of our reaching the mountains, much less of making a sojourn there.[13]

Griscom describes a number of adventures, from drinking *chicha* (the maize-fermented beer) to curing the illness of the local chief's wife with aspirin and a laxative. The chief then became their guide over difficult mountain trails.

> Penetrating the barrier of dense forest, we camped on the slope of the Cerro Flores at 3700 feet, and here we spent ten fruitful and fascinating days. . . . Every morning the party scattered in four or five directions, and it was very exciting to meet at noon, and see what the combined bag contained, and who had done the best collecting. Every day brought additional species, or another specimen of some choice rarity, such as a thrush, tanager, or quail dove. . . .
>
> One day a great flock of giant swifts was discovered darting around the summit of a bare peak, their wings making a humming sound, audible for a mile. The difficulty of shooting ducks on the wing paled into insignificance beside the feat of hitting these arrow-swift darters, which, as though shot from a bow, were carried by their momentum for several hundred

yards. That day we tried giant-swift pie for lunch, as every morsel of meat was precious. Although quite tender, it tasted like a cross between ashes and string, which I trust did not impair its nutritive value. . . .

The bird life was utterly unexpected. Not a single one of the mountain species found farther east occurred here. Instead, the fauna was obviously that of the Costa Rican highlands, but with this difference, that isolation and remoteness were accompanied by a certain amount of variation. Several at least of the birds obtained are new subspecies. Benson shot a new species of *Scytalopus*, small wrenlike birds of secretive habits, and I collected a very distinct new species of a peculiar finch (*Pselliophorus*), hitherto the only member of its genus. It was the reward of the explorer that, at the very least, every bird found automatically extended its range far to the east.

The highest point at which a camp could possibly be established was 4500 feet. Here Valentine and I spent two days, ascending to the cloud forest and collecting each day. An Indian runner carried our birds to the base camp to be prepared by those remaining below.

The situation deteriorated when the local natives decided that the Griscom party was up to no good. Short on food and with their guides abandoning them, Griscom and his party had no option but to leave as quickly as possible while they still could. They somehow made it back safely, thus concluding a grand adventure.

Griscom loved to tell stories of his adventures at dinner after a long day in the field, and after a martini or two, his recollections would pour forth, much to the delight of his birding companions. David Garrison recorded one such remembrance in his journal. "Griscom went up alone to the top of the continental divide, about 6000 feet, where he spent two nights wholly alone. At dawn the rising sun illuminated the Atlantic on his one hand and the Pacific on his other. He was in a beautiful and wild country, completely dependent on himself in any circumstances. Here he studied, and collected at each shot, birds new to science."[14]

Griscom described nearly a dozen new subspecies from Panama in a 1924 *American Museum Novitates,* and three new species, *Scytalopus chiriquensis, Pselliophorus luteoviridis,* and *Chlorospingus tacarunae.* All three were still recognized as species in Peters' Checklist, but *chiriquensis* disappeared into synonymy with *S. argentifrons* in the recent Sibley and Monroe taxonomy.[15]

Griscom started 1926 with a collecting trip, financed in part by the *New York Times,* to British Honduras (now Belize), Yucatan, and Cozumel Island. The expedition included Gregory Mason, the organizer; Herbert J. Spinden, an archeologist from the Peabody Museum at Harvard; Ogden T. McClurg, a commander in the Naval Reserve; and Francis Whiting, the youngest of the party at age twenty-one. Its aim was to collect ornithological specimens for the American Museum of Natural History and to discover Mayan ruins and associated anthropological and archeological artifacts. Although Griscom did not make detailed records of the various events, disasters, and associated anecdotes, we do have several letters written at the time of the trip or shortly afterward. Gregory Mason wrote a book about the expedition, *Silver Cities of Yucatan,*[16] which details the difficult conditions under which they were operating, the adventures they had, and the personality of Griscom, who at age thirty-five was still in his physical prime and ready for hardship and adventure. Despite the sometimes exaggerated prose of the probably apocryphal quotes, and a trend toward the dramatic, this book presents a reasonable picture of the trials and tribulations that beset adventurers in Central America during the 1920s.

Aboard the ship *Albert,* the conditions were close and uncomfortable, and Griscom slept on deck. He was opportunistic in his collecting and birdwatching, always keeping an eye open for something new.

> Griscom was elated. This was a new "farthest south" record for nesting fishhawks. This was the second time our ornithologist had scored, for he had already seen a herring gull in Belize harbor—a "farthest south" record for that species. . . .
>
> We armed ourselves with shotguns and gamegetters. The gamegetter is a very useful little implement, consisting of a folding, skeleton stock and two barrels, the larger 41 or 44 caliber and the smaller 22. Without the stock it is a pistol. With the stock it is either rifle or shotgun, for either ball or shot can be used in both barrels. Griscom says he has brought down game as heavy as large hawks with a gamegetter and he expects to bag most of his specimens with this tool. . . .
>
> The fourth time we poled her into a tiny ditch a native had dug through this grass-covered mud bank and pulled her out on the beach before his one-roomed hut. The man was out fishing, and when his wife saw us she ran into the woods with one child in her arms and another clinging to her hand.
>
> "You see, Griscom, you really ought to shave," observed McClurg.

Later, Griscom commented on a bird he had collected:

> "Here's something that makes our little shore adventure worth while, fellah," exclaimed the ornithologist, reaching carefully into a big pocket of his hunting coat. He pulled out an oriole.

"I can't be sure till I get back to the museum and check up, but I'll bet you a season subscription to the opera that that's a new subspecies!"

"It's beautifully shot." There was hardly a stain on the smooth golden feathers. "What's that between its beak?" I asked, leaning over the bird.

"A dried leaf to keep it from soiling itself." . . .

Griscom was below skinning birds and fumigating himself the while with his great curved tobacco burner. After half an hour he rushed top side, with his face a sicklier hue than any visage I have ever seen outside of a moving picture studio. . . .

His recovery was remarkable. . . . But he did no more skinning below decks. And he made no objections when Belize John, his apprentice in the art, announced he guessed he'd "quit sknnin" birds till the table's steadier. . . .

Eager as we are for Chunyaxche we decide to stay here tomorrow, dedicating the day to a gigantic bird hunt for Griscom's benefit. . . .

Griscom and I were to take the smaller boat to the nearest beach and hunt birds all morning. Whiting and McClurg with gamegetters, Gough and Nelson with Griscom's two sixteen gauge shotguns, were to take the larger boat to the farther side of the island. . . .

Griscom particularly wanted a rail. We heard these shy birds calling on every side but could not see one. . . .

They were covered with mud and sweat and the carcasses of mosquitoes, but their bearing was triumphant. For Griscom could cut another notch in the upper barrel of his gamegetter, he had shot another bird new to the catalog of ornithology. It was a flycatcher of obscure coloration. . . .

Birds of many sizes, hues and peculiarities of shape were arranged in rows on the sloping top of the engine room—just forward of that part of it which serves as our dinner table. Griscom went over them quickly. . . .

All afternoon Griscom skinned birds. So did Belize John, who seems to have a natural bent for this art. We others hunted again, but without getting another specimen of Griscom's fly-catcher or one of the rails he desired above everything.

The bird collecting continued.

Griscom said he would like to get one more skin. Now although these birds [egrets] were almost near enough to be killed with stones, they were perched over the very thickest part of the mangrove.

"Push around into the little bay and see if we can't pot a straggler where we won't lose him," directed the ornithologist.

"We've lost an oar," exclaimed Whiting. . . .

"Yes, let's look for it now," said Griscom, "we may need it yet." . . .

I saw an egret alighting on an outer branch of the clump we had left. If shot there he ought to fall where we could easily reach him.

"Look out, fellows," I cried, and shot, like an utter fool, with the end of my gun not two feet from Griscom's right ear.

The poor chap thought that his ear drum had been broken. He said he could hear nothing on that side. . . . McClurg and Whiting cursed me for the idiot I was, then we sat there in the gloom for an awful minute, while Griscom held his head in his hands.

At last he raised his head and said through his teeth: "Let's get the oar."

Whiting said that the egret which had offered the occasion for my asininity to be exercised at Griscom's expense had used its last strength to float into the heart of the maze of bow-legged mangrove roots.

But Griscom jumped overboard and gave an extraordinary exhibition of retrieving. After splashing through water and mud to his waist he climbed a mangrove and went from tree to tree like an ape till we lost sight of him. To our surprise he returned immediately—with the egret.

The hunters returned to the ship, eleven miles away, after dark. The engine wouldn't start and the sparkplug was dropped overboard, so they had to take turns rowing. At one point Griscom suggested the happy thought that if the boat sinks, "at least two of us can keep above water by standing on the other fellow's shoulders," and further suggested, "We might draw lots now to see who'll be the foundations." After a long and tortuous trip, they somehow found the mother ship in the dark. It turned out that losing the sparkplug hadn't really made any difference, since the gas tank was filled with kerosene.

They spent four days at Cozumel, where Griscom hired small boys to hunt birds, but malaria broke out among the group. Because of the various illnesses, and differences in interests, the group split up from time to time. In Cozumel, Griscom received the bad news from home that his grandmother was dying and that he should return home as soon as possible. He arranged passage to New York on a steamer, thus ending his involvement with the expedition.

Two *Novitates* in 1926 contain the descriptions of five new subspecies and a new species, *Elaenea chinchorrensis,* found during the trip. This species was reduced to a subspecies *E. martinica chinchorrensis* in Peters' Checklist.[17]

After his marriage to Edith, the tenor of his trips changed somewhat, but not the ornithological focus. She warned Ludlow that after they had children she would still be willing to go on trips but that she would always take the children.

She made sure that this was clearly understood. In addition, Griscom's mother had told Edith that Ludlow had suffered serious bouts of malaria on two occasions, and his doctors warned that a third case might prove fatal. Hence she insisted that Ludlow not travel to any malarial areas. The latter policy was not strictly adhered to, but that of bringing the children along was. For Ludlow these agreements had some merit. He maintained that when your children are born, you lost about 90 percent of your wife's companionship. In light of this inevitable loss, he tried to plan trips each year in which a governess or nurse was brought along to help with the children, so he and Edith could have some of their old companionship.

Griscom was certainly not one to let any grass grow below his feet. On 3 February 1927, he and Edith, now nearly five months pregnant, and Maunsell Crosby departed on an expedition to Panama, under the auspices of the American Museum of Natural History. In addition they had along a man to help collect and skin the birds collected. Edith wrote up the trip for the *Junior League Magazine,* and excerpts from the unedited manuscript and from interviews describe the primary localities visited and a few of the many adventures.[18]

They hired a skipper, "Big Bill," and his boat for a three-week exploration of the uninhabited Pearl Islands off the Panama Coast, which featured immense seabird colonies.

> San José was our first stop, a typical sandy beach awaiting us blazing in the sun and the cool forest behind. We roamed the hot beach and then with field glasses and "gamegetters" the men departed separately planning to meet for a swim in the nearby lagoon. That day land birds were being collected, brilliant little honey creepers and irridescent humming birds. . . . There were strange sweet little songs for the ear, flashes of bird-like color and clumps of gray-green Bromelia for the eye and tragedy following in the terse bark of the little game getter and a feathery being was added to scientific knowledge. . . . At mid-day we paused beside the bank of the lagoon and debated a cooling plunge, but suddenly a long brown form slid silently down the opposite bank into the water followed by five others and disappeared with a slight ripple. We left the crocodiles in undisturbed possession.

At Galera Island they found boobies breeding in large numbers and photographed them.

> We collected ten boobies at Galera, as the Museum did not have this species. It did not seem fair to leave them all to the young taxidermist, so all the bird men turned to work. We spread a sail above the deck as an awning and as the schooner chugged along peacefully on the calm water, the knives did

Ludlow Griscom, 1891, age one year.
Photograph courtesy of Andrew
Griscom.

Clement Acton Griscom, Jr., Ludlow
Griscom's father (ca. 1893). Photograph
courtesy of Andrew Griscom.

Genevieve Ludlow Griscom, Ludlow
Griscom's mother (ca. 1910). Photograph courtesy of Andrew Griscom.

Griscom's paternal grandfather, Clement Acton Griscom, Sr. (born 1831). Photograph by H. C. Phillips, Philadelphia, 1965. Courtesy of Andrew Griscom.

Ludlow Griscom's paternal grandmother, Frances Biddle Griscom, with Clement Acton Griscom, Jr., on her lap (1868). Photograph by Wenderoth, Taylor, and Brown. Courtesy of Andrew Griscom.

Griscom's maternal grandfather, William Ludlow *(right)* kneeling beside George Armstrong Custer *(center)*, Black Hills expedition, July 1874. Standing at rear is Custer's orderly, Private Noonan. The Indian *(left)* is Bloody Knife, chief scout of the expedition. Photograph courtesy of Andrew Griscom.

Griscom's maternal grandmother, Genevieve Sprigg Ludlow (ca. 1870). Photograph by Sarony, New York. Courtesy of Andrew Griscom.

Ludlow Griscom (*right*) with his brother, Acton, and father, Clement (ca. 1902). Photograph courtesy of Andrew Griscom.

Ludlow Griscom (ca. 1910). Photograph courtesy of Andrew Griscom.

Ornithology Department, American Museum of Natural History (AMNH), 1924. *Left to right, sitting:* Ludlow Griscom, Waldron DeW. Miller, Frank M. Chapman, Robert Cushman Murphy, James P. Chapin; *standing:* Charles O'Brien, Alice K. Fraser, Jonathan Dwight, Jr., Elsie M. B. Naumburg. Photograph by J. Kirschner. Courtesy Library Photographic Archives, AMNH, neg. no. 310800.

Southern façade of the American Museum of Natural History, New York City (1929). Photograph by Irving Dutcher. Courtesy Department Library Services, American Museum of Natural History, neg. no. 271681.

Ludlow Griscom in Montana, September 1927. Photograph by Edith S. Griscom.
Courtesy of Andrew Griscom.

Ludlow Griscom aboard the *H.S. Albert,* at Ascension Bay, examining the birds collected that day. Photograph published originally in *Silver Cities of Yucatan,* by Gregory Mason (New York: Harper Brothers, 1927).

Edith Sloan Griscom with children (*left to right*) Joan, Edith, and Andrew (ca. June 1934), in Connecticut. Photograph courtesy of Andrew Griscom.

their work, the big birds were turned inside out and the invisible sharks and barracudas received a share of the days work. Dried out with corn meal and treated with arsenic they were then stuffed with cotton and laid in a neat row to dry. . . .

From Galera we went to the mainland, where the men were happy on Cape Carachiné collecting some very interesting land birds. It was the first time the Cape had been visited by ornithologists and they made the best of their few days. There is a forest of Cuipo trees there, huge trunks up to ten feet in diameter and reaching skyward. Glorious macaws lit on their branches far out of gunshot reach and standing silent you could hear the trogons note booming through the forest. . . . they found their most interesting birds, a rare antbird, a South American woodpecker previously unknown in Central America, a tiny blue and yellow warbler, a glittering green humming bird, a blue honey creeper and a rose colored tanager—some of these new to science. Every evening the bright feathered birds were sorted on the deck and the thrill of a possible new species felt by everyone. All the woodpeckers, parrots, pigeons and tinamous were added to our menu, a welcome change from the inevitable beans and rice.

Edith outlined some of the hardships endured.

Food consisted of bread and butter and rice and beans, and birds shot for eating purposes. The diet Ludlow chose was outrageous. . . . The yellowlegs were particularly delicious. . . .

Eventually Ludlow decided to go up a small river, went up in a boat—his error. The tide went out and left the boat stranded on the mud. There were sick Indians camped along the river—probably malaria. Since I was pregnant it was important that I didn't get bitten, so they put me in a bunk and covered me, all but my head, with blankets, and connected a fan to the boat batteries to keep the mosquitoes from biting me. The men proceeded for the next three weeks to take quinine.[19]

A 1927 *Novitates* included the description of 5 new subspecies from the trip.

They arrived home on 21 March, none the worse for wear. No one had contracted malaria. On 29 June, Edith gave birth to a daughter, Edith Rapallo. The happy event did not long keep the family at home. With Edith and the two-month infant in tow, Griscom departed on 29 August for a month in Cameron, Madison County, Montana. A little over a month after their return they moved to Cambridge, Massachusetts, and established their home in a huge old house on Fayerweather Street. Griscom spent the winter and spring learning the birding localities around Boston, but the whole family spent three weeks in June out at Lake Owen, in Bayfield County, northwestern Wisconsin, and Ludlow took a short trip down to Charleston, South Carolina, in November. In 1929 the Griscoms vacationed in Dutchess County in May and June, and had a summer cottage at Cohasset, Massachusetts. Ludlow spent a good deal of time on Cape Cod and made five trips down Monomoy.

In 1930 he spent a month in Guatemala with Maunsell Crosby, on a trip instigated by Edith. Griscom was finishing up the writing of a book on the birds of Guatemala, and Edith was upset that Ludlow was writing this definitive book without ever having set foot in Guatemala. "You publish the book and people will ask when were you there, and you can't say, 'I've never been there;' it's just not done in society."[20] Unfortunately, Griscom did not write much about the trip, and as usual on these long collecting trips all that survived are lists of bird species encountered. Ludlow hated to fly, so although Crosby was willing to fly down, Ludlow insisted on going by train and boat. While they spent the end of June and most of July in Guatemala, Edith stayed home and made the index for the Guatemalan bird book.

In Guatemala the two men did a good deal of collecting, but Griscom's descriptions of more than three dozen new subspecies and three species had already been published from his studies of the Dwight collection of birds. One of the species he named, *Cryptoglaux rostrata,* has been reduced to a subspecies, *Aegolius ridgwayi rostratus.* The other two species fared better. The flightless Atitlan Grebe, or "Poc," is known only from Lake Atitlan and was named *Podilymbus gigas* by Griscom. The species still stands today, but unfortunately the bird is apparently extinct. The other new species (and new genus), *Xenotriccus callizonus,* the Belted Flycatcher, published with Dwight, still stands as a valid species.[21]

The Guatemala trip was to be the last major trip that Ludlow was to make without Edith and the children for nearly two decades. A son, Andrew, and a second daughter, Joan, were to join young Edith within three years. With these burgeoning family responsibilities, Ludlow settled into a more modest routine. His travel diary contains entries for Norway, Maine, and Myrtle Beach, South Carolina, as well as a wide variety of day trips around Massachusetts, and for the summers of 1931 through 1933 a "summer cottage at Peterboro, N. H. with family."[22] He also continued his trips to Tallahassee in 1933 and 1934. Ludlow did manage to get away for the International Ornithological Congress at Oxford, England, leaving aboard ship on 22 June 1934, and not sailing for the United States until 2 August. In February 1936 Ludlow, Edith, the three children, and a governess left on a six-week trip to Jamaica. As was apparently customary for him at this point in his life, Ludlow had six hundred Union

Club cigarettes sent ahead to the United Fruit Company ship *Calamaras* for the voyage. The Griscoms were accompanied by Frank and Louisa Hunnewell, who were close family friends.

Griscom's field journal from this trip provides a glimpse of their ornithological activities. In the course of his descriptions, he frequently commented on the land clearing and comcomitant habitat destruction that had already occurred on Jamaica and his keen awareness of it.

> *March 4th.* P.M. walk up Mt. Diablo, 4 miles along road. . . . *Jamaican Blackbird* 2—right in the thick forest; appear in a little clearing, silently explore a big bromeliad & melt into heavy forest; remarkable habits & habitats for a blackbird; long slender bill & glossy blue-black color & low flat crown profile very striking. . . .
>
> *March 11th.* To Dunrio River in A.M.; wind suddenly goes to n. w., hard rain showers & overcast all day; in p. m. trip by auto east of Mareaque towards Guys Hill as far as *retreat*—in mts. but country cleared. . . .
>
> *March 12th.* Walk up Mt. Diablo to summit & Holly Mount Hotel in a.m.; about 5 mile walk; best rain forest below, where I have so frequently been; nearer hotel all cleared away.[23]

Even with his family along, Griscom managed to rough it a bit. At the age of forty-six he was still in peak health, and a five-mile walk to start off the day didn't bother him a bit.

The following year another family outing was organized. The group sailed from Boston aboard the "S.S. Lady Nelson" on 13 March 1937. In a month-long grand sweep through the Caribbean, they visited Bermuda, St. Kitts, Nevis, Antigua, Montserrat, Dominica, St. Lucia, Barbados, and on 24 March arrived at Trinidad. From there they went to British Guiana, where they visited Georgetown and took a long trip east to Berbice River. Then they backtracked to Trinidad and continued on to Caracas, Venezuela, Curaçao in the Netherland Antilles, and then Port-au-Prince, Haiti, and thence back through the Bahamas home.

Ludlow's field journal is mostly composed of bird lists, but it does offer some insight into birding with a family. His rather harsh comments about some of the islands visited suggests that conditions weren't always optimal. He also once again makes frequent reference to habitat destruction.

> March 26–30; Georgetown, British Guiana.
>
> *March 26*—Brief trip in late P.M. to the very fine botanic garden, where there are lots of ponds covered with Victoria regia, & lotus of various kinds. These have islands with breeding rookeries of herons, egrets. etc.

March 28 (Sunday; Easter). Take car & picnic lunch, & drive up Demerara River to Covenden [?], 22 miles. Road goes along flooded sugar cane fields, teeming with Jacanas, Herons & Terns, & then enters country—miserable patches of scrub juniper. . . .

March 29. Country completely wrecked & denuded of forest. . . . Extensive savannahs & grassy marshes, interspersed with frequent mud flats & brackish lagoons. Herons, Jacanas & Everglade Kites almost incredibly abundant & all birds very tame. See an Agouti & a Water Possum. Only decent stretch of country near Macaripy River, where road dips inland for a few miles. On to Rossignol. . . .There wait an hour for ferry to New Amsterdam, where take car and go up bank of river [Berbice], & find Hoatzins in miserable mangrove scrub on bank of river. Astonishing they should be so local, as every river & creek just the same.

Venezuelan coast way off shore. [1 April]

Leach's Petrel 1 flies on board, dazzled by lights & is caught by a passenger & brought to me for identification. Threw it overboard & flops back on deck twice. I finally take bird & threw it with all my force as if it were a baseball & it disappears into the night! When held in the hand, it ejected an oily fluid from mouth.

April 2nd. At Carupano, Venezuela in A.M. . . .

Mainland a dreary desert, with cactus & thorny scrub, hot dusty & dirty. Margarita Island even more arid, but some forest on the mts.[24]

This was to be Griscom's last major overseas journey for fifteen years, and the last in which his health allowed him to exploit fully his adventurous spirit. From this point on he spent more and more of his time in Massachusetts, summering at Sears Point in Chatham, a habit begun in 1936.

In April 1938, David Garrison was invited to join the Griscom entourage on a Florida excursion and the following year joined Ludlow for the American Ornithologists' Union meeting at Berkeley, California. After the meeting they traveled to Monterey and the San Joaquin Valley. From there they went to Fillmore to look for California Condors, continued south to San Diego and the Imperial Valley, then turned north to Yosemite and Tioga Pass, the Sierra Nevadas, and on to Seattle and Vancouver Island. They visited Mt. Rainier National Park and worked their way east through the North Dakota refuges and the Turtle Mountains before heading home. Garrison related one of the highlights of the trip.

We got off the train in Merced. We wanted to go into Yosemite Valley. The only way to get in and out in reasonable time was to hire a taxi at the station. We drove into the floor of Yosemite, then up toward Tioga Pass. Ludlow wanted to see the White-headed Woodpecker, and we did. Then late in the afternoon we got up to the 10,000 foot mark, but missed the rosy finches because we ran out of time. The taxi driver had had it. Ludlow and I drove back, alternating driving—the driver asleep in the back seat. Got back to town about 1:00 A.M.[25]

The war years restricted travel overseas, but Griscom managed to get in the occasional trip within the United States. In 1943 he twice went to the South. His first trip began in earnest on 7 February when he entered the Singer Tract in Louisiana, looking for Ivory-billed Woodpeckers. He heard, but did not see one. The trip continued on through Houston, the Harris County prairies, and Eagle Lake to San Antonio Bay and Rockport, where he recorded 96 species, and ended at Aransas.

Apparently very taken with Rockport, he returned via St. Louis on 17 April. In the next three days, he recorded 141 species of birds. He then swung through the Rio Grande Valley, Laguna Madre, and Green Island, and in the Santa Anna Tract and Port Isabel area he recorded 170 species. Again he went to Rockport, and then finished the trip at Houston and Galveston Island, where he recorded 137 species. The inclusion in his ornithological diary of these species numbers, double underlined, suggests that he was excited by what he saw.

At Rockport, Griscom was shown around by Connie Hagar, known as the "Bird Lady of Rockport." Annette and William Cottrell accompanied Griscom on one of his trips there, and she sketched the lively times encountered. "When we came back from Corpus Christi and the Hagars met us, breathless, Mrs. Hagar jumping up and down with excitement with new back yard arrivals. A riot of flowers, cool shade of live-oak trees, with warblers, thrushes, elusive Indigo Buntings everywhere. Mrs. Hagar called to tell us of a Painted Bunting. . . . talk of woman who raised birds—a Limpkin in a bathtub. . . . suddenly a flock of Buff-breasted Sandpipers—Ludlow was so pleased and we for him, just what he wanted."[26]

Griscom's ornithological diary has a single entry for 1945–1949: "No trips away from Mas. Getting to be as damned provincial as the Bostonians!"[27] Except for two rather restricted expeditions after his health failed, Ludlow's peregrinations were at an end.

American Ornithologists' Union 7

Ludlow Griscom joined the American Ornithologists' Union (AOU) in 1908. He was elected a fellow in 1925, and for more than three decades after his election he exerted an influence on the inner workings of the organization. An outgrowth of the Nuttall Ornithological Club, the AOU was founded in 1883 and by 1925 had matured to become the premier professional ornithological association of the western hemisphere. Changes were then occurring in the structure of the AOU, as the "shotgun" school of ornithology, with an emphasis on museum collections, was being replaced by the school of scientists who dealt with living birds. Many of the old school were dying off and being replaced by a younger generation. Griscom had something to say about many of these changes. Before 1930 there is little correspondence by Griscom about the AOU, but in 1927 there is mention of Griscom collecting the life lists of birds of AOU fellows, and in 1930 a reference to his going over the galley proof of the fourth edition of the AOU Check-list. He was actively interested in the affairs of the AOU by that time, and he wrote to its president Joseph Grinnell about various problems in the union.

I am, of course, well aware of rumbles of criticism of various kinds against the A. O. U. The most serious element in this criticism, in my experience with the organization, is the ill feeling over election of members and Fellows. While in the so-called privileged class of Fellows myself, I must say that I take less and less stock in this division of membership as the years go by, and my conceit decreases. I have no particular respect for the basis on which either members or Fellows are elected, and I am well aware that human nature is bound to vote for or against a man for factors other than the pure merits of the case. . . .

Another unfortunate situation, which only time can take care of, is the fact that some of the founders and the older Fellows attained this position merely by being interested in birds at a time when almost nobody was, and the Union is, of course, full of associates and members who forget more about birds in a year than some of these surviving Fellows know. It is generally resented, therefore, by the younger elements in the membership that oldtimers of this sort should pass upon their qualifications. I should, myself, vote favorably for a proposition to abolish these three classes of membership. . . .

A final element of criticism which I have heard is with the programs of recent meetings. There is a general complaint that they are overcrowded and that anybody can put himself down for a title quite regardless of whether it turns out to be a perfect piffle or not. The probabilities are that there is some justice in this criticism and that we will have to follow the precedent of many other scientific organizations requiring the submission of abstracts of papers to be presented to a properly constituted officer or committee in advance, who selects those which are deemed worth presenting. This will, of course, make the amateurs very angry, and I have said before, we cannot escape the disadvantages of our assets.[1]

In 1932 Griscom sent some words of encouragement to Witmer Stone, editor of the *Auk*.

I know just how discouraging it is to have to everlastingly cut down and cut down and turn back perfectly good articles which we cannot afford to print. But please don't be discouraged, and don't throw up the job. Editing the Auk is indeed a wearisome chore, but it is perhaps the most important service that any one individual can do for the A.O.U., and I for one am glad to take this opportunity of expressing my appreciation. Heaven knows what will happen when you simply won't do it any longer, because the comparatively few people in the Union who show any signs of sufficient ability would not, so far as I know, touch the job with a ten foot pole.[2]

Griscom was elected to the Finance Committee in 1934, a position in which he served for many years. But all was not deadly serious, and for the 1935

AOU meeting he was asked by the secretary of the AOU graciously to allow some fun to be poked at him.

> We are asking three of the A. O. U. officers to make brief and more or less serious addresses [at the banquet], which will be tapered off into a more frivolous form of entertainment. . . . the toastmaster is giving some awards to outstanding personalities in the A. O. U. This brings me to the subject at hand. We should like to have him present you with a home-made dummy binocular with four objectives so that you can see twice as many birds. Will you please accept this at the banquet and make some appropriate remarks of two or three sentences?[3]

Humorous remarks notwithstanding, Ludlow was an active critic of many AOU policies and lobbied with a number of officials to try to implement some changes. He wrote Vice-President Arthur C. Bent to support an increase in the $600 honorarium for the editor of the *Auk*; strongly urged that the treasurer should be a business man, preferably with training in finance; and lobbied against giving the secretary or treasurer an honorarium. In a subsequent letter to Bent, Griscom offers opinions about the structure of the Finance Committee and asks for Bent's support.

> It seems to me that the Finance Committee of the A.O.U. is severely stymied by the fact that the Secretary and Treasurer are members of it, a most improper arrangement as regards most clubs and societies with which I am connected, as it effectually destroys the appearance of an unbiased committee. I take it as reasonably certain that my report will be a minority report, and perhaps the best thing for you to do is read it at the Council meeting as part of the Report of the Finance Committee. Even if you did not give my name, anyone at the Council meeting with a grain of sense would know that it was written by me. Somebody has got to have the courage of his convictions if the situation is to improve, but I hope you will do what you can to back me up.[4]

In an exchange of letters with Ernst Mayr, Ludlow's support is requested and Griscom elaborates his position on a number of issues. He is perhaps overzealous in his attacks on the AOU fellows and members, but Ludlow was often given to overstatement when he was trying to make a point. The first excerpt is from a 1937 letter from Mayr; the second is from Griscom's response.

> I was very pleased by your reaction to my proposals. I was pretty sure that you had sized up the situation in the A.O.U. and would be willing to assist a movement to eliminate the worst draw backs of the A.O.U.—I think you

have stated the whole trouble with the sentence: "The council has never had any collective 'guts' in my time." You are unfortunately not a member of the council, so far as I know, but you could raise your voice at the Fellows meeting, to which all proposals for amending the by-laws have first to be submitted.[5]

. . . I am now inclined, however, to write you even more frankly about the A.O.U., because I don't want you to stick your neck out and get your head bumped by your colleagues when doing so will serve no useful purpose. What you call the worst draw-backs of the A.O.U. are really technical matters of organization only. Back of them is a far more important human equation which you do not know at first-hand experience as well as I because you have not contacted these men for as many years as I have.

. . . The trouble happens to be that a group of ornithologists and bird lovers cannot help voting for candidates for these offices on the basis of their ornithological excellence, and the A.O.U. voter today is convinced that in so electing them he is conferring some sort of honor upon them. This should very properly be true of the presidency, which should only go to a distinguished ornithologist, but it is ridiculous when it comes to the treasurer, the secretary, and the council, all of whom if competent are doing the A.O.U. a favor, in the case of the treasurer and secretary a very great favor in handling such dull and unproductive chores as the secretary and treasurer of all organizations are required to do. . . . Similarly, I tried for years to campaign at the business meetings for Bob Murphy on the council, as a man with proved and obvious administrative and executive ability. Nobody would vote for him because (1) they thought he was too high-hat, and because (2) he spent too much time giving popular lectures, or because (3) he was interested in oceanography, geography, and kindred sciences, and therefore wasn't exclusively devoted to ornithology.

To my positive personal knowledge at least 50% of the Fellows and Members of the A.O.U. have pinheaded ideas and reactions of this sort and the other 50% are absolutely supine and dumb. As the voting starts for the election of officers they have no idea who the officers and council were last year and the names, by request, are always written up on a blackboard, and to spare themselves the effort of thinking, the majority will always vote for incumbents of the past year. In those years when the president retires the first vice-president is always made president, the second vice-president always becomes first vice-president, and the senior member of the council always becomes second vice-president, and in despair at finding an extra member of the council the voters look wildly around the room to see who is present for possible inspiration, and with 30 voters present I have seen 15 men get 2 votes apiece.[6]

In 1938 Griscom was invited to be on Herbert Friedmann's sub-committee of the Research Committee on Faunistics of North American Birds. In 1939 he was elected to the council, and early the following year became a member of the Endowment Committee, in charge of the work in the Boston region. The AOU annual meeting was held in Boston in 1940, and Ludlow was on the local committee, in charge of field trips. A letter from James Chapin suggests that Griscom's role was even more substantial. "I suspect that in view of Peters' illness the work of arranging for the A.O.U. meeting has fallen largely on your sturdy shoulders."[7]

In 1942 Griscom wrote a long letter to Alexander Wetmore about the editorship of the *Auk*. He was particularly concerned with selling the idea of a board to help the editor handle the increasing load that the *Auk* demanded. Two years later he again wrote to Ernst Mayr, this time blasting the AOU Check-list Committee and his close friend Alexander Wetmore.

What to do about the A.O.U. Check-List Committee is another matter entirely. Wetmore is actually the dominant personality on the Committee and is an arch conservative of the most old-fashioned kind. Friedmann is neither, but does not dare oppose Wetmore. Zimmer, Van Rossem, and Peters, while possessed with much common sense, have no real biological training worthy of the name. Most of the members of the Committee would not have you and me on it for the world and consequently I see no point in writing them letters of protest and I advise you to do nothing of the kind! If a majority of the Fellows and Members of the A.O.U. lack confidence in the Committee or feel that they are too preposterously old-fashioned all that they have to do is to prevent the publication of the new Check-List with the rapidly dwindling A.O.U. funds.[8]

A year later Griscom followed up with another letter to Mayr, reiterating a 1937 theme.

I heartily agree that it would be imminently desirable to get new blood into the Council and into the officers. But the Union is cruelly handicapped by an antiquated bylaw which automatically makes all past presidents members of the Council. Long years of experience in the A.O.U. has, however, convinced me that the major fault in the selection of Council members has always been that the voting members felt that they were honoring distinguished ornithologists in electing them to the Council.[9]

Mayr responded with a suggested course of action for Ludlow.

It seems that we agree in principle but disagree on some of the details.

I am planning to make a proposal for a change of the by-laws to be taken up at the 1946 meeting covering the election of vice presidents. Could we persuade you to make a proposal at the same time to eliminate the ex-presidents (except the retiring president) from the Council? The general sentiment seems to be entirely in favor of your proposal. There will be objections from Wetmore and a few others who have personal interest in this matter, but otherwise I think there is a good chance for such a proposal to go through.[10]

In 1946 Ludlow was reappointed to both the Finance and Endowment committees. A year later he gave one of his many talks at the AOU meeting, this time on redpolls. Largely because of his position on the committees, Griscom's advice was often solicited on AOU financial matters, here by Josselyn Van Tyne, at the time a vice-president of the AOU, who also suggests that Ludlow should be editor of the *Auk*.

I wish very much that I could discuss with you this financial jam in the A.O.U. It seems to me very bad management by the editor and treasurer. And how can the treasurer use endowment funds to pay current bills without any special authorization by the Council or Finance Committee? Is there *any*thing that can be done in 1949 except to cut the size of the *Auk* drastically (or "raise" several thousand dollars some where!)?

And what are we going to do about the *Auk* editorship? Could we persuade you to do it after all?

You are going to the meeting aren't you?[11]

In 1949 Griscom was again elected to the council, this time to finish A. J. Van Rossem's term. Despite being in uncertain health after suffering a major stroke, in 1950 he was elected second vice-president of the AOU. The next year, after recovering somewhat from his initial stroke, Ludlow was asked to be on the Committee for Publications by president Josselyn Van Tyne. In 1952 he was appointed to the Advisory Committee on Bird Protection. Van Tyne frequently consulted Ludlow on political matters within the organization, as excerpts from letters to him illustrate. They also show that Ludlow was perceptive in his choice of competent, deserving ornithologists and was involved in a good deal of political infighting in the committee structure of the AOU.

I have little that is original to say about nominating Honorary and Corresponding Fellows, and I do not think there is any mistake in nominating James Fisher. I note, however, what seems to me to be one outstanding omission, a man whom I know personally and whom I consider a brilliant student in the field of general biology of birds, David Lack.[12]

Thank you for your pleasant letter of December 15. I agree with you in being distressed at Gabe's [Ira Gabrielson] reaction. I still think that some of us did a good job in suppressing Mrs. Murphy and Mrs. Edge from the Conservation Committee of the A.O.U. How true it is in life that even if you try to do the best you know how it is virtually hopeless to please everybody and win universal approval![13]

Ludlow became chairman of the Brewster Awards Committee in 1953 and remained on the Advisory Committee on Bird Protection. The following year he became an AOU representative to the Council of the American Association for the Advancement of Science. He was still upset about the structure of the AOU meetings and voiced his complaints to the AOU secretary Harold Mayfield.

My usual gripe at all A.O.U. meetings is that the program of speakers is too hopelessly crowded. In spite of long and bitter experience, the Secretary can never realize that practically no ornithologist can speak on a time-clock schedule or can say what he knows about birds in the ten minutes that he reports, so that the program is hopelessly congested, the unfortunate chairman has to high-power it through, and there is never any chance for discussion worthy of the name, after each paper. So, for God's sake, if anybody puts himself down for fifteen minutes, allow him at least twenty.[14]

He was still railing at the Check-List Committee in 1955, when he wrote to Kenneth C. Parkes:

I thank you most warmly indeed for your most interesting and full letter of December 20. I certainly look forward to the continuation of your work on the systematics of certain North American birds. You may think me hopelessly old fashioned as my training in subspecies was primarily under Dr. Dwight and it is my private opinion that the checklist and the supplement are replete with unnecessary subspecies. For reasons which I do not exactly know, I must have been rude or tactless in expressing my opinions, as I am now completely sidetracked if my opinions, when published or expressed, are completely ignored. This was the complaint of my late colleague J. L. Peters, who, shortly before his death, complained to me that the checklist committee had voted his own recommendations down more often than anyone else. . . .

However, I hope you will play your cards more carefully than I have done and that you will be able to throw your weight against the present trend which, as Peters recently put it, consists in naming the intermediate between intermediates.[15]

Two years later he expressed to Eugene Eisenmann his continued dissatisfaction with some aspects of the new Check-list: " . . . In this respect the new A.O.U. Checklist is a great disappointment, for obviously Wetmore was able to override all possible opposition, and maintain his oldfashioned ways. The man who took a real beating was Ernst Mayr, as he was blanked 100%."[16] The next AOU Checklist accepted almost all of Ernst Mayr's proposals, particularly in regard to the new classification of the Anatidae and the removal of a large number of unnecessary generic names.

In 1953 Ludlow was elected first vice-president of the AOU. With the strong support of then president Alden H. Miller and Josselyn Van Tyne, in September 1956 Ludlow was elected president of the AOU. This was an extraordinary and generous gesture on the part of the council, since Ludlow was seriously ill at this time, and immediately resigned in favor of Ernst Mayr (see Chapter 16). His service to the American Ornithologists' Union had been long and substantial, and his election to the presidency was a fitting tribute to his efforts and performance for nearly half a century.

Nuttall
Ornithological Club   8

When Ludlow Griscom moved to Cambridge from New York City, the Nuttall Ornithological Club (NOC) was the most venerable ornithological club in North America. Founded in 1873 by William Brewster and seven other young men of the Cambridge area (it was originally named the NOC of Cambridge), it produced the first journal devoted exclusively to ornithology in North America, the *Bulletin* of the NOC. By the turn of the century, its corresponding membership included a veritable Who's Who of North American ornithology.[1] Brewster and Joel Asaph Allen, with the aid of many of the corresponding members, used the club as a springboard from which to launch a national ornithological organization, the American Ornithologists' Union (AOU). Established in 1883, the AOU took over the NOC *Bulletin* (which became the *Auk*) and its subscription list, and retained the services of its editor, J. A. Allen. The club, then, has at least partial claim to parentage of the AOU.

The club survived the loss of the *Bulletin*, and when Ludlow Griscom arrived in Cambridge in 1927, it had approximately eighty resident members. Eighteen of them, on the average, showed up at the two Monday night meetings a month, usually held at the Cambridge home of Charles F. Batchelder. A founder of the club, Batchelder had been its treasurer for more than forty years, and as host provided a touch of elegance and gracious hospitality. The NOC was then exclusively male, and the rather formal meetings reminded some of a Victorian men's club.

Ludlow was by this time a well-known, respected ornithologist and past president of the Linnaean Society of New York. It seemed only reasonable that shortly after his arrival he would be invited to become a member of the NOC. On 21 November 1927, Batchelder placed his name in nomination. The minutes of the council meeting of 5 December state, "On the motion of Mr. Bangs, duly seconded, Mr Ludlow Griscom of Cambridge was unanimously elected to Resident Membership."[2] This was an important day for the club, because in his thirty-two years of membership Griscom was to have a profound effect on nearly every aspect of the NOC's affairs.

Ludlow didn't take long to plunge into a variety of duties with his usual vigor and enthusiasm. In May 1928 he was appointed to a committee with Francis Harper and James Peters to make suggestions, on behalf of the club, to the AOU Check-list Committee. The same year he was nominated for the NOC council but was not elected. A year later he was nominated for treasurer, secretary, and councillor; he lost the first two but was elected to the governing council. At the next meeting he suggested changes to the bylaws that would simplify the election of members, but no action was taken. His successes were modest at first, perhaps because he was new to the club or because of personality conflicts, but he was confident and persistent, and better things were to come.

In 1930 Charles Batchelder decided that fifty years as treasurer were enough, and chose not to run again for a fifty-first term. Ludlow was ready, waiting, and duly elected treasurer, a post he held for a decade. This term in office was to be followed by three more years as a councillor, bringing to thirteen the consecutive years during which he was able to influence the decisions of the club in the council meetings. In 1930 he also joined Judge Robert Walcott and Batchelder on a committee to revise the NOC bylaws.

At various times Ludlow was asked to represent the club at important functions. In 1934 he was its official delegate to the International Ornithological Congress in England. Five years later he was the club's representative to the AOU meeting in Berkeley, California, where he was authorized to present to the union a joint invitation from the club and the Boston Society of Natural History to hold its next annual meeting in either Boston or Cambridge.

Ludlow was always interested in conservation, so when the Linnaean Society sent a resolution to the United States Biological Survey opposing the opening of a shorebird hunting season, it was Ludlow who was appointed to chair a committee to draft a similar resolution on behalf of the Nuttall Club. Along the same lines, Griscom later proposed a motion, which carried, that the club again strongly protest to the Biological Survey the proposed opening of a hunting season on yellowlegs and plover.

Perhaps the greatest influence that Griscom exerted during his first decade or so of membership was on the field notes section of the club meetings. He is credited by many with leading, or at least popularizing, the transition from "shotgun" ornithology to field ornithology using binoculars and spotting scopes. He certainly perfected the art of rapid and accurate field identification faster than anyone else. He was practicing these methods while most ornithologists remained, at best, skeptical of this new field approach. By 1930 the field notes section of the minutes had become long and detailed, perhaps the influence of the secretary taking the notes, but more likely because the infectious enthusiasm of Ludlow for field identification had placed new emphasis on this section of the club's activities.

In 1931 the minutes indicate that Griscom was commenting at length on the migrations, and in the second meeting of May, Griscom "outlined the advance of the spring migration to date."[3] These analyses of the seasonal changes in bird distribution were to evolve into a series of regular programs by Griscom. From all reports, they became a much-lauded and respected part of the club's tradition. He also included a discussion of the Christmas bird counts as part of the field note section of the meetings, which is still a feature of the January meetings of the club today.

In the minutes of the second May meeting in 1933, the Griscom field notes tell of 101 species seen on a single day. "Big Day" birding was underway in the club. The field notes were taken seriously, and species were covered in systematic order. There were, however, occasional light moments. The minutes of a 1933 meeting read: "It was reported that the manager of a staid and somewhat exclusive inn on the Cape recently admitted with some misgivings, and over the apparent but unspoken objections of his guests, a group of rough appearing characters, two of whom were subsequently identified as Mr. Griscom & Judge Walcott."[4] And several years later one finds: "Dr. Allen, under the prerogative of Club gossip, read an article which had appeared recently in the Traveller and other newspapers describing how (our eminent member) Ludlow Griswold had collected a European Godwink, at Chatham. Mr. Griscom explained how the story had leaked out through the treachery of the driver of a hired beach-wagon."[5] Apparently there was a good bit of warm humor within the club at that point, especially, according to some reports, over the traditional and famous New Year's Eve punchbowl at Charles Batchelder's home.

Judging from the minutes of the meetings, Griscom and the entourage of birding enthusiasts that had gradually developed in the club tended to dominate the field notes and discussion. Ludlow's effect on the club dovetailed with the appearance of the field guide concept, thrust so dramatically into everyone's consciousness by another club member, Roger Tory Peterson. But certainly Griscom was the guru for the new generation of the club's birders.

Griscom gave nearly fifty talks at the regularly scheduled meetings. The presentations were of two basic categories: ones relating to his experiences with birds on his many trips, both foreign and domestic; and ones dealing with local bird migration or distribution. The minutes of club meetings where he was the featured speaker attest to his success: "Ludlow Griscom gave an enlightening talk," "masterly review of events in the field during the summer months and autumn to date," "Ludlow Griscom . . . giving a brilliant review of the unsatisfactory birding season," "Mr. Griscom in his usual inimitable style described a trip to Louisiana and East Texas."[6]

His first talk to the club was in January 1928 on birds of the Yucatan, and in April he gave one on the birds of Montana. The following year he talked about summer birds in Wisconsin, stressing habitat changes and their effects, and on another occasion he compared the birdlife around Boston to that around New York City. In February 1930, he gave a vintage Griscom talk, one that illustrates his field identification philosophy.

> The paper of the evening was by Mr. Griscom on the "Field identification of Gulls." The speaker stressed the fact that apparent size is not a reliable field character unless the bird is seen under unusually favorable conditions or when an actual comparison between species is possible. Of great value are first—the pattern formed by the amount and distribution of white and black in the primaries, color of the under surface of the wings, colors of soft parts and especially in immature plumages the presence of darker markings on the upper parts of the body. . . . In conclusion Mr. Griscom gave an account of the capture of a black-headed gull (*Larus r. ridibundus*) by himself and Mr. Emilio in Newburyport harbor on 27 January.[7]

Most of his early talks described the birds of areas he had visited, including Arizona, Guatemala, the Texas coastal prairie, the prairie region of southern Texas, and Jamaica, to name a few. They were more than mere listings of birds, however. In his 1931 talk on additional notes on Guatemala, he stressed life zones and their birds, and illustrated his talk with "lantern" slides. When he gave a talk on field identification, as in his 1934 talk on the field identification of Brünnich's (Thick-billed) and Atlantic (Common) murres, he used skins to illustrate his points.

Griscom's field notes usually went far beyond a list of unusual or vagrant species that he had observed since the last meeting. He often discussed the effects of cold, wind direction, and other weather effects on bird distribution, and he looked for patterns in bird abundance rather than for a simple listing of rarities. In June 1935 his extensive field notes, "reviews of the seasons," were elevated to the status of featured talk of the evening, in this instance described as a "resume of the migration this year during March, April and May, as observed by him."[8] He gave more than twenty-five of these reviews over the course of two decades, and the concept was to carry on long after that. Though serious and detailed, his discussions sometimes included a touch of humor, as the June 1941 minutes report:

> The paper of the evening was presented by Mr. Griscom who gave his analysis of the spring migration in his usual interesting fashion. In brief, he mentioned that winter returned during March, but summer weather came in suddenly for the last half of April. Though the temperatures were record-breaking migrants arrived in only normal numbers. The first week in May was cool, but May 6 brought heat, with a wave ensuing on May 7 and 8. After this, the weather remained warm and fine and the birds trickled through and were hard to find. By May 17–20 the late warblers and flycatchers began to appear and it seemed that no late wave would develop. These conditions held through May 28 and Mr. Griscom became so bored that he went to New York. While attending a meeting of the Linnaean Society on May 29 he discovered that the migration had started all over again in Central Park on May 27 and 28, so he left the meeting at once and took a train home hoping to beat the birds to Essex County. In this he scored a tie and discovered a tremendous wave on May 29 especially on Plum Island. He was unable to advance a theory to explain the lateness of this last wave.[9]

> Griscom gave his last review of the spring migration in June 1955.

> He spoke first of the effects of the 1954 hurricanes in dispersing migrants and that the winter visitors were early in arrival and extended farther south than usual. Old Squaws in flocks reached the Gulf as did Siskins and Evening Grosbeaks. Brown-capped Chickadees, White-winged Crossbills and Pine Grosbeaks moved unusually far south.
>
> The spring started early but frosts in late March disrupted part of the early movement. Reports from the east in the later spring indicate a usual weather pattern, but very erratic movements of birds in general and in the south and east reported only a late and poor migration or a complete failure. Certain places in the Southern Appalachians and central Great Lakes area seemed to have had a good migration, though late.[10]

He was still looking for distributional patterns of birds and their causes.

Griscom was a controversial figure in the history of the NOC. When he joined, the average attendance at meetings was fewer than twenty, and the majority of those present were definitely of the old school or "bird in the hand" persuasion. The study of bird behavior in the growing fields of ethology and ecology was on the ascendance. Nevertheless, the boisterous, superconfident, somewhat dogmatic Griscom did not promote a quiet and peaceful transition between eras. Many were either unfamiliar with his field identification techniques or simply didn't trust them. Some, no doubt, were irritated by the fact that Griscom, with his tendency toward overstatement in his pronouncements, was so often proven correct in his identifications. In addition, he nominated a number of men for membership, including Richard Eaton, Richard Hinchman, Hustace Poor, and Tudor Richards, who tended to be of the new school. When, in 1933, Roger Tory Peterson's nomination had been tabled, it was Ludlow who moved to untable it, leading to Peterson's election. New members, whether nominated by Griscom or not, were often attracted by his ideas. As the sport of birding emerged, Ludlow tended to develop a following, which did not sit well with many of the old guard. There were personal and professional disagreements, and changes that occurred in the club were often blamed on Griscom, whether he was responsible for them or not.

As usual, Ludlow did not make the situation any easier. Reports have it that he began to test the waters of the club about the possibility of nominating a woman, one of his protégés, for membership. In 1936 the members apparently considered this idea a heresy. In fact there had been two female corresponding members in the nineteenth century, who, if they had been in the area, would have been invited to the meetings, according to the constitution and bylaws of the club. Those bylaws did not preclude election of a woman since they required only that potential members be "persons" interested in ornithology. The backlash, however, was swift and forceful. At the council meeting of December 1936, with Ludlow present, "It was unanimously voted to recommend to the Club members a change in the wording of the By-Laws in order to clarify and indicate definitely the original intention of these laws, namely, that members should be men. The use of the word 'persons' at present might at some future date be interpreted to permit women to be members."[11] Not wishing to make a fight out of it, Griscom apparently voted for the recommendation. With only six dissenting votes from the thirty-five members present, the motion to make the change was carried at the January 1937 meeting. Ludlow was obviously a bit ahead of his time.

A bitter personal feud developed between Griscom and Wendell Taber. They had been good friends and constant birding companions for years, but the relationship rapidly went stale. Taber viewed himself as a member of the old guard, although in many respects he clearly was not, and this allegiance may have started the difficulties. The break came, however, over a single incident in which, it was alleged, Taber accused Ludlow of showing too much interest in one of his female birding companions and protégés. The date of the falling out is uncertain, but it occurred sometime in the late 1930s or early 1940s. That things were not going well between them emerges from the minutes of the club meetings, which were written by Taber as club secretary (ironically, he had been nominated by Ludlow for that post). Little digs—"A very short distance away Hagar also found and collected a bird, possibly overlooked by Griscom" and, in the same minutes "A so-called Western Willet seen by him, Griscom et als."[12]—suggest that all was not well between them as early as 1937. As long as the meetings were held at Charles Batchelder's house, the feud did not markedly affect Ludlow's participation in the club. As Batchelder's health began to fail, Taber took over the responsibility for hosting the meetings. By 1942, Taber was holding a few meetings each year in his home, and within five years he was hosting about half of them. After mid-1949 until the end of 1952, Taber hosted virtually all of the meetings. Ludlow's attendance and participation in club affairs began to wane in 1943, when he attended only five meetings and gave no talks; he went to only three in 1944, although he gave talks at two of those. The club records are missing for 1945 and 1946, but he attended only two meetings in 1947 and none the next. He attended only three meetings in the succeeding three years. The feud with Taber had significantly interfered with his involvement with the club.

In 1952 James Peters, who had been president of the club since 1942, died of a heart attack and precipitated a crisis in the club. In the May meeting following Peters' death, the members decided to postpone voting on a new president until the annual meeting in December. In October vice-president Charles Blake announced the appointment of a nominating committee consisting of Richard Hinchman, Wendell Taber, and Alva Morrison, who reported to the club in November: "The Committee was unable to agree on candidates for President and Vice President. Two members of the Committee nominated for President Charles H. Blake, and for Vice-President Stuart K. Harris. One member of the Committee nominated for President Ludlow Griscom, and for Vice President Charles H. Blake."[13]

Almost certainly it was Richard Hinchman, a birding companion whom Ludlow had nominated for membership, who held out for Ludlow. Griscom had previously been nominated for vice-president in 1938 and for president as well as vice-president in 1942 (after the death of Glover Allen), but he had yet to be elected to either office. Now Griscom expressed his reservations about the pending election in an October letter to Josselyn Van Tyne.

The trouble in the Nuttall Club and the reorganization involved and just who will turn out to be president, is another difficulty and I know nothing of how it will be resolved. I certainly do not want to become president as feeling is running very high and so far as I can see whoever does become president will automatically involve a considerable lot of resignations. I have not got the personal popularity to unite all factions and differences of opinion so I see not [sic] reason to stick my neck out. Another reason would be the meetings would have to be in my own private home and my wife does not want them there.[14]

On 3 December 1952, forty-two members were present, the largest turnout in the club's history for a regular meeting. The assembly was held on "neutral ground," away from Taber's house, at the Biological Laboratories at Harvard University. The vote was 28 to 13 in favor of Griscom, apparently dividing somewhat along the old guard–new guard lines. Wendell Taber, in a letter years later, traces his "uncontested divorce from the bird group in this state" to that date.[15] All indications are that the political jousting had been intense, but the more active "birders" had clearly carried the day. It was amazing that a man who had attended only four meetings in the preceding five years, and who was not present for the election meeting, should have won such substantial endorsement. Griscom assumed office and presided over the next meeting, delivering the talk as well, a report on the fall migration. There was an attempt to pull the club's factions back together, as a letter to Ludlow from Judge Robert Walcott makes evident.

It is a pleasure to see your star in the ascendent, due to the great success of the dinner at the Harvard Club and to your election as President of the Nuttall Club last night by a vote of better than two to one (28 to 13.)

We were spared the presence of Wendell Taber. Charles Blake's conduct thru the evening was altogether admirable in a rather difficult position.

I am of the same opinion as Russell Mason and Henry Parker in thinking it would be inadvisable to make any address or speech at your first meeting of the Club, and in believing it would be better to have the next two or three meetings at the Biological Laboratories before having the regular place of the meeting at your house, — if that is convenient to Edith and agreeable to you. I have in mind that it might be difficult for Hagar and Austin to go immediately to your house, and that it would be easier for them after one or two meetings had been held at the Biological Laboratories.[16]

Nevertheless, the year of Griscom's presidency marked a watershed for the club. No longer would the meetings be held in the informal setting of a private home. The change probably resulted primarily from the Taber-Griscom rift. Surely, it was not caused by lack of private homes of appropriate size. The average numbers of those attending meetings had not increased since the 1930s and in fact was declining slightly. Griscom (despite Edith's objections) and Taber both offered to hold the meetings at their homes, and there were doubtless others who would have done the same. Charles Blake described the situation:

> I don't know whether you remember that during the war the NOC did meet occasionally at the Audubon Society. It helped the transportation situation for some people at that time but the general feeling was that it was much less pleasant than a private home. We could secure accommodations without charge at at least three places and possibly four but I don't hear any lively demand from the brethren as a whole to change our custom although I recognize the existence of certain frictions which would be alleviated if there were more meeting places.[17]

The move to the Biological Laboratories was to be permanent.

Griscom's presidency produced a burst of activity and vigor in the club. A Program Committee of Ludlow, James Greenway, and Russell Mason arranged an excellent slate of speakers, more than half of whom were guests. This established a trend of increasing numbers of guest speakers that continues in the club today. The committee was granted funds to pay up to $50 for a speaker's expenses in an attempt to enhance the programs.

As a response to discussions of the qualifications for membership, the club voted to retain a membership limit of 112. This was another attempt to maintain or promote the quality of the NOC. There was a flurry of discussion concerning the various ornithological projects that the club might undertake. The members agreed to sponsor the continuation of the work of Bent's life history series should he be unable to carry on the work and extended an invitation to the AOU to hold their 1954 meeting in the Boston area. The bylaws underwent a major overhaul for the first time since 1899, and the term of the president was limited to three years, thus ending the virtual life tenancy of the position that had been the case since the club's founding in 1873.

In poor health as the result of a series of minor strokes, Griscom was unable to attend the last five meetings of the year and chose not to run for a second term. He was clearly not happy with the internal politics, and although the club was headed in new directions, Ludlow felt that he was not able to provide the necessary leadership. In a letter to Charles Blake, who succeeded him, Ludlow expressed his concern.

This gives me a pleasant chance to write you a friendly and personal note. Carried away, obviously by enthusiasm, a group of my friends precipitated what I regarded at the time, before many witnesses, as a most unfortunate incident [presumably getting Ludlow elected President]. With some months reflection I was unable to see that this incident paid constructive dividends in any way. I, therefore, made it a point to appoint a chairman of the nominating committee so far as I knew, personally friendly to both of us, and I immediately disqualified myself. I warmly congratulate you on becoming president of the Nuttall Club and hope that you will have much more pleasure and satisfaction in your term than I did.

As you must undoubtedly be aware, I have been needling the Nuttall Club for years about having no activities. Here, I am irreconcilable as I have little interest in any club that does not possess them. I gather that at the last meeting of the Council some discussion of possible activities took place, but the meeting was called without my knowledge and I had a date to talk to another bird club. Believing as I do that some form of activity is of vital importance to the Club, it occurs to me that possibly the best way to foster it, is to keep out of it. It seems, therefore, the most courteous thing to do under the circumstances is to not attend the annual meeting.[18]

The events that occurred during Griscom's brief presidency set the course for the club along new paths. The Nuttall Ornithological Club was irrevocably changed. Not all of this can be attributed to Ludlow, but it is certain that his influence on the club had been substantial. He left an indelible stamp on the club and provided impetus and direction that is still evident in the NOC today.

Museum of Science 9

When Ludlow Griscom became an associate member of the New England Museum of Natural History in 1927, it is doubtful whether he had any inkling of the enormous influence he was to have on the museum or that the museum would have on him. For the remainder of his life, he would be intimately involved in its affairs, and in particular, its evolution into the Boston Museum of Science. This evolution was a tortuous one, which taxed Ludlow's administrative abilities, occupied an enormous amount of his time, brought scathing criticism down upon him, and eventually contributed to the deterioration of his health. But through it all he held steadfastly to the principles he believed to be correct, and today there are few who would fault his judgment.

In 1937 Griscom became involved with the inner workings of the museum when he was appointed chairman of the Budget Committee by the president of the Boston Society of Natural History, which sponsored the New England Museum of Natural History (as it was usually called). The following year he was designated to head the Walker Prize Committee, which was responsible for choosing the best memoir in ornithology for that year. He was also involved in upgrading the museum bulletin. Major changes were in the works at the museum, including the possibility of constructing a new building, and Ludlow was intimately involved, as we see in a letter to John K. Howard.

I have your interesting letter of December 29th, and I am entirely willing to accept an appointment as a member of your new Committee on Exhibits. The future will show just how much time will be involved.

With regard to other items in your letter about the general ground plans of the proposed new museum building, it is obvious that the architect must have some idea as to what the building is to contain. I agree heartily that a modern public educational museum should have a good auditorium, adequate quarters for a good educational department, and regard these two items as intrinsically more important than proper quarters for the staff.

The exhibits should most certainly include a good sound collection of North American material, and probably a general collection of at least the higher groups illustrating the fauna of the world as a whole.

I am very strongly of the opinion that anthropology and archaeology should be completely left out. . . . In other words, would it not be advisable to confine our work to present-day living material? I am also inclined to raise, at least for serious consideration, the abandonment of botany for the same general reasons that we agreed on leaving out anthropology and archaeology. We have ample precedent here with the American Museum in New York, and exactly the same reasons apply. The Boston Society's collection and library in botany do not amount to Hannah Cook. In exhibition work we would be competing with the absolutely unique and irreplaceable and world famous glass flowers and the Botanical Museum at Harvard.[1]

An enormously fruitful relationship began in 1939 when Bradford Washburn met Ludlow during a dinner interview concerning the directorship of the museum. The process had begun the preceding November on a plane flight to Philadelphia, when Washburn had met John K. Howard and been offered the directorship by him. Washburn was at that time assistant director of Harvard's Institute of Geographical Exploration, not far from the Museum of Comparative Zoology (MCZ). Washburn had made a number of trips to Alaska, was an experienced lecturer, and was well known to people at the MCZ and the members of the Harvard Traveler's Club, of which Howard, Washburn, and Griscom were members. In addition, the preceding year Washburn had given a fundraising lecture for the New England Museum. Not long after the plane flight to Philadelphia, Washburn dined at Howard's apartment with Wendell Endicott, Ralph Hornblower, and Griscom. According to Washburn, these four prominent citizens explained that the museum was in need of a young leader who could come up with some bright ideas and plans, and what a wonderful opportunity it was for him, despite the fact that the museum was one of the "most

God-awful Natural History Museums in the world."[2] They suggested that he would not have to concern himself with fund-raising, though in fact, he did spend the rest of his professional life doing so. The august group persuaded Washburn to take the job.

One of the first things that Washburn and Griscom did was to try to decide on the name of the institution. Ludlow wrote to the new director: "As regards the name of the Museum, the present situation seems to me to be both confusing and awkward. Speaking ideally, the name New England Museum of Natural History is reasonably short, definite, and conveys the proper information to the modern public, whereas the name Boston Society of Natural History would suggest to the modern public a group of cranks and specialists interested in the study of natural history."[3]

The museum was then lodged at 234 Berkeley Street in downtown Boston. It was in serious financial difficulty, balancing its budget by using money from the meager unrestricted funds. If any major changes and improvements were to be made, a new source of income would have to be uncovered. Harold J. Coolidge, Jr., of the MCZ, suggested the idea of raising unrestricted funds through the sale of duplicates from the New England Museum's library.

At that time, the museum's library was one of the top five natural history libraries in North America. The MCZ at Harvard was also in that elite group, and Coolidge, backed by Ludlow, argued that it was immoral that two such collections should be in the same city. There was an enormous overlap in their holdings, and those duplicated resources should be somewhere else where they were needed. Ludlow became closely involved at this point, because he fully understood the dangers of an adverse public reaction to the proposed liquidation of a major part of the museum's library. In 1941 rumors were beginning to spread, and Griscom, vice-president and on the board of trustees at this point, moved to squash them. Nonetheless, the proposed sale stimulated some fairly serious reaction.

We are all having a great deal of trouble with Miss Cobb at the N. E. Museum. She has developed almost a psychosis about the terrible things that are going to happen to the library, most of which exist in her imagination only. Apparently there was some meeting of the Library Association in Boston recently. She wrote them a lurid report of our plans for the destruction of the N. E. Museum library and tried to get them to start an official protest. Naturally some really first class men did not allow themselves to be carried away, and nothing came of this plan, but Miss Cobb did start a good deal of excitement. Various people wrote letters of protest to the papers and the Museum got some very unfortunate publicity. Washburn and Young have, of course, the handicap of youth in dealing with Miss Cobb, and, Glover, bless his sweet soul, will do nothing except keep on pleasant relations with everybody. But Miss Cobb actually seems to be a close parallel to the reactions of Ned Wigglesworth in recent years. She is automatically against any change of any kind whatsoever in the library and, so far, shows no capacity for adapting herself to any changes.[4]

As part of the fund-raising effort, Griscom backed the sale of some of the New England Museum property:

I am heartily in favor of the sale of twenty feet of our land to the New England Mutual Life Insurance Company at Sixty Thousand Dollars, and I do not favor the refusal of this offer on the ground that, some uncertain number of years in the future, we could presumably sell this land at substantially more per square foot. . . .

We live in difficult times of increasing financial stringency and need money desperately. I wish to point out that a bird in the hand is worth very much more than two in the bush. Assuming that our treasurer can get between four and five percent income on this Sixty Thousand Dollars forever, and adding this income to the principal over a ten year period, we will approach at least the theoretically larger sum that we could get ten years from now. My vote is, consequently, cast for immediate sale.[5]

Coolidge, Griscom, and Charles H. Blake of MIT joined together and discussed the matter of the library sale with Thomas Barbour, director of the MCZ. Barbour agreed with their position, and an appraisal of the library was begun in which Griscom became heavily involved. Well organized and precise, Ludlow was responsible in many areas for seeing to it that commitments made by the MCZ administration were carried out. Hence it fell to Griscom together with Blake to recruit subcommittees of experts in all fields of natural history for the appraisal, which involved dividing the collection into three categories: books that the museum should retain, consisting of special books like the Audubon Elephant Folio and the Gould series, together with enough professional books to allow it to maintain its function as a research library (the MCZ was not interested in becoming a public research library); books and reprints that were not available at the MCZ or elsewhere in the Boston area (nearly 1,000 items); and books that duplicated the MCZ collection or other collections in the Boston area. The latter group would be sold. Griscom did the assessment of the ornithological books himself. Later he oversaw the trimming of the extensive bird-study skin collection at the museum, with the transfer of much of the collection to the MCZ.

Negotiations were proceeding in the sale of the library to the University of

Southern California, Los Angeles. Two letters in March and April 1943, from
Irene McCulloch of the university to Harold Coolidge of the museum, suggest
that the deal was ready to be closed.

> This morning the President suggested that it might be advisable for him to
> go to Washington shortly, to have you join him at the expense of the Univer-
> sity and for the two of you to travel to Boston where he is going to be very
> much interested in seeing the library before it is disturbed. *He is going to buy*
> *that library and he will want everything in the way of reference material that your*
> *organization has to sell.* The fact that he tentatively thought of one figure and
> you have thought of another means that both of you are about ready to find
> a suitable compromise.[6]

> In many ways I am hoping that the President will give me an opportunity
> to return to Boston to work with the proper people there, to go into the
> collection of books which Mr. Griscom intimated would be available for sale
> at a subsequent date. There is every reason to think that if the initial
> agreement can be made mutually satisfactory to your group and to our Pres-
> ident that your institution will have a steady customer for all of your subse-
> quent offerings.[7]

During World War II the books that fell into the third category were sold
for more than a quarter of a million dollars, the bulk of the purchase to USC.
Criticism of this library liquidation was widespread and bitter. According to
the general reproach, Washburn, together with Griscom and company, had
destroyed the museum, destroyed the library, and perpetrated a total disaster.
Ludlow and Barbour took the brunt of the tidal wave of this censure. Most of
it came from the older, more conservative echelon, either because they opposed
change in general or because they felt that this was the first step in the destruction of the entire museum. Griscom and Washburn attempted to assuage the
situation by arranging for anyone who needed reference to any of the books
that had been sold to have free access to the Harvard University library system.
But the criticism was fierce, and Ludlow received it from more than a few of
his birding acquaintances and friends.

The difficulties, frustrations, and criticisms all intensified as the idea
emerged that the old Natural History Museum had outlived its usefulness and
that one which included sciences other than natural history might better fulfill
the needs of the community. This idea surfaced dramatically in 1945, when
Brad Washburn was offered the directorship of the Rochester Museum in New
York and presented what amounted to an ultimatum to the board of directors
of the New England Museum. He essentially said that he would not remain as

director unless the board agreed to change the name to the Museum of Science, find a new location for the museum, and build an integrated science museum, with medicine, astronomy, and technology taking their places alongside natural history. It was a dramatic proposal, since no such science museum existed at that time anywhere in the world. In what was in essence a conservative society, this was a bold and futuristic concept, one that met strong resistance from all levels, including a segment of the board of directors. The die was cast, however, in a momentous board meeting on 14 December 1945, convened in the living room of trustee Barbara Danielson. The proposal for these changes was made, and the treasurer indicated that if it were approved he would resign. After about a minute of stony silence, Thomas Barbour, who was presiding over the meeting, said "Sir, your resignation is accepted, let us proceed with the meeting."[8] This was the beginning of a new institution.

There was a pervasive fear that broadening the base of the museum would detract in general from the focus on natural history, and in particular from the study of birds. Washburn, with Griscom supporting him, argued that natural history could hold its own, and that a broader base would attract more people and provide the natural history with a wider audience. Griscom was pictured by those opposing change as the renegade who was selling the natural history museum down the river—not an easy burden for him to bear. When Barbour died in January 1946, Ludlow was left to shoulder the burden alone.

The next five years were crucial to the success or failure of the venture. There were a series of critical decisions to be made: finding a place for the new museum; negotiating with the legislature once the new location had been chosen; selling the old museum to provide part of the funds for building the new one—to name but a few. Some of the plans were set forth in a 1946 letter to the trustees:

LAND: On June 7, an agreement was signed with the New England Mutual Life Insurance Company which, it is expected, will lead to the ultimate sale of our Berkeley St. property for the sum of $775,000. . . .

LIBRARY: An informal agreement has been reached, and formal papers are now being prepared to consummate the sale of another section of our library to the Allen Hancock Foundation of the University of Southern California.[9]

The strength and leadership of Ludlow Griscom during these critical years can be seen reflected in the letters of people connected with the emerging new museum. Typical is a memo from Terris Moore, at the time president of the museum, who expressed his appreciation in 1946.

Ludlow—you are a real comfort and help in keeping me on the track! I stewed around with this problem for days—but your suggestion is of course the orderly way of handling it.

Yours with admiration.[10]

With Griscom as president, the cornerstone was laid in 1949, and the east wing of the new Museum of Science opened its doors in March 1951. However, the acute financial problems that had plagued the transition period continued even after the new museum had opened. The new building cost almost exactly the amount received from the sale of the old one, so there was no unrestricted money left over to use for operating expenses. At one point, the museum was raising money in December for the February payroll. The problem was somehow to survive the period of deficit financing until there were enough people visiting the new museum to render admissions income a significant part of the operating budget. It took time, as well, to gain enough public acceptance to make major fund-raising viable.

Bradford Washburn states that Griscom was a tower of strength during this period. They lived several blocks away from each other in Cambridge, and after breakfast Washburn would drop by Ludlow's house, which he referred to as "the Griscom coffee shop," and have long strategy sessions before he went to work. There was severe criticism of both men from all quarters, and since Ludlow was well acquainted with most of the people involved, and was wise in the ways of politics and diplomacy, the two would plan how to pour oil upon the various troubled waters.

Washburn's recollections of these difficult years offer many insights into Ludlow's character, remarkable executive ability, and his difficulties, as well as strengths, in interpersonal dealings. Griscom tended to be peremptory with people and to present things in a black-and-white way, never in shades of gray. Washburn was apparently of similar temperament, and thus applauded this approach because he felt that the situation called for someone who would stand up and fight in a straightforward way. This bothered some of the trustees, who didn't like such a direct route to decision making, and often preferred a path of greater flexibility and compromise. Ludlow often saw no point in compromise. "After all if it's true, why back away from it?"[11] Yet he also was circumspect, didn't stick his neck out when he was unsure of a situation, and often would suggest getting other advice. Judging from the results, his combination of wise caution and frankness served him well. According to Washburn, when Ludlow went to a board meeting he knew exactly what he wanted to get out of it. Many of the trustees leaned heavily on Ludlow's counsel, and if Washburn put forth a suggestion, many of the them would ask Ludlow his opinion.

"I had no stature," recalled Washburn, "so they would ask Ludlow what he thought, and he would say 'I think that's a fine idea,' then my idea would sail. . . . we never, never, never, could have done the things in the four or five year period that we did, without Ludlow saying 'that's great—I'm for it.'"[12]

Griscom was not all bluster and aggression by any means. Beneath his brusque exterior was a skilled political tactician who thoughtfully planned the strategy for each board meeting. Washburn's description of a typical meeting illustrates Griscom's patient, carefully planned methods.

> He was wonderful at meetings. We would sit down at breakfast in the "Gris-com coffee shop" and we would plan the agenda of the meeting. Then we would parcel out that I was to talk about this, and he would cover that, and Charlie Blake would be assigned this package, and it was my job to get ahold of Charlie and say that this is what we want him to cover. Ludlow would preside, and he did a wonderful job of presiding. We used a system that I wish more people used in board meetings, a system which Ludlow and I shared. If you have a controversial issue, and if both you and your Director are convinced that you are right—that this is what should be done—then it is better to present it and say where you stand, and then say, "Well, now has anybody got any comments?" Usually, unless it is very controversial, nobody will respond because people don't like to respond. Then what you have to do is wait for just a moment, and if it is clear that nobody is going to respond, then you have to be ready and say "Charlie Blake, I'm sure you know a lot about this, wouldn't you like to say something?" Then Charlie says something, then somebody else says something, and then when the decision is made, everybody's been involved. If the two of you say, "This is what we want, we hope you'll go along with us on it," and you vote yes, then you've got the whole thing on your back if it doesn't work. You have to know who has something to say and will respond. Ludlow was a master at that. The whole process of involvement is vitally important. The board gets bored if all they do is rubber stamp things. The other way, with discussion, it's "our" decision. . . . I can't overemphasize the importance of Ludlow to this organization in those critical days.[13]

Early in 1950 Ludlow suffered the first of a series of major strokes that were to plague him for the rest of his life. Washburn was convinced that it was the pressure associated with the museum that brought about the deterioration of Ludlow's health.

> He was a very, very, fine fellow. He was very sensitive. People didn't see this. Many people who appear to be peremptory and a little tough, often have very thin skins. Ludlow was like this, he didn't like having his ornithological

friends saying nasty things about him, because he was working on that project with those guys who were "ruining the New England Museum of Natural History." We owe him a prodigious debt of gratitude. If it had not been for Ludlow's strength and persistence, this museum would not exist today—there is just no question about it.[14]

In a handwritten letter of 1950, Washburn thanked Ludlow for his efforts.

God bless you for all that you've done to carry us forward to this point. The time has now past when two or three of us can do the job—unless we get real team-work for at least a few months this winter we'll have to do some royal figgering to balance our books!

When the campaign is done & we have our old ship back on a steady course again, you'll be able to have a keen sense of satisfaction that without your help, counsel and leadership we'd never have had a new Museum of Science worthy of the name—and by this I don't merely refer to your presidency, but to the years when you were on our executive committee and patiently guided and taught me as well as most of the others on the committee, when few, if any, of us had the slightest idea of how to run a museum.

Nobody knows better than I what a magnificent & unselfish contribution you've made during these many years—I only hope that we will all have the strength and the determination to put this job through in such a way that you'll be proud to say that you were one of those who started the plan for the new museum a dozen years ago.[15]

The Boston Museum of Science was the first "hands on" integrated science museum in the world, and it remains the model and showcase for such museums to this day. It brings in more visitors in two weeks than the old New England Museum of Natural History did in a year and provides an educational function for all the sciences that transcends even the wildest expectations of its founders. The natural history exhibits more than hold their own, and in fact, the most popular exhibit in the museum is still the chicken incubator.

Its 1991–1992 budget exceeded $22 million, it has a paid staff of 371, 652 volunteers, and it greeted 1.6 million paid visitors—a brilliant outgrowth of the 1940 budget of $44,000, a paid staff of ten, a handful of volunteers, and a slightly more than 40,000 visitors who entered its cavernous and squeaky old halls, paying no admission fee at all. "Ludlow Griscom's contribution to these thrilling figures was incalculable," Washburn said in 1993. "Boston would have no Science Museum at all today if it had not been for his extraordinary courage, his strong leadership and his wise counsel to those of us who were in the front-line trenches forty-five years ago!"[16] His devotion is commemorated by a plaque there that reads: "Ludlow Griscom, who almost gave his life for the Museum."

Part Three

IN THE FIELD

From Shotgun to Binoculars 10

Ludlow Griscom spanned two eras in scientific ornithology: the "shotgun school" era, where systematics and distribution were virtually what constituted ornithology; and the field ornithology era, in which the emphasis shifted to the ecologically based study of live birds. He also was a central figure in the explosive development of the sport of birding, a pursuit that led him into a paradoxical situation. He loved birding and surrounded himself with amateurs in the field, but he took scientific ornithology very seriously. A conflict arose between the two. The problem of sight records—from the "horde of amateurs" for whom he was largely responsible—and how to handle these observations became a constant source of concern. His amateur friends were hurt when he rejected their sight records, and his professional colleagues accused him of being a dilettante. This chapter documents Ludlow's influence in both professional and amateur circles, and the development of his field identification techniques. The problems of sight records and bird collecting are presented in Chapter 12.

Late in his career, Griscom laid out his ambivalent view of the two worlds of bird study in a speech he gave at a testimonial dinner given for him in Boston in 1952:

This dinner is an appropriate occasion to discuss the role of the amateur versus the professional bird student. It is impossible here to stick to the strict dictionary definition of these terms, as very few ornithologists support themselves wholly by a paid job (there are too few), others like Dwight and William Brewster, and most Englishmen, had ample independent means, and their museum curatorships were without salary, while still others like Townsend, Elliot Coues, Bent and Brandt had to do something to make some money to afford the luxury of devoting full time to birds.

The only valid criterion that remains is time. Some people manage to devote full time to birds, while with most of us it is an interest or a hobby for a carefully regulated amount of *spare* time only, and they have to exercise a certain amount of character and control (like Frank Chapman) to see that their interest does not impair their success in their main job of earning a living.

Whether or not a man becomes by reputation an ornithologist depends not so much on money, advanced degree, a museum or academic connections, but how he spends his time, the degree of his interest and his accomplishments in research. This is bitterly disputed by some professionals. In my youth all ornithologists were technical systematists or taxonomists and had to do some work along these lines to qualify. . . .

But so far as I know the increasing horde of amateur birders don't want to go professional, they wisely wish to keep a healthful and recreational hobby in its place, have no burning urge to add to knowledge or make startling discoveries and if anything comes of their time, work, or efforts it depends upon whether they fall under the baneful influence of myself or some one equally dreadful. Most professionals pray God to steer clear of them. . . .

It was consequently my great good fortune never to lose my interest in local faunistics. It is common sense that most amateurs can only be interested in local faunas, no other outlet is available for their hobby. It was my business to try and make something out of it; it was my business to try and enthuse and point up their interest. My success—companionship.[1]

Many who knew Ludlow from the early years, and who had made important contributions to ornithology or the sport of birding themselves, considered him influential. Thomas Barbour wrote that Griscom "had raised field ornithology to the dignity of a science and become unquestionably a master of this science which he has made so completely his own."[2] Joseph A. Hagar, who was not a great supporter of Ludlow, described him as really the first practitioner of the field glass phase of ornithology.[3] Roger Tory Peterson has written of Ludlow's influence on a number of occasions. He once said that Griscom "did more than anyone else in America for birding with binoculars."[4] Later, in the introduction to Norman Hill's *The Birds of Cape Cod, Massachusetts,* based in part on the field records accumulated over the years by Griscom, Peterson wrote: "More than any other man he bridged the gap between the shotgun naturalist of the old school and the modern field biologist. Although he backed up his field work with a bit of judicious collecting, he demonstrated that most birds could be recognized instantly, even at a distance, by their *field marks* and that it was seldom necessary to resort to the collecting gun. A whole generation of students now owe their skill to his pioneering."[5]

That Griscom was "riding the wave" is equally clear. Ornithology was maturing as a scientific discipline and rapidly becoming more diverse. Birds had become study animals for biologists other than taxonomists and systematists. Ethology had been launched in 1914 with Huxley's *The Courtship Habits of the Great Crested Grebe,*[6] and ecology students were recognizing the advantages of using birds as subjects for their investigations. In 1923, when Griscom's influence on ornithology and birding was on the ascent, Witmer Stone, editor of the *Auk* for more than twenty years, provided an excellent summary of the changes that had been occurring in ornithology:

> . . . From these comparisons I select as perhaps the most striking differences between the ornithology of today and of the yesterday of fifty years ago:
>
> (1) The immense increase of ornithologists, using the word in its broadest sense, and their differentiation along special lines.
>
> (2) The great decrease in collecting and collectors and the increase and improvement in the study of the live bird.
>
> (3) The taking up by ornithologists of broader philosophic topics and their participation in discussions of general biological problems. . . .
>
> While we all realize that the collecting of specimens in the more remote parts of the world is still of the greatest importance, and the collecting of specimens for special research purposes, in any locality, or for certain critical cases of identification, is still a necessity, we also realize that it is unnecessary for every student of birds to be a collector today, and that a local museum collection of skins easily accessible for examination seems to serve the same purpose as many private collections. Furthermore we are today in need of vast stores of records for work on migration, distribution, etc.—far more than could possibly be obtained by collecting,—and a similar stock of observations on behavior, courtship, etc., not only for life histories but for discussing broad biological problems,—observations of a character which are obtainable only from the study of the live bird.

These desiderata have already resulted in attempts to further the field study of live birds and to bring their identification, by observation alone, as nearly as possible to the degree of absolute accuracy that is attained by the collecting of specimens. The binocular field-glasses furnish the means of bringing the bird close to the observer, and what is now needed, and what is being supplied, is a series of descriptions of our birds based on field characters observable under such conditions, in place of descriptions drawn from a bird-skin in the hand. . . . The difficulties now presented by sight records will largely disappear when we have a standard of observation for field students so that they, and we who have to accept or reject their records, will know what characters they *can* see, and what characters they *ought* to see to render an identification acceptable.[7]

Some of the changes for which Griscom receives credit were already becoming part of the mainstream thinking in ornithological circles, but Peterson's field guide was more than a decade away, and the person who would emerge in the succeeding two decades to decide what can be seen and what ought to be seen was Ludlow Griscom. His ability and the efficiency of his methods were often put to the test. Peterson recalled one of the stories about Griscom in his early Linnaean Society days: "When Ludlow Griscom was a young man developing his field glass technique he was challenged by one of these old boys who made all his own identifications through the sights of a shotgun. Griscom pointed out a female Cape May warbler in the tip of a sycamore. The old boy blazed away. He picked up the bird. It *was* a female Cape May. After several repeat performances he became convinced that Ludlow knew whereof he spoke."[8]

This story, with a number of variations as to the species of warbler and location (usually Central Park), is so commonly recounted that it may well be true. Apocryphal or not, it suggests that as a young man Griscom, with his usual aggressive manner, was influencing the New York City crowd in a substantial way. What were these new field techniques that were purporting to make the shotgun a relic of the past? Edwin Way Teale, after a considerable interview with Griscom, reported an interesting story that sheds some light on Griscom's approach:

A few years ago, for example, he was leading a field-trip during a warbler wave. Seventy feet overhead, a small bird flicked from one treetop to another. Griscom called: "A magnolia warbler!" The rest of the party was frankly incredulous. How could he be sure when he had seen the bird for only a second so high overhead? During that second, he had seen that the underside of its tail was marked with white and jet black. No other warbler in North America is similarly marked. Handling skins of warblers in the museum had fixed this detail in his mind. He didn't need to see any more. He was sure.[9]

Griscom kept field journals, recording his observations in large ledgers after each day in the field. He began this practice in 1907 and continued it up to the time of his death. In 1949 he described his method of keeping field records.

Roughly speaking, my notes and records are on a much more simple basis than those of William Brewster, which in part seem to be sunk by overcomplexity and detail. I keep a daily record book which enters the field trip, the list of birds seen, careful counts or estimates of the number of individuals of every species and sufficient notes on the weather and migration as are pertinent. I do not stop with the weather of the day of the trip, but have kept a weather diary for 40 years by which I can even now perfectly reconstruct the history of the spring or fall migration wave by wave in past years when the details have completely escaped me. The most important aid to fact finding from this daily journal is a series of ring binder ledge[r]s in which every bird of North America is arranged in systematic order, and my observations are filed under each species by years and states. From this it is a simple matter to draw off the data from any particular area in which I am interested or working at the moment.[10]

The sixteen volumes of ledgers, which contain entries for virtually all of his several thousand North American trips and many of his foreign birding adventures, are housed at the Peabody Museum, Salem, Massachusetts. They contain a remarkable record of Griscom's bird lists (state, year, and life), and his observations of field marks and behavior. It is from the latter that we can gain insight into the development of his field techniques.

In 1914 Griscom recorded pages of field notes on the identification of ducks. One extensive entry, excerpted below, follows the usual list of species recorded during a day in the field, under the title of "notes."

7. Pintail — Was pleased to find that this species is easily told from other *Anatinae* at any distance. At long range the tail-feathers of the male are invisible, so that it appears no bigger than the female & neither sex appears as big as a *black duck* or a *Mallard drake*. In fact at long range it most closely resembles the *Baldpate* and the *female Mallard*. From all other *Anatinae*, however, it is easily distinguished by its shape, the body very slender, the neck very thin, the best characters being the width of the wing in flight at its junction with the body. In no other *Anatinae* is the wing so narrow at this

point. As a result it tapers gradually to a point instead of quickly as in other *Anatinae.* . . .

I was fortunate enough to see all three species in the same flock. About 8000 duck got up 1/2 a mile away and Wilson was able to tell the 3 species apart at that distance with the naked eye, and what is more to the point he was right. The *Canvasback* can easily be told at long range by its long bill & head. This gives it the effect of having the wings placed far aft. In the *Scaup & Redhead* the wings are in the middle. Furthermore the *Canvasback* appears slim in proportion to its length and is noticeably larger than the other 2 species when mixed in with them. From the *Merganser* apart from shape it differs in that the bill, head & neck & body never form a straight line, which is invariably the case in the Mergansers.[11]

A modern observer may disagree with many of the details of duck identification, and question the bold assurance of Griscom's pronouncements, but he was cutting new ground, looking for field characters that could effect rapid species identification under a variety of field conditions. He drew generalizations from these field observations and in 1915 completed his Master's thesis, which was largely on the identification of ducks. It included four plates on the shape of the Anatidae in flight, the wing arcs of ducks, flocking habits, and bills and heads. The concept of critical field marks was beginning to emerge.

The following series of excerpts from his field journals exemplify his new approach and demonstrate the care with which he made his observations in the field. First we see Griscom's comparative approach, helping to tease out the characters among similar-appearing or closely related species:

The *Sandhill Crane* stands about a foot shorter than the Whooping Crane and about 6 inches taller than a Great Blue Heron, which I have seen once very near some Cranes. There is a strong superficial color resemblance. The Crane is uniform, however, not distinctly lighter below, and the wing tips are deep brown rather than distinctly blackish. Shape however and outline is an excellent and infallible distinction. The bills of the two birds are approximately of equal length, consequently proportionately shorter in the Crane, the bigger bird of the two. It is at least *twice as deep* at the base. The neck is *twice as thick,* though equally long. The wing spread is at least 25% greater. The crown and forehead rises abruptly in a rounded curve as in sea ducks, while in Herons the head scarcely appears any deeper than the bill at base. These characters are readily noticeable when the bird is a mile away.[12]

Even before his move to Massachusetts, Ludlow was striking ornithological pay dirt around Boston.

The *Barrow's Goldeneye* male a very conspicuous bird, identifiable a quarter of a mile away. Black bar on side forward of wing; top half of wing black with longitudinal row of 7 white rectangular spots, decreasing in area backwards. White of lower half of wing continuing backwards as a narrow line separating black flanks from black back & tail, the forward line of the flanks distinctly in advance of the black above. Crescent shaped mark on side of head, really a curved tear-shaped mark, distinctly secondary in importance; head peculiarly shaped, purple. Bill very stubby, culmen rising very steeply. Female with dark gray spots in white wing patch, head perhaps a slightly darker brown; bill stubby & yellow at base; not a satisfactory bird to identify alone.[13]

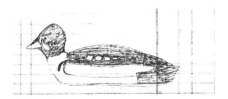

Sometimes, Ludlow would let a bird go unidentified, and often did so after long and careful observation:

Gull sp. 1 in juvenile plumage Newburyport, sitting on boat off Joppa Flats with 1 imm. & sev. ad. Herring Gulls, 50 yds. Differed from Herring Gull in following points

1. Very dark general coloration, fuscous, with small & more sharply defined lighter markings on back and wing coverts.

2. Head not lighter than body, with a solid blackish area on side of head, giving masked effect.

3. Primaries apparently solid blackish.

4. Tail conspicuously mottled with lighter basally, a conspicuous, broad, blackish, terminal bar.

5. Bill noticeably longer & slenderer than Herring, solid black, flesh color at extreme base only.

6. Legs longer & slenderer than Herring.
These characters would appear to correspond to the Lesser Black-backed Gull of Europe.[14]

He was always alert for patterns in migration. In this entry, he contrasts what he heard migrating at night with what he observed the following day.

Sept. 8 (Frid.) Sharp drop in temp. with w. & n.w. winds produces tremendous night migr. Out from 10.30 — 1.*oo am*. Warblers & 3 species of thrushes overhead every few seconds. Only a few Veeries; *Olive-back* 1 every 5 seconds = *1800* +, as often 6+ could be heard in a 5 sec. period . . . At least *3000*+ warblers. . . .

[September 9] During a long day's field trip . . . a record list of *112* species, and a record list of 15 species of warblers.

1) We did not see 100 Warblers!

2) We did not see a single Thrush!

3) The grand total of Olive-back & Gray-cheek thrushes seen by me in 37 spring & fall migrations does not exceed 3000 individuals![15]

With an abiding interest in bird behavior, as well as in field identification, he took every opportunity to record interesting behaviors as illustrated by this 1946 entry.

Clap hands & start night Herons out of reeds. Notice them flying wildly about, squawking hoarsely. Suddenly register the Gyrfalcon stooping at them. It finally cuts one immature out, which constantly rises, squawking hoarsely. Gyrfalcon gets above it and stoops 7 times. Each time night Heron squawks desperately, & does a remarkable "falling leaf" act; didn't know a night Heron could do it. At one time the two birds came within long gun shot range of me. Have strong impression Gyrfalcon only fooling; feel sure it could have struck Heron if it had chosen. In the meantime all ducks, grebes, coots, etc. disappear.[16]

Griscom would spend considerable time studying a rare bird. The field notes of a trip to South Carolina, when he visited John Henry Dick at Dixie Plantation, provide an interesting example. The purpose of the trip was to see a Bachman's Warbler. He ends one journal entry, "Have with us Newton Seebeck, a live-wire, energetic 18 year old, the discoverer of the warbler. In all 116 species,"[17] and two days later reports:

114.* *Bachman's Warbler* 2 males at Fairlawn Plantation [an asterisk signified a life bird]; study one of them from 5.30–7.15, and have one male under continuous observation, with Seebeck's help, for 75 mins. The most *persistent singer* I ever saw, 40–50x per. minute. Only 3 times did he stop, drop down to the undergrowth & grab a worm. He never went to the female, as I had hoped, and she never appeared. The *song* is loud for a good ear, audible at a considerable distance, but is quite ventriloquil, & it is often difficult to locate the singer, who occasionally shifts perches in his territory, for no apparent reason. The song is a rapid, monotone trill, most nearly resembling the Worm-eating, but the quality & timbre suggest that of a Parula, without any rise. The song has a slight *roll* in it, less buzzy & dry than the Worm-eater.

In *appearance* the bird suggests a dwarf, dingy, Hooded Warbler gone wrong. The olive green above is much grayer, the yellow below duller & oilier, the black breast patch duller. It is obviously a *Vermivora*, & the yellow chin & forehead are readily seen. The white patches on the tail are readily seen, only when the bird is moving about. The long, decurved bill is a character very difficult to see, only at close range, with a proper background. It *feeds* like a Blue-wing.[18]

Ludlow's development of an emphasis on field identification of live birds, the analysis of definitive field marks, and his love of the sport of birding (with its inevitable listing), had a marked effect on the ornithological community. New York City was the first center of critical field birding, and according to Roger Tory Peterson, the methods of field study were more or less developed by Ludlow.[19] In a 1960 article he reflected on the influence of Griscom in those early days.

"Ludlow Griscom was the first ornithologist I ever met, when as a lad of 17 I came to New York in 1925 to attend my first meeting of the A.O.U. . . . I was to see him in action the following Saturday when he led the field trip to Long Beach on Long Island. On that day 13 new birds went down on my life list, and I particularly recall the Brünnich's Murre that flew over near the inlet. It was the first record, Griscom stated, since the days when Eugene Bicknell worked the beach with his hand-held telescope.

Returning to New York a year later to take up my art education, I often saw Ludlow Griscom at the bimonthly meetings of the Linnaean Society which he dominated. He was always a good show and just a bit austere in keeping a group of young upstarts in line, a half-dozen eager-beavers known as the Bronx County Bird Club (Joseph Hickey and Allan Cruickshank were charter members). Although he had a particular fondness for these boys, his cross-examinations were ruthless when they reported three-toed wood-peckers and other unlikely finds. This was good training and only a few years later I witnessed both Joe and Cruicky giving similar merciless grillings to other upcoming youngsters at Linnaean meetings.

I became the first non-Bronx member of the very select Bronx County Bird Club, mostly because I hung around so much. Griscom was our God and his "Birds of the New York City Region" our Bible. Every one of us could quote chapter and verse. We used his terminology and even his inflection when we pronounced something as "unprecedented" or "a common summer resident." The leader of our little group, Jack Kuerzi, even parted his hair in the middle in the approved Griscom style.[20]

Griscom's influence on the younger bird enthusiasts can be seen in a letter to Peterson from Joseph J. Hickey.

Dear Tory,
My usual apology for being so tardy in forming a reply. I missed the last Linnaean but have been down to all the others. In reply to your "what's doing?" I can only inform you that Griscom has resigned his presidency of the society, and has left New York to accept a position at Harvard. Can you imagine the loss we of the younger generation feel? I don't suppose the old timers mind it as much as we do but L. G. certainly was the greatest single help and inspiration the B.C.B.C. ever had.[21]

Peterson, when recalling this era, added that he felt that Griscom's influence had not been lost, and that there had been a "chain reaction" right down to the present time. Hickey, in an interview, reiterated Peterson's description of the important role Griscom played in the Bronx County Bird Club, stating that they had memorized Griscom's master's thesis on duck identification and worn out his *Birds of the New York City Region*. Hickey suggested, however, that this influence was not always of a positive sort. He noted that Griscom inspired a sporting interest in birds, leading to a "list-crazy" focus, and that many young men under Ludlow's sway experienced difficulty going beyond the field identification stage to concentrate on more broadly based scientific work.[22] This is the great paradox in Ludlow's effect on the bird community, the poorly defined area of overlap between ornithology and sport birding. In later years Hickey came to view Ernst Mayr as his inspiration, but he thought that Griscom had always remained Peterson's inspiration.

The event most responsible for the explosive increase in the popularity of the sport of birding was the publication of Roger Tory Peterson's *Field Guide to the Birds* in 1934.[23] The field guide series, together with other guides that have appeared in competition with them, has shaped the development of both a widespread interest in all natural history and the ecological awareness that is the hallmark of the conservation movement of the present day. It may well be that Griscom's greatest single contribution to ornithology and conservation was the influence he had on the creation of that first field guide. Peterson has acknowledged, "My *Field Guide to the Birds* owes much to Ludlow: certainly the philosophy and the fine points of field recognition I learned from him."[24] In a 1980 article, he elaborated on Griscom's importance, beginning with the New York days.

I fell in with the seven young men of the Bronx County Bird Club to nurse the seeming impossible hope of sighting 100 species on the Christmas Count. We soon reached that number and more, thanks in large part to Griscom.

A genius at field identification, Griscom used his encyclopedic memory for "field marks" to identify birds. That phrase, which Edward Howe Forbush featured in his authoritative text, *The Birds of Massachusetts,* was already part of the *lingua franca.* But in print "field marks" usually meant the complete catalog of a bird's features starting with every raptor's talons and every tern's black cap. Griscom developed the practical habit of looking for distinguishing marks in the field—the visible signs that separated one wren from its almost identical cousins.

I left New York in 1931 packing all the ingredients of my new synthesis: Seton's boy protagonist sketching stuffed ducks; Reed's rustic book; Forbush's felicitous paragraph heading; Griscom's attention to the unique combinations of features which identify almost every species at a distance, whether afoot, abranch, or awing."[25]

In 1931 Peterson went to the Boston area, where he renewed his friendship with Griscom, and taught natural science and art at Rivers School. During the next three years, he put together his field guide, at the original suggestion of William Vogt. By 1933 the manuscript and plates were finished, and it was time to find a publisher, no simple task during the early years of the Great Depression, as Peterson describes:

In the belief that Bill [Vogt] had written a letter of introduction to Francis H. Allen at Houghton Mifflin in Boston, I went to call at his Park Street address. Allen liked the idea of the book immediately (he was an expert amateur birder). He said he'd like to consider it though he hadn't received Bill's letter. There was a catch, of course. Houghton Mifflin considered the project such a gamble that they could not afford to pay royalties on the first 1,000 copies.[26]

What Peterson did not know (until shown the following letter in 1982), was that part of that "consider it" would be to test the book plates on Ludlow Griscom. Richard J. Eaton of Houghton Mifflin recalled:

I had recently taken a job in another department of the company, & was invited by him to look at them [sample paintings and text] as a matter of interest. He asked me what I thought of them and did I have any suggestions? In reply, I offered to invite Griscom's opinion from a technical point of view, he being a recent Cambridge neighbor. This resulted in a session in

H. M. & G's conference room at #2 Park St. with me as a silent spectator. We seated Griscom on one side of the room, while Francis Allen showed the paintings one by one about fifteen feet away, thus approximating the equivalent of viewing the bird in the field through 8x glasses. The paintings passed the test with high marks. In due course Peterson was offered a contract based on the acceptance of completed text and paintings, thanks to Allen's confident judgement as an ornithologist in the commercial possibilities of Peterson's innovative idea.[27]

Griscom's expertise was valued by more than Allen and Eaton for, in a 1933 letter, Peterson asked him to review the book before it went to press.

No doubt by this time you have heard through some source or other of my projected Field Guide to Eastern Birds. Houghton Mifflin has agreed to put it out so I am very busy now trying to polish it up. . . .

As we all agree that in matters of field identification you are without question the court of last resort, I wonder if you would be willing to give the manuscript the final check-up? That is all that is needed to put the little handbook beyond too much further criticism. . . .

The illustrations are calculated to simplify things a good deal. They are not pictures or portraits but pattern charts devoid of feathering and modelling, making possible quick easy comparison of the species that are most apt to be confused with each other.

Some day soon I will drop in at the museum with the material and then we can talk it over.[28]

Ludlow gladly complied with his request. The book was published shortly thereafter and soon passed the "ultimate" test as an authoritative field guide. Fred M. Packard, a protégé of Griscom, remembers the incident: "I have a fond memory of a trip to Plum Island, shortly after Roger's first guide appeared, when he and Ludlow got into a hassle about the field marks of some bird before us. Finally, in fury, Ludlow reached in his pocket, handed Roger a copy of the guide, and snorted: 'Here, look it up for yourself.'"[29]

The field guide was a huge success. Peterson continued to ask Griscom's advice whenever a revision of the field guide was in order, as in the following 1937 letter.

Perhaps you already know I am planning a revision of the FIELD GUIDE. Such things as range, song, etc., will be dealt with more adequately, without enlarging the size of the book.

If you have any views, comments, or specific suggestions that might be profitably acted upon, I would be very indebted if you would send them on to me. Your counsel in these matters is always extremely valuable.[30]

When yet another revision was underway in 1946, Ludlow expressed his willingness to help and gave a few criticisms.

I am delighted that you are about to bring out a new, better, and revised Eastern Guide. You are probably right in having an increased number of colored plates and you are certainly right in doing over again most of the illustrations.

As a matter of fact, I have given some thought to ways and means of being of help to you. After all, there are so many species involved and the amount of factual detail is so enormous that it exceeds my capacity to read through your book and think of additional and worthwhile points, species by species. I can't begin to say how often I have dipped into your book, only to notice at the end of five years that some character in the identification of some species or some qualification in the use of a character might have been put in. Don't ask me why it took me five years to register. I have only three general suggestions at the moment.

1. You are obviously weakest on those birds with which you have had inadequate personal experience in the field. You might even consider the possibility or advisability of having some experienced expert prepare the text for such species. It did not detract in the least from Chapman's Handbook that various other ornithologists contributed sketches of certain birds.

2. You are exceedingly erratic and inconsistent in your treatment of immature plumages. If you reflect on it, you will find that quite a list of birds of eastern North America apparently don't have an immature plumage, according to your text.

3. The major fault of your guide is over-simplification of the identification of many difficult groups. Notable examples are the gulls, the terns, the two shrikes.[31]

In a 1946 letter Griscom suggests that Peterson took some of the advice.

I have had a most delightful correspondence with Roger. He first asked me to prepare the manuscript for a small list of special species and then sent me the manuscript of some fifty others for approval or correction. I was delighted to do this for him, and as a matter of fact, worked on this manuscript until two a. m. two days in succession. The net result is that I am enormously impressed with the caliber of the new book. It will be immeasurably superior to the last one and commands my unbounded admiration and respect.[32]

Griscom wrote the text for the Pacific Loon, Eskimo Curlew, Ruff, Black-headed and Little gulls.

At a meeting of the Nuttall Ornithological Club following Griscom's death, Peterson was quoted as saying that Ludlow had been the primary factor in stimulating the field guide.[33] For him, writing in memoriam,

> Griscom symbolized an era, the rise of the competent birdwatcher. . . . His influence spread like ripples on a pond. When he moved to Cambridge, Massachusetts, in 1927 . . . he created a second center of influence and Massachusetts ornithology has never been the same since. Today, wherever one goes in all parts of our country one finds that the sharpest local field observers were trained either by Griscom, his protégés, or his protégés' protégés; or they can be traced indirectly to his influence through some eastern club in New York, Boston, Philadelphia, or Washington where his influence was felt most strongly.[34]

Griscom's importance to birding in general extended beyond his contribution to Peterson's work, as he took his methods into the field and shared the joy of birdwatching with others.

Birdwatching with Griscom   11

In this chapter we turn to another component of Griscom's field ornithology, the sport of birdwatching. His great success at this activity, and his popularization of it, earned him the title "Dean of the Birdwatchers." Ludlow's success was measured in part by the size of the list of species seen, and it was this aspect of Griscom's field outings that got him into the most trouble with his professional colleagues. Certainly, Griscom did keep track of species seen in day lists, year lists, and, of course, a life list. He was proud of them and published his annual list for many years in the *Bulletin of the Massachusetts Audubon Society*. But as correspondence with fellow birders reveals, for all his pride in his accomplishments, compiling the largest list was not usually the goal or even the most satisfying part of birdwatching.

I was indeed pleased to get your letter and was most interested in your statistical bird report. I appent [sic] mine below by way of comparison but would add the observation that I have never yet tried to see how big a year's list I could get:
   1. Life list 2141 [includes some subspecies]
   2. North American list 941 = 640 species + subspecies
   3. Best year's list 660 in 1917

4. This year's list to date 589, certain to cross 600 even though I remain in Massachusetts the balance of the year.[1]

I was, possibly, a little more in the field than ever before but never have I had so many observations of interest to share with choice friends and companions. It was this last fact, rather than the size of the list, that made it a pleasant year's birding.[2]

We find in Ludlow an overwhelming love of the chase. He marshaled around him a group of devoted protégés, who followed him into the field, obeyed his orders, and dashed through the poison ivy flushing birds, like so many soldiers rushing off into battle. "Charge!" The general was not to be trifled with. Henry Parker, who spent many days afield with Griscom, stated:

> You brooked no nonsense with him. Some people got quite irritated with him because they claimed that he was very dictatorial in birding, but common sense and some understanding of human nature would make you realize that this man was the authority, he was doing this on a professional as well as pleasure basis. If you went birding with Mr. Griscom, you went birding the way Mr. Griscom wanted to, where he wanted to, and when he wanted to, and you were stupid, in my view, if you didn't recognize that before you went. He is still missed by those of us who were with him and we still remark on his extraordinary ability to con the birds out of the air, and tell what they were just about as far away as you could see them. . . . "I'll meet you . . . in Harvard Square at 5:30, breakfast inside" (you'd better have eaten), and if you were late he was gone—if you wanted to go with him, you'd better damn well be there (this irritated a few people).[3]

Birding was a social outlet for Ludlow—one in which he reveled. Behind that gruff exterior was a patient, kind, and sensitive person, who, if you were willing to play the game his way, could provide very satisfying and profitable days afield. He had a fine sense of humor, and, according to those who accompanied him, if you looked closely, you could always catch a marvelous twinkle in his eye. The recollections of those who went with him capture some of the flavor of these expeditions and provide a portrait of the man, his personality, and his skills in the field.

Dorothy Snyder, one of Griscom's frequent companions, and his co-author on *Birds of Massachusetts* (1955), documented Griscom's prodigious number of field trips in Massachusetts:

> His favorite spots were Cape Cod where his summer home was in Chatham, and Essex County. From the former he went to sea on 57 occasions and

drove down Monomoy more than 300 times. These were often exciting excursions. . . .

In Essex County there were more than 500 trips, sometimes from dawn to far into the night. These included some twenty sea trips, even in midwinter. Griscom made numerous, sometimes daily trips during migration to Mt. Auburn [Cemetery] and the Sudbury Valley, and took parties regularly to Berkshire County and the Connecticut Valley.[4]

Ludlow had a flair for the dramatic. He was a born showman, who capitalized on every opportunity to display his abilities, often with a slight touch of arrogance (prompting one detractor to call him the only man that he had ever seen who could strut sitting down). Roger Tory Peterson remembers him on a field trip back in the New York days: "He was a great leader. I remember there was a problem with crossing a stream in ankle-deep water, and he very gallantly picked up one of the ladies in his arms and carried her across the stream (he was a single man at the time)."[5] Peterson also wrote of Griscom:

A day in the field with the master was always punctuated with his characteristic phrases and pronouncements which became cliches to the clan: "Let's stop here and flap our ears . . . Check me on that one . . . Well, we bumped that one off . . . That's just a weed bird . . . Now someone find a bird with some zip in it . . . Just dribs and drabs left . . . What's the tide schedule? . . . First record for Massachusetts! . . . Unprecedented! . . . Please lower your voice to a howl . . . I don't like the look of that bird . . . Put it down to sheer ignorance, incompetence and inexperience . . . We got skunked on that one . . . That's a 10 cent bird . . . Well, we didn't do so badly . . . Having a good time?"

For many of us, these phrases and a hundred other Griscomisms bring to mind some of the richest hours of our lives, hours that usually started before dawn at the cafeteria on Harvard Square and often ended at Newburyport, Cape Ann, or Cape Cod.[6]

After Griscom's death, Annette Cottrell, who, along with her husband, William, were frequent companions of Ludlow's, compiled a list of "Griscomisms," wove them into an essay, and added the following to the list presented by Peterson:

"Just coming up for air," says LG, proposing a field trip . . . "Total waste of time. It just continues to be cold and backward . . .

"We have a good chance for a wave. We'll meet in Harvard Square at 4:00 AM with breakfast on board . . . " LG's searching eyes rake my extra top coat. "What are you going to wear when it gets *really* cold? . . . Cut the motor, please . . .

"What is this—a Yellow Warbler? Yes, just a ratty female . . .

"We'll beat the bushes here . . . Well, we ticked that one off . . . Who are those birders coming down the track? . . . What's your report? . . .

"Another cup of coffee, please . . . This is a good mug-up . . . Now gang, let's have a council of war. Clark's Pond? An avian desert this time of year. Fay Estate? Total waste of time. Not what it used to be. Besides, we've got to catch the falling tide at Plum Island . . .

"I don't like the look of this bird . . . Well, that was better than a belt in the rump with a spade! . . .

"Let's get out of here, it's getting dull! . . .

"Let's g o o! Bailey's Restaurant next stop. My sides are clashing together! . . . It's a whisker . . .

"Now gang, don't take too long over this; We're running behind schedule . . . A double martini, clam chowder and fried clams, please. Oh yes, and coffee. No, I never eat goop" (dessert) . . . "Thank God for that little bite . . . You have a clam chowder flush . . .

"Guess we wiped their eyes that time . . .

"Twit bird . . . that bird must be checked . . .

"A vast inland sea" as the tide floods the marshes on our right. "Yes, it's bursting full." We gaze apprehensively ahead at our road—submerged. "Charge! . . . Well we muffed that one." . . .

"With what I'm pleased to call my mind . . . What did you put over on us? . . . Accidental straggler—Good for *you*! . . . A golden day gives benediction."[7]

Juliet Richardson was a close family friend as well as birding companion. Her detailed recollections provide interesting insights into Griscom's character.

It so happened that he liked me and he liked David Garrison, so when the [Harvard summer school] course was over he began to invite us on his trips, and, of course, he only liked to go with people he liked, he would eschew other groups. But if you were included in the charmed circle—I can't tell you what it meant, my life was just transformed—I didn't care how early I got up in the morning, and I'd often wait if I was invited to something else to see if I was going to be invited on a field trip. . . . If the wind suddenly changed he could call up and say "We have to leave at four." He didn't waste any time and he knew right where to go. . . .

He was always the King and people did what he wanted. . . . Often I'd be the only woman and there would be Wendell Taber, Dick Eaton, and Gil Emilio . . . so I got to go through the poison ivy to flush the warblers—I was much younger—and I wouldn't dare not to do anything he would ask me to do, not possibly. He would have this enormous breakfast either at the Waldorf in Harvard Square or at a restaurant in Union Square in Somerville, where we would meet in the spring no later than 4:30. . . . First he would have orange juice, then wheatena, and he always had cream because as a boy his parents had cream but a boy never got cream, maybe a slice of orange, usually dropped eggs and three cups of coffee. Then off we'd go. We always stopped at a restaurant for lunch, he didn't like picnics, and it might not be until one or two that we got lunch. If you ate anything in between you were a creampuff (one of his pet terms). Annette [Cottrell] used to sneak raisins. Out on a ocean trip from Gloucester, we might get back as late as 3:00 for lunch in a restaurant and he always used to tease me about my "chowder flush." . . .

In those days you would never see anyone on Plum Island from Labor Day until Memorial Day, two little ruts, and in some places you'd churn. Twice he went walking off and when he got back the salt water was over the floorboards. Once when I was alone with him, we were half way down the island and we had to walk back to Newburyport and make arrangements to have somebody come and tow it back. Then we took the train to Boston. He wouldn't stop and think what the tide was at all, that maybe it would ruin his car, he wasn't practical, he wasn't a mechanic. . . .

One funny time with the Fosters and Griscoms and Richard Curtis, we went to Pittsfield for the weekend. He had rooms all arranged at the hotel. We had particularly to go to Lake Onota because it was the one place in the state then that you could get a Florida Gallinule. Then he had the idea that we should go up to Mt. Greylock to get the Winter Wrens and juncos, and Gray-cheeked Thrushes. So we arrived there just in time for sunset, and then he said, "Oh, I think we had better stay here and see the sunrise." It was a warm late spring, and I had on a linen dress. Judge Walcott was there, and someone had a Nash that became a bed, so Judge Walcott and Richard Curtis slept in that. The Fosters had two sleeping bags and slept on the ground. Ludlow had good quarters [?] which left the car for me and Edith Griscom. She took the back seat and I had the front seat with the steering wheel. It was a gorgeous sunrise. . . . Ludlow was like an English lord, and everything he did was right. We had reservations at the hotel, so that was where we were going to go for breakfast. You can imagine me in my linen

dress (which needed ironing)! We had to walk right into the dining room—
just follow him and everything was O.K.[8]

A number of Griscom's field companions came from the Outer Circle Bird
Club, which included Maurice and Ruth Emery, Arthur and Margaret Argue,
Cora Wellman, Rosario Mazzeo, Henry and Edith Halberg, Sibley Higginbotham, and several others. When Griscom heard about the OCBC, he insisted
on belonging. He became the mentor of the club and each year encouraged
little projects, usually something he was working on, thus recruiting a small
army of helpers. They changed the group's name to the Old Colony Bird Club
not only to give it a bit more respectability now that Griscom was a member
but also because Russ Mason wouldn't allow it to be the Outer Circle Bird Club,
when publishing its records of bird sightings in the Massachusetts Audubon
Society *Bulletin.*

The range of experience and scientific expertise of those who ventured into
the field with Griscom varied widely. When Ernst Mayr moved to the Boston
area, Ludlow took him birding. Mayr, perhaps the world's leading evolutionary
biologist, is critical of some of the professional aspects of Griscom's career
(thinking that Griscom was brilliant but not achieving his potential in scientific
ornithology). He nonetheless remembers with warmth their time together in
the field, during which Ludlow showed him a number of life birds (which
rather amused Mayr, who is not a birder in the sporting sense).

It was one of Griscom's great virtues that he always took the time to teach
the novice birders, answering their questions without irritation and making
sure that they enjoyed the outing. Annette Cottrell recalled her first such trip:

We reported [a Glossy Ibis] to our friend Dick Eaton, and he said, "Oh, you
must tell Ludlow Griscom about this." I said, "I haven't met him yet," and he
said, "Never mind, just give him a ring, he likes to get reports." So I did,
and he was very courteous, and thanked me warmly and asked me some
more questions about it, and at the end of our little discussion he said, "I'm
going to be birding down in Essex County this weekend and if you and your
husband would like to join us, I'd be happy to have you come along." We
did join him, and that was the beginning of joining him for years on week-
ends. His patience with newcomers was to me a very striking characteristic.
Whenever someone interested in birds would come to town they would hear
about Ludlow Griscom, and we often had young people, sailors, or people
just passing through along. We tried to keep our automobile cavalcade
down to as few as possible, but sometimes we would get up to six or seven
cars. But he didn't become impatient, he wanted everybody to learn, he

wanted to share his enthusiasm, which was infectious, because he was so obviously having a wonderful time himself. . . .

The end-of-the day rite seemed imperative—no matter how late or tired we might be, he'd sit down at that card table and write up every single bird. He would set up the card table and put out that book and write them all down. He would check around and say, "Well, I remember 20."[9]

Ludlow often took his son, Andrew, with him on birding expeditions, and Andrew recalls his father's proficiency and the warm strength of personality that contributed so much to the success of the outings.

The Brookline Bird Club mob would have been at Newburyport for a half hour looking at the obvious birds, and Dad would pull up, look around and within thirty seconds he'd say, "Say, have you noticed that?," and nobody would have seen it. Things always happened when he was around. He had an intuitive, almost gut-level feeling of where a bird would go—the suitable habitat. Over and over he'd take us over to some dune area and sure enough an owl or a hawk would fly out of that particular pocket of the dunes. It wasn't at all clear why he decided to walk in that direction, as opposed to any number of sand dunes, and I've walked over many sand dunes that don't have hawks or owls. . . .

He would be very entertaining after a long day of birding. The crowd might stop for dinner, and the inevitable cups of coffee that my father was always drinking, people slumped from fatigue around the table, and he'd get a burst of energy, get people perked up, start talking, get the whole table completely revitalized with his sense of humor. He was quite aware at some level of how other people were feeling, and would want to do something to improve the scene.[10]

Griscom's remarkable powers of identification extended beyond avifauna. John Baker, president of the National Audubon Society, related a botanical story about Griscom in a 1959 article.

One day Ludlow and Dr. Robert Cushman Murphy were traveling east toward Montauk, Long Island, at some 50 miles an hour. Murphy suddenly said, "Ludlow, what is that white flower we just went by in the shoulder of the road?" Ludlow, without stopping the car, still doing 50 miles an hour, looked through the back window and said, "That is (such and such) indigenous to Switzerland and that is the first record of it in this country." He stopped the car within a quarter-mile, backed up, and verified his observation.[11]

The anecdotes concerning Ludlow in the field are legion. One of Griscom's freshman advisees at Harvard, Chandler S. Robbins, said, "I don't ever remember his making an identification error [in the field]. I can't say that about anybody else."[12] He also recalls the brash side of Griscom, who had been known to take a group of the "HOC boys" (Harvard Ornithological Club) to some fancy estate and say to the owner, "I'm Ludlow Griscom and I've got some students to show birds to and I want to go on your place." Griscom was rarely turned away.

Douglas Sands, a Nuttall Ornithological Club member, recollected a typical bit of Griscom showmanship.

> Wherever Ludlow went, others were sure to follow. One spring morning in Mt. Auburn he had his usual "gang" keeping him company and he stopped at the intersection of two of the little roads there. He had a flair for keeping excitement in the chase. He pronounced that if everyone would look around, they might find a Screech Owl watching them at the moment. Frantic looking ensued with eventual success. Then as he strolled (he was seldom in any obvious hurry) down one of the roads, he swung his big head skyward, and pointed with a finger to the zenith, exclaiming "Gavia immer immer [Common Loon] going north." All I could see was a faint speck against the blue. Seems as though his eyes were comparable to Ted Williams of the Red Sox. He was unique, one of a kind.[13]

Garrett Eddy, another Nuttall Club member, reports one of a number of stories, many apocryphal, about times when Ludlow was caught off base.

> We were sitting around a fire on the beach totalling the species seen. As the list was being finalized, some one casually mentioned the addition of a Dovekie to the list. Mr. Griscom paused, shook his head, and said he thought that was highly unlikely. In fact, it had been hazy over the ocean and a small bird way out over the water seen through a telescope would be very difficult to identify with certainty. No records had ever been made of a Dovekie in May this far south. "No, we better not include it," he said. With that, Roger T. Peterson lifted the wooden box he had been sitting on and a Dovekie waddled slowly out into the firelight.[14]

Some of the great birding shows that Griscom sponsored were the sea trips for pelagic birds and ducks. Sometimes in winter when the alcids were around, he would rent a fishing boat in Gloucester, and head out around the Salvages, a group of offshore islands. In late summer and fall, the trips left from Chatham and concentrated on the pelagics—shearwaters, petrels, and jaegers. In the winter the Cape Cod trips were aimed primarily at the enormous flocks of sea ducks that overwintered in that area. Griscom described one memorable trip in a 1936 field journal entry.

21. Surf Scoter perhaps 50

One of the greatest concentrations of sea-fowl I ever saw; in the tide rips around Stone Horse Lightship; water covered with scattered flocks of Scoters over several square miles, also one huge flock 1/4 mile deep by 1 1/2 miles long, most of which got up at once, when 2 motor boats went through it. A very fine spectacle.[15]

A bit of the character of the sea trips and weekend accommodations is found in the recollections of Ruth Emery, a protégé of Griscom's.

We were on a sea trip and I picked up my glasses because a bird came along that looked different to me. Ludlow said, "What are you looking at?" He would sit down there and let the rest of us do the work. He knew immediately what they were. I said "Oh, don't bother it's just a Laughing Gull," eye level, dark head coming right at me. By the time it got around to him, he said, "What do you mean, that's a Sabine's Gull!" I said, "It is?" I had never seen one before. He used to call up and say that it's going to be a good weekend—call up a group and fill the house— no more than six people who were good campers. Down at Chatham, the boys would start the furnace—it would take an hour—and I'd be assigning rooms. Everybody brought their sleeping bags. . . . We went there in the fall and winter. You'd go to sea in November and it would be darn cold, and you'd get in and have a rum swizzle, Meyer's dark rum, and an open fire, nothing more pleasurable. We used to have great arguments around that open fire.[16]

Wallace Bailey, the first director of the Massachusetts Audubon Society's Wellfleet Bay Wildlife Sanctuary and a birding companion of Griscom's, also shared the boat trips.

Harold Claflin was the only person Ludlow would go to sea with off of Chatham. He was just a fisherman, later Harbor Master. Some trips had very few birds in summer, on others there was great abundance. We would always catch some cod or other fish, get the livers, and Harold Claflin would squeeze the liver out, making a slick on the water to pull in petrels and shearwaters. It was a small boat that fishermen would use, you could take six so the party was always small. Claflin used to know where the fish were—we used to leave it up to Harold since he was going out about every day. Back in those days there were very few people who went out on an organized trip except for Ludlow. Once or twice a year or more—it was always a long day.[17]

Ludlow even had his own recipe for bringing in the pelagic birds: "Replying to your recent inquiry, the only slick that is really sure fire for ocean birds is cod-livers, and apparently the riper they are, and the more the nasty stuff stinks, the better! This is the only fish gurry that has enough oil to float on the surface of the water. The combination of bread crumbs and ordinary salad oil will often attract Petrels, but nothing else."[18]

A typical Griscom itinerary was a trip to Monomoy, the sometimes peninsula, now a series of islands, off the south side of Cape Cod near Chatham. In the early years, Griscom would rent a beach buggy from the Eldredge brothers, Norman and Clement, who ran the Eldredge Garage. Norman often acted as driver. Eventually, Griscom owned a series of his own vehicles, the most memorable of which was a wooden-sided stationwagon called the "Sandpiper's Rest" or just the "Sandpiper." The vehicle had to be ferried over to Monomoy by barge, which was a precarious undertaking, and after arriving safely, there was always the threat of getting stuck in the sand, or encountering some other misadventure. Generally, Ludlow would invite people for the weekend, doing Monomoy one day and Nauset Beach the next. The hundreds of trips that he led down the island, with innumerable guests, produced some great adventures and some great misadventures. As Wallace Bailey remembers, when Ludlow was driving he was thoroughly reckless, and he expected whoever was driving to be the same.

> He drove wildly on Monomoy, there's no question about that. It was a horror scene. Edith would try and get Henry Parker or one of the other boys, or me, in the driver seat if she could. But Ludlow was pretty determined that he wanted to drive. He had an old vehicle which he called the Sandpiper, which he bought from the Eldredges. It was a Model A Ford, old wooden stationwagon with huge balloon tires. He used to always get stuck. We always dreaded it when he would get stuck because he would grind it in good, and it would take us a couple of hours of wasted time, and he always counted the minutes when he was down there, he wanted all the time he could get to be at a certain place at high tide, and the flats, and watch for jaegers when the tide was low.[19]

Allen Morgan, executive vice-president of the Massachusetts Audubon Society, also frequently accompanied Griscom on Monomoy trips.

I can remember on Monomoy in August, *Empidonax* flycatchers all over the place, and Ludlow identifying Least from Traill's. I said, "Ludlow you can't do that," so he said, "All right, let's collect a series." He was right in every single instance. On the same day, I think, driving down Monomoy, warblers would zip across the road and he would say Cape May, Bay-breasted. From one plum bush to another across the sand road, in flight while he was driving, in August! We'd stop, and damnation, he was right.[20]

One annual activity that helped promote birdwatching was the Christmas count, an occasion that had been started in 1899 by Frank Chapman of the American Museum of Natural History in New York. This event was still in a developing stage when Griscom did his first Christmas count in 1908, in Bronx Park, with one other person. The following year he did the Long Beach census by himself. Today thousands of people engage in the annual counts of fifteen-mile-diameter circles, located mostly in North America, usually with dozens of birders covering each circle. By the time he reached the Boston area in 1927, the Christmas counts had become a bit better organized, and Ludlow started one on Cape Cod (reporting the tally in *Bird-Lore* in 1928), and became a regular on the Essex County census. Under Griscom's direction, by the mid-1930s the counts had become well-oiled machines, with large groups deployed to make sure that few birds got away uncounted. The following excerpt from the 1935 field journal of David Garrison tells of Griscom's army of twenty.

> The method was to divide the above posse into four parties, each to search a clearly defined area of the general territory. The closeness of the search that resulted amazed me. Low and Whitman . . . covered Nauset and thereafter poached in the Brewster Lakes region. Hinchman's troop did from Nauset Heights southward, land & sea, though not to the very end of South Beach. Scott, Taber & party had the Brewster Woods and shore. Griscom's party, where I was assigned, had Eastham & Chatham, starting along the A.O.R. [Austin Ornithological Research Station], crossing to Chatham & doing the southern boundary, i.e. Morris Island, then returning along the North Chatham waterfront; with a hoot for owls ad lib. after darkness set in. Well, we looked the territory over right and proper.[21]

Griscom had to deal with the common problem of the occasional over-zealous person coming up with improbable species or numbers of birds. Since he took the collection of Christmas count data seriously, he tried hard to minimize these "problems," putting inexperienced people with more experienced ones, and if he anticipated difficulty with a particular individual, he was not above assigning a specific individual to "shadow" the potential problem person. His best-laid plans didn't always work, though, as sometimes the problem person got away. Ruth Emery reported that on one occasion a young man had been assigned to cover an older birder who had a habit of finding some pretty fancy birds when he was alone. Griscom said to the young man, "Whatever you do, don't let him out of your sight. Now that's an order." Back at the inn that evening for the tally the poor young man sat there, too scared to move. The older man announced a find that no one else had reported, and the sad young man looked over at Ruth and said, "I only left him for a moment."[22] Sibley Higginbotham confirmed this account, remembering that when the older man at the tally announced the only sighting of a particular species, Ludlow gave the young man a look, and the boy just shrugged—the older man had gotten away![23]

When you were in the field as many times, with as many people as Ludlow Griscom was, things were bound to happen. The stories about Griscom on the Christmas censuses are numerous, and it is difficult to sort the real events, embellished or not, from the apocryphal tales. But they all speak to the mystique of Ludlow Griscom. Many stories relate the rather dogmatic tendency that Griscom had, and on many occasions he was drawn into traps by his friends. A case in point was related by Tom Davis in a 1979 memorial article on birder Robert W. Smart.

> As a college student, Bob became a protégé of former Linnaean Society President Ludlow Griscom. Bob proved to be one of Ludlow's better understudies and injected his own style of Falstafian wit to expose the foibles of his fellow birders. Bob loved to relate how he found a Virginia Rail on the Cape Cod Christmas Count one year. When compiler Griscom gruffly responded to Bob's claim by saying, "Mr. Smart, one does not find Virginia Rails on Cape Cod in the winter," Bob removed from his coat pocket an injured Virginia Rail—which immediately ran to Ludlow![24]

Griscom had a hand in making another event a part of North American birdwatching. The Big Day is a grueling event in which a team of birders attempts to see as many species of birds as possible in a single calendar day. Griscom's field journals have entries as far back as pre–World War I, which, although not called Big Days, have all the earmarks of them. He ran them in Rhinebeck County, New York, with his close friend Maunsell Crosby, and many others around New York City and New Jersey. After he had moved to Massachusetts, he often invited some of the New York crowd, including Roger Tory Peterson, to come up and join him for his Essex County to Cape Cod Big Days. He sometimes traveled south to New York or New Jersey to repay the favor.

An excerpt from Griscom's 1931 field journal gives insight into the schedule, pace, and territory of his early Big Days.

Elizabeth at 3oo a.m.; arrive Troy Meadows, 4.30 *am* to 7.30 a.m.; Boonton, reservoir & hills, about 3 hours; across country through Morristown, & Bernardsville to Lamington . . . thence through Princeton & South Trenton to Atison & Hammonton in the Pine Barrens to Atlantic City & Brigantine Beach (5.30–7.30); up the coast to Tom's River (where pitch dark about 9 p.m.). . . .

We left Troy Meadows at 7.30 *am* with 104 species in three hours, and had 142 species before reaching the coast. Weather conditions ideal the whole day, warm & muggy & overcast until 6oo a. m., clearing cool from the northeast but without any high wind; lovely morning generally (temp. 72° max.), became overcast & cooler with shift to very light northeast wind about 3 p.m.; birds consequently active all day & more or less singing all day. All factors combined produced the *world's record list* of 163.[25]

By 1933 Griscom was establishing his Big Day route in Massachusetts.

May 21st. New census route in eastern Mass.; left Cambridge at 2*am,* arrived *Boxford* 3.15 *am* in pouring rain; try for owls a failure as a result; left Club camp at dawn & arrived Lynnfield Meadows at 5.15 *am.*; *West Peabody, Fay Estate* (brief stop for specialties only), *Nahant* (brief tour only & left at 9oo a.m.); *Cambridge & Mt. Auburn Cemetery* (left at 11.45); to *South Carver* via Route 58, with stops for pine barren specialties; *Wareham* (left at 3.30 p.m.); *Chatham & Monomoy* (4.30 - 7.30 p.m.); *Pleasant Bay & Town Cove, Orleans* (brief stops for stray ducks); *Eastham golf club* (8.30 p.m.); *Great Pond, Eastham* (no luck with owls); home via Route 6 with frequent stops Brewster to Barnstable for night birds; arrive Cambridge 2.15 a. m. . . ; Eaton, Wendell Taber & Peterson.[26]

The Griscom-led Big Days were very popular, and a number of people have written up their accounts of adventures experienced on them. Roger Tory Peterson described the general strategy and detailed some events from a particularly interesting Big Day. The references to the military, and the military language, suggest that Griscom was the boss, the general of the army, in a war of limited objective: to compile the largest list of species seen in a single day. We also witness an example of Griscom's brash confidence.

This all-out May-day tournament was something I had never heard of before I came into contact with the birdmen of the big cities along the East coast. New Yorkers and Bostonians call it the "Big Day"; the New Jerseyites the "Lethal Tour"; Philadelphians the "Century Run," and Washingtonians the "Grim Grind." . . .

The evening before we held a council of war over the telephone. Griscom had studied the weather maps and the tide tables. He had outlined where we would stop and when, but each of us offered amendments. Even though the trip was planned as precisely as a train schedule, we left some room for flexibility. . . .

Like a magician, plucking rabbits from a hat, Griscom pulled out the two "fanciest" birds of the day. Ordering the driver to stop, he put his glasses on a lone bird swimming beyond the surf. Quickly appraising, he called out "Brünnich's murre." The telescope was brought to bear on the piebald swimmer and without a hint of chagrin, Griscom retracted the first guess. "Sorry!" he apologized, "just an old-squaw." Even Griscom makes mistakes, but he is usually the first to correct them.

We had hardly gone several hundred yards further down the beach when another lone swimmer caught our attention. Griscom squinted, hesitated and blurted "Brünnich's murre." We respectfully reserved judgement while he tensely hauled out the telescope again. In a moment he relaxed. "Don't you believe me?" he queried. "Look for yourselves!" We did. There was no doubt about it; the bird was a murre, that black-and-white sea bird that reminds one so much of a penguin. It was in changing plumage and the proportion of the bill and the light-colored mark along the gape showed it to be a Brünnich's! This curious coincidence did much to increase our ever-growing awe of Griscom. No one but he would have dared cry "Brünnich's murre" again so soon after making a blunder.

The payoff came a short distance further down the beach when a third lone sea bird was spotted, bobbing up and down in the wave troughs. With hardly a moment's deliberation Griscom electrified us with "Atlantic murre!" That was too much! To get both murres in one day was an extremely rare event in Massachusetts even in the dead of winter. It was next to impossible in May. Surely Griscom was getting tired—probably he had too much sun. But the telescope backed him up. The bird *was* an Atlantic murre in winter plumage. The thin pointed bill and the dark line behind the eye left no doubt about it. . . .

Dinner never tasted so good. When the apple pie had been followed by coffee and we had taken out our check-list cards, we counted the day's total.

It came to 148! This was a new high for Massachusetts and for all New England.[27]

Accompanying Griscom and Maunsell Crosby on a Big Day in Dutchess County, New York, were Francis Lee Jaques, a celebrated wildlife artist, and his wife, Florence. Whereas he was an accomplished ornithologist, she was something of a neophyte. She recorded her impressions of the Big Day with humor, and produced a marvelous portrait of Ludlow while she was at it, in her book *Birds Across the Sky*.

Soon we came to a pleasant old mansion surrounded by thorny locust trees, whose trunks were veiled in pale green. On the steps we met the other guest, Ludlow Griscom, a noted ornithologist from Boston. He was a square man with black and silver hair, strong decided features and equally decided opinions. Lee told me, as we went into the house, that Mr. Griscom was supreme in identifying birds in the field, "all known sub-species at ultimate range."
. . .

Maunsell and Mr. Griscom were evidently intimate friends, and their railleries, humorous and easy on one side and caustically witty on the other, sparkled like fireflies through their tales of trips taken together through Florida, Texas, Panama and Guatemala. But it was easy to see that in spite of the interest Maunsell had in far places, it was Dutchess County which he passionately loved.

After dinner, we had coffee in a yellow drawing room and Mr. Griscom played Bach for us, while our host showed us his daughter's poetry. A little after ten, Maunsell suggested that we might like to get some sleep. "We get up frightfully early, you know, Florence. I hope you won't mind."

"Oh, I won't mind at all." (What statements do we make for courtesy's sake!) "When do we start?"

"Half past two."

After the before-dawn start yielded a Barred Owl as the first bird of the Big Day, the trip progressed.

"But you seem to go to a certain spot and find the exact bird you want!" I said to Maunsell. "I thought birds went their own sweet ways, here, there, and everywhere."

"Not at all. Birds are closely tied to their special environment," Mr. Griscom said. "Just as you'll find a banker in a bank and a mechanic in a garage, you'll find a jacksnipe in a boggy field and an oriole in an orchard." He proceeded to tell me about bird distribution in North and South America. I was flattered by his casual use of Latin names when I didn't know half the English ones I'd heard.[28]

The list for the day was 120 species.

When there was a chance for a record, Ludlow would pick up the pace a little. He really did enjoy the challenge. Sibley Higginbotham was along on one such occasion.

> Ludlow knew that Bill Cottrell was keeping the list, and he was measuring it all the time to see if we had a shot at the 160. Ludlow would say, "Let's not relax, let's continue." (Cottrell was giving him the statistics). He would have continued on anyway, but not with the intensity or excitement as if he knew there was a chance to break the record. I can remember one important decision he made. We were in Newburyport, and there were some pegged down [not literally] Blue-winged Teal seven miles away in Ipswich, and he decided not to go, figuring that we might lose two species to pick up that one. He was making those administrative decisions all the time. At Crooked Pond we were after Barred Owls. Ludlow called and called, I never felt so sorry for anyone, he really wanted to impress Guy Emerson that day, he was trying so hard. Then all of a sudden two started, and Ludlow turned around and looked at everybody with this big smile on his face. It was dark but we could still see it.[29]

In 1942 Ludlow Griscom was asked to accompany President Franklin Delano Roosevelt on a morning of birding.

According to James L. Whitehead, who eventually published the story of the trip, Roosevelt had been keenly interested in birds as a boy, but his passion had been curtailed in later life by his political career and his debilitating polio paralysis.[30] The idea for an outing originated among a group of birding friends—Allen Frost, Whitehead, and Margaret Suckley. The two men had participated in a Dutchess County Big Day the previous May, and Suckley was to be included in the event in 1942. She was a good friend of President Roosevelt, whose Hyde Park home was in Dutchess County. As early as February, she had inquired of the president whether he would be interested in such a birding trip, and he apparently had been enthusiastic about the idea. They all knew Ludlow's love of Dutchess County and mastery of its bird life, and so Ludlow was duly invited to accompany the president and the others on this excursion.

Edith Griscom stated that Ludlow was at first not at all taken with the idea. In political matters, Ludlow was a Republican. He considered FDR's "shenanigans" outrageous, and in 1940 had strongly supported Wendell Wilkie's nomination for president. She recalled:

> This man [Allen Frost?] got in touch with Ludlow and asked him if he would take the President on an early morning birding trip. Ludlow said "No!" he didn't like the man, was against Roosevelt politically. . . . So I said "Ludlow, this man happens to be the President of the United States, there's a war on, a very serious war, and he is absolutely exhausted. He's back there at Hyde Park resting. Its your patriotic duty to go and do anything that can relax his brain in any way, shape, or form." So Ludlow said he would do it. . . .
>
> Ludlow took the train to New York, then on to Daisy Suckley's house. They went over to Hyde Park—there were flares along the driveway. Roosevelt was brought down the stairs by two men and greeted Ludlow. He had a big car with the top down. They placed Roosevelt in the back seat and he told Ludlow to get in the back seat with him. The librarian got into the front seat. There were handgrenades on the floor. Roosevelt said to Ludlow "We call this car the Queen Mary." The sides of the car were bullet-proof. The Secret Service man had said to Ludlow "Where are you going?" and Ludlow replied, "Off into Thompson's Pond, but I'm not exactly sure where we are going." It was dark and the Secret Service men were in a tizzy over it. Off they went to Thompson's Pond, birding by ear. A big searchlight went on and four Secret Service men ran up and stood beside the car. All the birds got very quiet. Ludlow said to Roosevelt "Please tell them not to put that flare-light on, and not to come rushing up noisily like that." Roosevelt said to Ludlow, "There is one person that the President of the United States can not tell what to do, and that is a Secret Service man. If you want to go back and plead with them, go ahead." So Ludlow went back and talked to them, and the light went off, but two men on each side of the car continued. Daybreak came, the sun was up, and at seven A.M., Daisy, Ludlow and the Secretary [Frost] were out sitting on the running board eating breakfast."[31]

Andrew Griscom related a final anecdote: "One incident included my father standing beside the car doing his usual chirping to call the birds in close. At that moment a chickadee landed on his hat and explored it for a few seconds to the President's delight."[32] Certainly it had been an unusual way to start a Big Day, one that ended successfully with a total of 108 species seen. Ludlow had thoroughly enjoyed himself and sent Margaret Suckley a note of thanks.

> I have been meaning for some time to drop you a few lines of thanks and grateful appreciation for hospitality and shelter under most appalling and unusual conditions. Seldom, indeed, in my life has it devolved upon me to thank someone for supplying an excellent breakfast at 2:30 A.M. . . .

I am, of course, keen to hear, if you are permitted any gossip, about the President's reactions to the trip, not to mention that of your own family. I hope he was not worn out and sorry he did it.[33]

Griscom's virtuosity in field identification of birds is legendary. But what his field companions remember most about Ludlow was his enormous enthusiasm, his brusque sense of humor, his vitality, and his immense satisfaction in initiating others into the pleasures of birdwatching. As Allen Morgan wrote in a letter to Dorothy Snyder, "But really he dominated his era as a *person*."[34]

Sight Records and Collecting 12

There has been much misunderstanding of Ludlow Griscom's attitude toward collecting, sight records, and the role of the amateur. Griscom created, or found himself, in a difficult and paradoxical situation. On one hand, amateurs were shocked by his criticism and failed to understand his goals and his standards; on the other, professionals, likewise uncomprehending, chided him for dilettantism.

Griscom viewed himself as a moderate when it came to the problem of sight records. He stated his position unequivocally in a 1954 letter to Harold Mayfield, secretary of the AOU, in which he supports the philosophy of having symposia at the AOU meetings.

I think a suitable topic for a good symposium would be the problem of sight records. The following people should be asked to speak: (1) somebody like Van Tyne who, no matter how polite, really has no damn use for sight records; (2) somebody like Alexander Sprunt, who has obviously adopted the unfortunate modern slogan: "Modern techniques in field identification have so greatly improved, so many people are acquiring first-hand experience with birds all over the United States, the censoring of records is disagreeable, often embarrassing; let's believe everybody." Finally, you might select a middle-of-the-road man like myself, who has more or less proved that he can see two sides to this question.[1]

The pressure on Griscom concerning sight records versus collecting came from all directions. At the Nuttall Ornithological Club meetings, Griscom was quickly criticized by the "old boys" in the club, for whom collecting was virtually the only acceptable means of bird identification. Richard J. Eaton described the kind of pressure new sight identifications received from another club member, Charles W. Townsend.

> He was of the old school which profoundly distrusted sight records of rare birds, even his own. Griscom told me that shortly after his move to Cambridge, he reported as a field note some bird, I forget which, that is exceedingly difficult to identify in the field, let's say a Long-billed Dowitcher, a bird he had studied carefully and had been able to prove his field identification by subsequent collection. Townsend hauled him over the coals for making such a report. "How do you know you saw a Long-billed Dowitcher" etc. etc. Griscom took it on the chin without a murmur, but later brought in a specimen of the bird in question which he had happened to report.[2]

Griscom claimed that he averaged collecting one bird per year between 1928 and 1945 (but he did collect fifteen during 1941). He was judicious in his selection, usually collecting only those that were distinctly state records or had odd plumages. This is well illustrated by his annual report for 1941, which listed six horned larks, including three of the Hoyt's subspecies, two of the Alaskan subspecies of the Red Crossbill, a second state record of the Nelson's subspecies of the Downy Woodpecker, a first record for the Labrador subspecies of the Savannah Sparrow, the first Massachusetts specimen of the Little Gull, a hybrid tern, and a Newfoundland subspecies of the Yellow Warbler.[3]

His acquisition of the Alaskan Red Crossbills made for some interesting reading. Ludlow had originally tried to collect one on a Sunday in Cambridge but was denied permission by the police because it was Sunday (no hunting allowed) and because it was Cambridge (no discharging firearms within the city limits). This was wonderful fun for the local press and articles appeared with the headlines: "Sergeant and Sabbath Cross up Science" in the *Boston Herald,* "SCIENTIST CAN'T SHOOT RARE BIRD" in the *Boston Post,* and "Law Blocks Science, Saves Rare Finches" in the *Boston Globe.* Later, Ludlow managed to get police permission, and the local press responded with: "Great Cross-Country Crossbill Hunt Is On," "Alaskan Crossbill, Rare Specimen, Found Dead," "Professor Griscom Gets Crossbill," "Crossbill Finch! Beware of Harvard Zoologist's 'Pouf,'" and "Crossbills Now Birds in Hand; Science Flinches at Finches."[4] The humor of the press accounts apparently rubbed off on Ludlow, who described the collection of one of the crossbills: "P.S. Just back from lunch. The 12th visit to the Nash Crossbill pines, resulted in finding the birds there, & I have just popped off an Alaskan male on Samuel Eliot's front lawn!"[5]

Griscom's field journals yield many examples of times when he thought it necessary to collect a bird, and the disastrous mistakes you can make in identification of a difficult bird unless it is collected.

> *Dec 9th* Plum Island . . . *Steller's Eider* - Watched all a.m.; return after lunch at 1.30 p.m. Bird's habits quite regular; feeds off tip of breakwater & then drifts out into rough sea, where tosses about, preens etc., after a while swims or flies back to breakwater & resumes feeding. . . . The Eider never comes in to feed again, but flies north over breakwater with Mergansers. Hagar had perfectly good shot, but no point in shooting bird into rough sea & tide current running out, as could never retrieve it. Get fine views, & can see characteristic bill & feather processes as per specimens examined Monday. No doubt of identity. . . .
>
> Dec. 22 & 23, Hagar at Plum Island working on Eider. As result of studies in field last week & study of specimens at museum, begins to doubt bird is Steller's Eider, as bill & process not right, nor can he find any specimen colors which correspond exactly to pictures of bird in the field. . . . Hagar can land on "pinnacle" & shoots Eider at easy range.
>
> 1) *King Eider* 1 imm. — proves to be remarkably small bird of this species, with a plumage not to be matched exactly in M.C.Z. series. . . . The matter of size very interesting. When Hagar is on "pinnacle," this Eider as usual with Scoters and Mergansers, & there are also 2 *changing male King Eiders,* blackish birds with some white on chest & neck & white wing patches forward. These latter, just as expected, obviously larger birds than the White-w Scoters, & our puzzling Eider obviously smaller.
>
> The whole incident is as fine an illustration as any in my experience of the risk in "sight records" & the value of collecting the specimen![6]

Some birds simply cannot be satisfactorily identified in the field, as in the following two instances.

> *Jan. 24th.* Notes on remarkable Oriole. . . .
>
> Today find bird in 5 minutes & after a while it flies to apple orchard & feeds on frozen apples. . . . Go to museum at once & look at skins.
>
> *Jan. 26.* Hagar arrives Dedham 7.30 a. m., Garrison & Touseys at 8.30. Bird arrives at 10.55 with only Touseys present. At 11.30 after watching it on ground with sparrows don't know what it is, but think too large & too dark above for Orchard. Hagar returns & all watch it in apple tree at 15 yds. Tousey says "why not Baltimore"? Hagar says "no; it is an Orchard" too

large, say Touseys. All 3 proceed to M.C.Z. & looks at skins. Hagar inclines
to Baltimore (abandons Orchard theory), but admits bill & color below off.
Richard Tousey strongly inclines to Scott's, and Ruth thinks Baltimore ±
Scott's with doubts in either case. Summary — no identification!

   Jan 27. . . . Take Francis Allen to Dedham & meet Hagar there at 11 a. m.
Find Oriole in nearby yard on ground with sparrows & have perfect studies
of it for well over half an hour. Thanks to study of skins, obvious there was
no such Oriole in real life, & conclusion that bird was freak of some kind
obvious. Theory that it was a freak Baltimore gains ground on general *pattern* of coloration, waiving exact color & shade. Leave at 1 p. m. with Allen,
leaving Hagar behind. He collects bird & arrives M.C.Z. with Allen & me.
Careful exam shows that bird is . . . *Baltimore Oriole*—wings *adult,* tail *immature;* bill largely bluish ivory gray; coloration strongly melanistic throughout, but (also?) a strange olive wash throughout, completely distorting color
of front half of bird above & whole surface below. Wings practically normal,
tail normal, merely darker throughout. The light & striking bill, makes bill
appear longer & proportionately more slender than it actually is.[7]

Henslow's Sparrow First flushed by R. Emery, who called Winter Wren! Then
she saw it perched & saw yellow & chestnut & called Dickcissel. Then dove
[?] & she said some kind of a small sparrow. They then proceeded to call
the description, I realized they had something unusual; never bothered to
look at it, & went & got gun & at once shot it at close range. Could not
recognize it when saw it to aim, & couldn't tell when in hand! Could not be
named from plates & description in Peterson or Pough! Interesting moral. If
it had not been shot, no argument could have identified this sparrow & an
unexpected & remarkable record would have been lost![8]

Oftentimes, however, scientific study did not require shooting the bird.

March 6th (Thursday) [1941] *Hoary Redpoll* 1 female or imm. . . . Today we
find a flock containing 1 Hoary very easily & get fine comparative study at
very close range, while feeding in birches. Not a single male ad. in flock, so
that plumages were perfectly comparable. Easy to see whiter, less streaked
underparts, almost confined to sides, gray rather olive-brown tone to
back & fortunately got excellent glimpses of extensive pure white un-
streaked rump! . . . The bird could easily have been collected, but it did not
seem necessary, with this identification confirmed 3 days in succession by
different observers.[9]

When he thought he had seen a Bridled Tern north of Boston, at Clarks's Pond, he described it in his journal, and counted it for his own personal records, but ended his journal entry, "*Not a publishable record,* of course!"[10]

Ludlow occasionally ran into trouble with neighbors when he was collecting. "*Northern Hairy* Woodp. 1 female coll. — astonished to have a party report a migrant Hairy at Little Nahant of all places! An enormous, white bird, exceedingly tame and dumb. Finally get permission of owner to shoot & and damn near cause a riot with neighbor. Haven't been so 'bawled out' by anyone in years!"[11]

Not always correct in his field identification, he did not hesitate to admit his errors, and even went back through his field journals and expunged sight records he later decided were unconfirmed by reference to museum specimens. Occasionally he made an error of identification in bird calls, but as usual, did not seem the least embarrassed or bothered by these occasional revelations.

When someone challenged Griscom about collecting birds, though, he could be rather abrupt in his defense. We see this in his response to a letter that questioned his collecting a vagrant bird.

Dear Mr. Griscom:

You may remember about two months ago that a Long-billed Curlew was reported as having been collected by you. . . . I was interested in this at time & finally decided to write & ask you about it. . . .

Of course there was very little chance of this bird's ever finding a mate (it was a female, I think) and breeding in the spring. But I wondered if this chance was so slight as to justify collecting the specimen, even though the bird is extremely rare.

Was particularly puzzled as I knew a zoologist of your experience wouldn't collect such a rare bird unless he had a good reason for it. Would appreciate your enlightenment on the matter.[12]

Dear Mr. Richardson:

. . . We now come to the stray bird which was found on the 14th of June at Chatham, in other words, at the wrong season of the year and 2,000 miles east of its present breeding range at the height of the breeding season. Thirty years experience with selecting [?] purely accidental stragglers has proved, thanks to dissection and post mortem study, that unless their occurrence can be accounted for by a violent hurricane they are invariably diseased and defective individuals, and as a matter of common sense it is reasonable to infer that they never would conceivably get to where they really belong. In the case of this particular Long-billed Curlew which I collected on June 15th, careful study and inspection of it beforehand showed that it was in a very frowzy condition of plumage, that it had never succeeded in molting into the breeding or summer plumage, and when collected dissection showed that the ovaries were minute and diseased. While you say that "there was very little chance of this bird's ever finding a mate," I consequently point out that even if there had been a male Long-billed Curlew on the same marsh this particular female could never have mated with it and laid eggs.[13]

The situation did not always lend itself to such simple, clear-cut resolution. For example, on another occasion Griscom was sure that he had seen two Eskimo Curlew in Ipswich, Massachusetts, and in answering a letter inquiring about the sighting, he ended with an interesting question. "It would be inexcusable to collect an Eskimo curlew to validate a sight record, and on the other hand, when a bird is practically extinct is a sight record any good?"[14]

A number of Griscom's letters deal with his philosophy of sight records of birds. In some cases, Griscom writes of the importance of collecting selectively. In others, he concentrates on the problems of the censoring of sight records of the "hordes of amateur bird watchers and their list-crazy fringe," which he had been so influential in creating.

In the course of a letter to O. C. Bourne, Massachusetts Division of Fisheries and Game, endorsing Wendell Taber's permit application, Griscom champions a discriminating approach.

I am quite aware of the fact that Mr. Kenney and you are endeavoring to cut down on the collecting permits issued in this state and to scrutinize very carefully the record and performance of those who now hold them. Without wishing to appear presumptuous, might I say that I have nothing but the highest commendation for this policy.

However, considerable experience in field work in the eastern United States has convinced me that while the general collecting of specimens is no longer in the slightest degree necessary, there is, of course, a small residuum of cases where the securing of the specimen, either for exact identification of rare stragglers or for the enrichment of the local highly educational exhibition collections of the museums properly devoted to this purpose, does do real good and serves to advance the interests of science in general. In most of our northeastern states today we have ever-increasing hordes of opera-glass amateurs and list makers who clutter up the ornithology of their state or region by a mass of unverifiable records of rare and casual stragglers which cannot possibly be properly sifted or the accuracy of the identification definitely determined. There are, however, a mere handful of such amateur students who have a genuine scientific interest and spirit in this subject, and who consequently are competent to collect with some judgment.[15]

Griscom's aversion to the proliferation of sight records in the literature—even his own—is a persistent theme.

> I acknowledge your inquiry of October 13th with pleasure. You are quite correct in thinking that I spent my honeymoon in the Mogollon Mountain region of northern Arizona and observed a number of birds which are not yet recorded from the State of Arizona. As a matter of fact, I never did publish any paper on these observations, though I perhaps should have done so in part, at least, as we seem to have very little information about water fowl in the State of Arizona. On the other hand, I don't believe in additions to state avifaunas being based on sight records only, and as I collected no specimens of any of these birds I deliberately refrained from publishing them.[16]

> I happen to know Swainson's Hawk in life very well indeed and to the best of my knowledge and belief, the Swainson's Hawk which four of us saw last August 23 was correctly identified. My own conviction is that there is indeed a plague these days of exceptional sight records and it behooves the professionals to fall backwards in not rushing into print with their own observations. You may notice that I have not had a general note in the Auk for many years about a sight record of an accidental straggler and it is by no means because I have not seen such birds annually. Eliot and many other people in Massachusetts are fit to be tied because I will not publish such records and I will not allow them to appear over my own name in either the Bulletin of the Massachusetts Audubon Society or the Seasonal Report in the National Audubon Magazine.[17]

Griscom did censor sight records, and in a light-hearted 1952 letter he commends this practice. "I must say that I had to laugh and laugh at your letter of June 24th, as I have been in the same hellish jam with these goddamned Blue Grosbeaks for three decades. Of course you did just the right thing to throw them out. . . . P.S. Beware also of Connecticut Warblers!"[18]

An earlier letter suggests the contradictory position Ludlow was in. He was so fond of sport birding, and perhaps did more than anyone else to promote it, and yet he denigrated the people who practiced it.

> Thanks to the automobile, super highways, fine binoculars, a horde of guides and text books, bird watching instead of being an adjunct of natural history is developing into a game or sport. A score is now kept; and just like

a game of golf where the fan is only interested in lowering his total score for eighteen holes and keeping a list of each one of the holes in which he has scored a par or a birdie, the modern bird watcher is interested only in the size of the daily maximum list of species observed, the maximum scores for the month and the year. He is consequently a record chaser, and somebody in Massachusetts will win the 1949 amateur championship by scoring 297 species of birds for the year, with the disappointed runner-up only 295.[19]

The paradox of the sight record phenomenon was beginning to haunt him.

In a 1965 article, Cora Wellman, a birding companion of Ludlow's, states that "we saw his enthusiasms and developed our own. He let us think that our birding efforts, however humble, were still significant."[20] In truth, this is exactly what Ludlow Griscom did *not* think. The confusion over his great pleasure in, and support of, the *sport* of birding and his professional views of the scientific value of the results of sport birding is here apparent. Griscom had an enormous amount of fun birding and enjoyed the company of rank amateurs as well as professionals. But he grew irritated when sport birders tried to publish their sight records, which in his view cluttered up the literature with false, or at least unverifiable, sight records. His position was made more difficult because he took his own records of birds, seen on his birding trips in the company of amateurs, very seriously.

While Griscom consistently strove to maintain the integrity of the professional literature, his reactions to the efforts and claims of amateur birders ranged widely in intensity. In the following exchange, we see him at his kindest, attempting to influence or cajole individuals into proper behavior regarding bird identification or the publishing of records. C. Brooke Worth, a naturalist, wrote to Ludlow concerning his fear that he may have misidentified some sparrows.

Dear Dr. Griscom:
. . . I'm sure in an awful mess now. If my bird was a Cassin, then, as I mentioned in my last letter, I am a poor ornithologist for having called it a Botteri in the first place. If, however, it was a Botteri, I am a doubly poor ornithologist now for not having stuck to my guns and being so afraid to stick to my belief that I made a somewhat rare record, that I backed down because I had no proof, such as a collected specimen.

This is probably the last chapter, so I won't pester you with any more letters. The way things stand now, I am not going to call my bird either, but strike the whole business from my records, as I probably saw both species, identified neither, and was too dumb to collect the one I had.[21]

Dear Mr. Worth:

I have your interesting letter of August 25th regarding your misidentification of Botteri Sparrow. There is nothing particularly dreadful in all this and I would not feel badly about it if I were you. It does not matter in the least how many errors we make as long as they do not get into scientific print.

As a matter of fact the main difference between a good observer and a poor one is the ability of the former to catch himself at mistakes before it is too late. In my experience the ordinary socalled amateur has an idea that the professional ornithologist does not make mistakes or does not believe he does and thinks that the amateur is constantly doing so. As a matter of fact, this is not true. The professional ornithologist, whose field experience is far more frequent and wide than that of the average amateur, if anything makes more mistakes than the amateur but catches himself in time to avoid publishing an error. The average amateur tends to think that he does not make mistakes and this should arouse the suspicion of the socalled professional.[22]

His tone could sometimes be more critical, and even a bit austere, but his remarks are constructive. Here we find the experienced scientist giving authoritative counsel.

Now with regard to the Bohemian Waxwing. I think that all I can do is to give you my own point of view about the type of observation which is required to establish a sight record worthy of serious consideration of any bird so exceedingly rare in the eastern United States as this particular species. . . . No sight record of so rare a bird as this is worth a hoot in my humble opinion unless *all* of the possible diagnostic points are noted, and it has been my rule for more than twenty-five years to say nothing about very rare birds that I have seen in various parts of the country in constant field work unless I succeeded in getting what we professionals term a really satisfactory observation. I consequently do not consider anybody's records more seriously than I do my own when it is apparent from their account that they had an unsatisfactory and incomplete observation and were apparently, in addition, entirely unaware that there were several good characters in addition to the one they noted.[23]

My advice in any case, however, would be not to write a note for The Auk [about the spring sighting of a possible Forster's Tern]. My reasons for suggesting that you do not do so are exactly the same as in my own case. It happens that three years ago in late May I was convinced that I saw a Forster's Tern at Monomoy Point, and I, too, have had ample previous experience with this species. It never occurred to me to publish a note in The Auk about it for the very simple reason that in so critical and much misidentified a group of birds as these terns the occurrence of this particular species in the spring on the New England coast requires far better substantiation to be of real scientific value than any sight record, no matter how competently made by how experienced a person. I trust, therefore, that you will appreciate in all friendliness that I am advising you to act on just the same severe standards as I have actually applied to myself.[24]

Griscom was easily irritated when an amateur, no matter how well-meaning, nor how much he appreciated or enjoyed his or her company in the field, was put forth as a professional, or claimed to have accomplished things Griscom didn't feel had been done. In the following letter he blasts Connie Hagar of Rockport, Texas, and his best friend, Guy Emerson. If you overstepped the boundary between the professional and the amateur when Griscom didn't think it was justified, it didn't matter who you were. Griscom felt honor-bound to say something blunt about it.

The first reason I am writing is to say, for God's sake go slow. By all means have a write-up of Connie Hagar, but don't get stampeded by Guy Emerson into glorifying her unduly or making out that she has made all kinds of contributions to Texas ornithology along the lines outlined in your letter, because she hasn't done anything of the sort. Actually, she has done marvelous and intensified field work in a little section of the Texas coast, from which previously there were no data. The enormous variety of species that occur and, above all, the spectacular numbers of many of them during the period of migration, are valid and true. She is, however, the rankest kind of an amateur, handicapped by inadequate text books and complete lack of experience of birds anywhere else in America, nor does she know anything whatsoever about the past literature on the birds of Texas. Many of her remarkable discoveries, consequently, exist only in her own imagination and that of other amateur but admiring friends, like Guy Emerson, who doesn't know anything about these things either. In certain other cases of very difficult and variable birds, like the hawks, her ideas on their identification are preposterous and must never be allowed to enter print.[25]

Ludlow was capable of compartmentalizing his life. He could be a harsh professional critic of someone whom he otherwise treated with genuine warmth and affection. Such was the case with Samuel Eliot, a professor at Smith College, who was a solid friend and birding companion. Most of Griscom's correspondence with him is cordial and helpful, but when Eliot got out of line on sight records, Griscom lowered the boom. In 1935 he wrote to Witmer Stone:

> . . . As regards the two notes for The Auk from Sam Eliot, which I return herewith, I have, of course, consulted with Pete [James Lee Peters] about them, and our independent reactions were, naturally enough, unanimous. My opinion of these two observations is that they are preposterous bunk, and I thoroughly disapprove of such poorly endorsed stuff being published in The Auk, or anywhere else, for that matter.[26]

After the publication of *Birds of the Connecticut Valley in Massachusetts* (1937) by Eliot and Aaron C. Bagg, Griscom felt ambivalent about rendering an opinion of the book because of his friendship with the two men. Ultimately, however, this feeling didn't keep him from heaping criticism on both authors, particularly on Eliot. You had to be a bit thick-skinned to be a friend of Ludlow's and disagree on sight record philosophy.

> I hardly know what to say and am torn in two between conflicting emotions. I know you well as two honest and sincere gentlemen, for whom I have a strong affection and with whom I have had many a happy hour in our favorite pursuit of bird study, but our intellectual approach and our premises to such a work as yours is so profoundly different that it is a complete waste of your time, as well as mine, for me to tell you what I think of your book. We must face the fact, Sam, that I am utterly unable to appreciate your point of view and you are equally incapable of grasping mine. In your note you say 'you will not fail to notice the fruits of some of our conversations in your car'. My own impression in reading the book last night was that I had completely failed my friend in every possible respect. While you abstract in a commendatory manner my paper on Problems of Field Identification, and while you are so kind as to state that my Birds of the New York City Region and Dutchess County had been used in part as models in your own work, to me it seems as if you had never once applied the spirit, rather than the purely technical side of the principles of sight records, you have paid no attention whatever to every one of the ways in which my two local avifaunas have been deemed to have merit, and if I were not so fond of you, Sam, I would recoil in horror and indignation at the idea that any work of mine could possibly have been regarded as a model for the production of your own volume. I am reminded of Kipling's wise and famous lines, "East is East and West is West, and never the twain shall meet." There is a profound intellectual gulf between us which cannot possibly be bridged and which I, on my side, am glad to accept and forget, with the same honest and loyal spirit with which you have obviously tried to deal with me in your volume.

Bless your heart, Sam, and I hope that soon again we can join forces for a pleasant trip in the field, preferably here in Boston so that you may see an interesting bird or two that you cannot reasonably hope to get in the Valley.[27]

Years later his professional opinion continued to have sway over his personal attachment. In 1952 he wrote to the editor of the *Bulletin of the Massachusetts Audubon Society:*

I am embarrassed by your letter of January 29 about continuing the series of articles entitled "Ornithologists Alive!" Perhaps the first and most important thing is to clarify a matter of editorial policy about when somebody interested in birds becomes an ornithologist. In this category comes my friend and companion Sam Elliot [sic] who is generally regarded as a list-crazy amateur, chasing records and rarities and whose book on the Birds of Connecticut Valley was regarded as one of the outstanding flops of the century. It would make [James Lee] Peters foam at the mouth as [if] Sam Elliot write-up came right after his.[28]

Griscom wrestled with the problems of sight records and censorship throughout his career, and they continue to plague the ornithological community, both professional and amateur. Many states, organizations, and journals have set up some sort of "rare bird committee" in an attempt to screen reported sightings. There does not seem to be any completely satisfactory resolution, and people still get their feelings hurt when their sight records are rejected or ignored.

Part Four

CONSERVATION

National
Audubon Society 13

Ludlow Griscom seemingly could not resist the temptation to join every organization he encountered and then be "persuaded" to contribute his time and professional expertise. He claimed at one point to belong to forty-two professional and charitable organizations. Among those that drew most heavily on his time and energies was the National Audubon Society (NAS). Its conservational ethos matched his own, and for more than two decades he dedicated himself to maintaining and improving the society's practices. In carrying out his administrative responsibilities, which are the primary focus of this chapter, he made major contributions to the strengthening of NAS structure and leadership. Much of his correspondence was conducted at the Museum of Comparative Zoology, on museum time, and it seems clear that these professional activities were considered, at least to some extent, as an extension of his MCZ responsibilities.

The concept of the Audubon society emerged in the late nineteenth century as part of the protectionist movement. In 1886 George Bird Grinnell started the first group, the Audubon Society for the Protection of Birds, and for two years published *Audubon Magazine*. This phase of the movement was short-lived. In 1888 few of the membership of 50,000 subscribed to the magazine, and Grinnell shut down the society, largely for financial reasons.[1] During the following decade, the resurgence of interest in protectionism produced a flowering of local (mostly state) Audubon societies, and Frank Chapman's *Bird-Lore* became the unofficial organ of the Audubon movement. Three dozen such societies existed by 1901, when William Dutcher engineered the formation of the National Committee of the Audubon Societies of America. Incorporation in New York followed in 1905, and the National Association of Audubon Societies for the Protection of Wild Birds and Animals, with a promised endowment and a salaried executive position, was born. T. Gilbert Pearson took over the leadership of the organization in 1910, when Dutcher became ill and continued in power until 1934, when he was replaced by John Baker. An aggressive executive, Baker changed the name of *Bird-Lore* (acquired by the society from Chapman) to *Audubon Magazine,* and the name of the organization to the National Audubon Society. Griscom had to deal with the fiery and less-than-tactful Baker when he joined forces with the society.

Griscom's connections with the NAS started in 1908, when he began to submit Christmas census accounts to *Bird-Lore,* and he knew William Dutcher and T. Gilbert Pearson at least by reputation. He first wrote to Baker in 1934, and they met often in New York City, where the society had its home office. He corresponded with Baker throughout their respective careers with the society, with Griscom supplying professional advice on ornithological matters, discussing society political matters, and giving thumbnail sketches of his acquaintances about whom Baker expressed an interest. Their letters were usually straightforward, but occasionally the accounts were amusing but rather harsh:

> I have your inquiry this morning, and the man that you inquire about is Henry B. Durant of 71 Larch Road, Cambridge. He is a brother of Aldrich Durant, now Business Manager of Harvard and my very good friend. I know the young Nash boy, and I also know Dr. Lombard Carter Jones, an old cluck of an amateur about water birds, whose general ignorance of the subject is compensated for by his sublime unawareness of it and his ideas of his own knowledge and information. I am in constant correspondence with Jones, who is a much older man than Henry Durant. The latter is a well esteemed business man of Cambridge, of the old-fashioned stuffy, small town type, whom I absolutely never heard of before as interested in or really posted on wildlife conservation matters.[2]

In 1935 Baker asked Ludlow to consider a summer position at the proposed Audubon nature study camp on Hog Island, Maine. Ludlow politely refused, citing the probable conflict with his summer ornithology course at Harvard. He then followed with a few comments about the proposed camp.

> A person of your acumen and experience will, of course, see that the National Association would lose prestige unless your camp was run on a higher

basis than several other Audubon, or nature study propositions of the same sort already afloat in New England. . . . In propositions of this sort, just as in a University summer school, the success of the enterprize does not consist merely in supplying a teaching staff of the proper degree of scientific reputation but it also involves, to a quite surprising extent, the caliber and type of person who comes to the camp to receive the instruction. It is here, I think, that you will find your chief difficulty.[3]

The following year Baker recommended Ludlow to the Nominating Committee as Massachusetts representative to the advisory board, and he was duly elected. In his letter soliciting Ludlow's consent, Baker gives some insight into why Griscom did not actually become a member of the board of directors until five years later. "Personally, I would be more than pleased were you a director of this Association. I think, however, you would be the first to recognize the fact that while Dr. Chapman is an active member of the Board and present at most of our spring, summer and early fall meetings, it might not be entirely wise to have you at the same time a member of the Board."[4]

In 1936 Griscom was asked by William Vogt, editor of *Bird- Lore,* to become the "Seasons" editor for the Boston region. Griscom accepted the volunteer job and thus began an editorial association that would last two decades, first with *Bird-Lore* and then *Audubon Magazine.* His initial contribution was to point out to Vogt that there was far too much emphasis on rare birds and stragglers, and not enough on the common birds.

I am perfectly willing to undertake the editorship of the Boston Region "Season" if you really want me to, but it will be on a trial basis, say for six months, until I can find out definitely (1) just how much time it takes, and (2) whether I get the necessary amount of cooperation from the local gang. . . . I should appreciate from you, however, as editor-in-chief some instructions or some platform, if you have one, on which "The Season's" report should be written up. It is my impression from the past that too many of "The Season" reports have primarily consisted of as long a list of abnormal migration dates and casual records as space would permit. In other words, far too much stress has been laid on this side of things and far too little on the status of the more regular species, the varying abundance of which seems to me to be much more worth while following in detail.[5]

By 1941 Griscom had taken over the organization of "The Seasons" reports on a national basis.

Ludlow was responsible for answering complaints about publication delays. In the following 1949 letter, Griscom makes a rather impassioned defense.

No one can be more exasperated than I at the delay in the appearance of the Christmas census, and it is true that each number of Audubon Field Notes is appearing later than formerly. You are, however, a little uncharitable in concluding that the delay is inexcusable. The editor of the Audubon magazine was carted off to the hospital in the middle of March fatally stricken, and a new and competent editor for the magazine cannot be grabbed out of the United States like a berry off a bush. Miss Manning, who handles the makeup and layout of Audubon Field Notes, has come down with epilepsy. The printer with whom we have a contract was tied up by a strike that lasted six weeks. The slowness in appearance of each issue of Audubon Field Notes is due to the fact that we now have nineteen regents [regions?], all work being done on a 100% volunteer basis by regional editors and their collaborators; and they just won't or can't get all their reports in and the write-up completed within a week after the close of the period date.

There is no use writing John Baker as he is not interested in Audubon Field Notes, and the project is being kept going at an increasing annual deficit only by my own personal influence. So wish me luck, old fellow.[6]

For the most part, Ludlow seems to have had a fine working relationship with the editors of *Audubon Magazine* and *Audubon Field Notes*. This was particularly true for Eleanor A. King, whom Ludlow usually addresses as "Grabcat." Her correspondence displays a similar tone.

You are a nice bear—either on the telephone or off of it! And what was that you called me—greedy gizzard? What a delightful "pet" name. Mr. Sanderson has some choice ones too—Vinegar Liz, Susie Sour, Whistle Breeches, and a whole bunch of others that I can't remember. Shall I get a complete list to send you, or are you satisfied with your own repertory?

Now all this freshness is because you are so obstinate about writing an article for me! I've tried to be winning, and it hasn't worked. Now I'm going to have to try some other method. I can't think of a good method, however, because of course you are right. You are already doing two articles a month, and only a greedy gizzard would ask you to do another! But don't you appreciate being in demand? . . .

Sincerely,

Greedy Gizzard[7]

But it was not all harmony between Griscom and the Audubon publishing contingent. Ludlow was all for censoring regional reports, and he could take a bit of constructive criticism in stride, but when someone tried to censor one of his articles, he left no room for doubt about his level of dissatisfaction.

Dear Grabcat:

I have been meaning for a couple of days to drop you a line of warm and friendly appreciation for your letter of October 24. Never in my life have I received better or more constructive criticism, and in re-writing the article for publication I shall adopt every single one of the points raised in your letter. At least I will try to do so.

On the other hand, I am forced to advise you that Audubon Magazine will not get the article. I have a very astounding letter from John Baker who thinks that the article should not be published until every member of the Board has been polled and a sampling of the hostesses of various tables at the dinner who are not members of the Audubon Society. Moreover he seems to feel strongly that a 100% biological and realistic approach is dangerous to the society. . . .

Two other organizations have offered to send the article to press at once just as is, verbatim, and various organizations have asked for a total of 7,500 reprints. . . . My Professional integrity makes it impossible for an emasculated article to appear in the Magazine over my name, and I am afraid that you will have to go without articles on conservation from me until such time as I am perfectly free to say exactly what I think, without submitting to the censorship of incompetent amateurs.[8]

Despite these occasional difficulties and outbursts, Griscom was able to write dozens of articles, notes, and reviews for Audubon publications, and he published more than one hundred regional reports and summations. By example and influence with the editor, Griscom strongly shaped the development of the regional report concept, which still continues today in the society's *American Birds.*

By 1941 an aging Frank Chapman was presumably less active with the society, for Guy Emerson, then its president, recommended Griscom for a director position. In May 1941 Baker approached Griscom on the subject. With his customary enthusiasm, Griscom wanted some responsibility, and Baker responded. "Now the point is that we need to establish a proper standard in initiating a series of Audubon research publications. I think that you are the ideal person to assume responsibility for the recommendations as to such standards and the editorial policy with regard to our publication of such research reports. I would very much like to be able to look to you for the editorial revision."[9] Ludlow was soon involved in policy decisions, and his advice was sought by both Emerson and Baker, who as executive director actually ran the organization.

In a 1943 letter to Emerson, Ludlow discusses the possibility of the society's publishing Harry C. Oberholser's volumes on the birds of Texas.[10] He not only analyzes the situation but also blasts Oberholser in the process.

> I have, of course, your long and very interesting letter embodying your excellent and fruitful reflections on the role of the Audubon Society in bringing out Oberholser's book on the birds of Texas. I am inclined to agree heartily with your arguments as to why it is a legitimate interest of the Audubon Society and why it might be feasible to do something about it in relatively slack times like these. I have the following comments to make:
>
> (1) I happen to have known Oberholser very well indeed over a long period of years. While I have every esteem for him as an ornithologist, as a man and a human being he is a mean spirited hypocrite and, in spite of his scientific distinction, got himself detested by every ornithologist in the United States. For years his colleagues in the National Museum and the Biological Survey looked forward with keen anticipation to the happy day when he would finally reach the retiring age, and all of them would enjoy writing a sonofobituary address. One of his outstanding characteristics in this connection is that he is never wrong and that he must always have everything his own way. If he can get it by double crossing you he will, and if he can't double cross he says to hell with you.[11]

Ludlow remained a director during the war years, when the society felt the pinch of resources, both financial and manpower, as did the Museum of Comparative Zoology. He outlined some of the difficulties they faced.

> The National Audubon Society has not as yet sustained anything but the most trifling decrease in membership, but the personnel problem is rapidly assuming insoluble proportions. It proves to be impossible to maintain a staff adequate for our activities of, say, two years ago, for the very simple reason that the people are unobtainable. Roger Peterson went off to the army last week and Allen Cruikshank will leave next Friday. We long ago lost Robert P. Allen. . . .
>
> Applying the repercussions of this fact [that the War might last for five more years] to the Audubon Society, there will be no Summer Camp on the coast of Maine; the Season Supplements and the Christmas Census Supplements of Bird Lore will fold up first; and secondly there will be no National Audubon Magazine at all as we know it.[12]

A major struggle developed in the power structure of the society, and Ludlow was caught right in the middle. John Baker's forceful personality and lack of tact produced a variety of problems since he was the society's major spokesman in the day-to-day conduct of business. Emerson heard much of the criticism of Baker from the community, both inside and outside of the organization, and felt an obligation to try to restrict the executive director in those areas in which he thought Baker's faults produced the most damaging effects. In a 1942 letter to Griscom, Emerson made his position clear.

> I still have the stubborn feeling that we can either improve John's public relations ability, or supplement him in some way in that field. . . .
>
> I hope you will find occasion to talk with him before long. But, as I say, I think we can work out some program that will be satisfactory, even without the extremely difficult step of asking for his resignation. . . . My feeling that his negative qualities are basically injurious to the society is not a conviction based on a lack of affection for him, but is based purely on my feeling of obligation to the Audubon Society. . . . He does not take criticism too easily, but he is enough of an organization man to recognize the fact that I have duties and obligations to the Society, just as definite as his own and that I would be failing in my trusteeship if I saw a major defect which threatened the whole future of the organization and refrained from doing anything about it.[13]

Ludlow sympathized with Emerson to some extent. Although Ludlow had a strong affection for his friend Baker, he, like Emerson, was basically an organization man who took his responsibilities seriously.

> There is only one impasse in the affairs of the Society which it will take time to resolve. If the Society is to continue to grow, I hold strongly to the view that it must cease to be a one-man show as it now primarily is. No scientist, no conservationist, no personnel manager, and no public relations expert has ever run his department successfully and happily under a president who longed to be a one-man show. The question consequently is, will John be able to grow to this stature or must the Audubon Society wait for its second reorganization until John passes from the scene?[14]

Baker was feeling the pressure from Emerson and complained about it to Ludlow, thus putting him in the center of the dispute between his friends.

> The difficulties that we have recently experienced with regard to the waterfowl matter go back in my opinion to Guy's expressed desire, with which you are familiar, to show me that I was not the whole show, or something to that effect. . . . The Executive Director can get along first rate with any committee of reasonable members of the Board, but it is an impossible situation when the Chairman of the Board wants to handle the matter himself.[15]

Ludlow responded to Baker by giving him advice on his handling of the rather outspoken conservationist, Rosalie Edge, and providing what might be interpreted as an implied threat. This letter offers insight into Griscom's methods of handling people.

> It happens that I have some ideas about how to handle Mrs. Edge myself, and one of them is never to get into discussion with her, but to have every statement of position in writing. As a matter of fact· I had two long and friendly chats with her at the Annual Meeting at the conclusion of which she patted me on the shoulder and said she had known for years that I was a "fine man" but that I had not been on the Board of the Audubon Society long enough to realize the outrageous goings on. She went so far as to say that the real outrage was that you were the Director and that when she showed you up as a liar and crook it was outrageous of the Directors not to boot you out of the building. Now, I may be frightfully conceited, but I do not think you can tell me anything about Mrs. Edge worth knowing that I don't know perfectly well, but in any scheme of yours for handling her, you are getting off inevitably to a bad start. . . .
>
> There is probably much in what you say about the difficulties between the President and the Executive Director. It is only natural that it should be easier for you to see difficulties caused by the President [Emerson], but I side with him also in feeling that there are other difficulties caused by the Executive Director. If I might generalize for a moment, we have here what is primarily a personnel difficulty. This type of difficulty takes some time to work itself out at best, and at worst one person or the other has to leave the organization.[16]

As it turns out, both Baker and Emerson remained in positions of power.

In 1944 Emerson decided to step down as the president of the National Audubon Society. The year before had begun to sound out Griscom as a possible successor, an offer Ludlow firmly declined. Emerson renewed his suggestion—"I recall the pleasant talk we had on the general subject one evening a year or more ago, so you know that I have never had but one candidate in mind to succeed Guy Emerson as head of the Audubon Society"[17]—and society treasurer Carll Tucker wrote to Griscom laying out their reasoning:

> Then comes the selection of a man to fill the head position in the Society, in the eyes of the public and conservation-minded people generally. Here, there should be a combination of personality, recognized scientific attainments, and not merely a hobby interest in birds, no matter how deep the interest is; and, lastly, there must be a warm community of interest and personal appreciation and liking between our admittedly able executive director and the head of the organization. This last is most important and

without any doubt whatsoever, a consideration of these required conditions points to you and only you as the new head of the Society.[18]

Griscom remained unpersuaded by their proposal. He summed up the situation in a letter to Thomas Barbour, director of the Museum of Comparative Zoology.

Now for my problem: It transpires that Guy Emerson simply will not consider being President for another year. He has consequently appointed a confidential nominating committee (all very fine and high class men) who have between now and October to dig up a new President. Guy Emerson wrote them an able letter in signing off, making various recommendations and suggestions that the Committee might find helpful. He considered that I was the only logical person to become President but correctly reported the talk he had with me last July in which I made it clear I would not consider it for a moment on personal grounds and that I did not think the President of the Audubon Society should be a 500 mile [round] trip away from New York and the offices. His alternative suggestion was that the office of Executive Director, now held by John Baker, should be abolished; that John Baker should become President of the Society; that he should not be a member of the Board and that I should become Chairman of the Board of Directors who, so to speak, would be John Baker's boss and able to fire him if necessary.[19]

He also wrote to Emerson stating his objections to the plan.

You should have heard nice simple Dave Aylward compare John and you at the Washington meeting last January and deplore the fact that you couldn't and Carl Buchheister wasn't allowed to represent the Society more to handle certain types of controversial public relations where disagreement is inevitable, a fight the sign of failure. The moral of all this is that the National Audubon Society needs John and gains greatly from his able services in many discussions, but it also needs an able and distinguished man as President, who with the aid of every competent, knowledgeable, and really interested man on the Board, can hold John down and compensate for his defects. This requires a New York man. I consequently strongly disapprove of the proposed organization.[20]

After considerable maneuvering, however, the intricate compromise was struck.

I yield to the two gentlemen from New York at the present time. Let John Baker be given the title of President, and I am prepared to be called Chairman of the Board, provided it is understood that (1) I am dubious of the propriety of making John Baker President; (2) I have no more time to devote to Audubon affairs than I have given in the past; and (3) I will be unable to come to New York more frequently.[21]

Ludlow became chairman in October 1944. He took the train to New York, where he presided over the meetings, visited his mother, and stayed overnight at the Union Club.

Griscom had strong thoughts about the nature of committees and committee work, and he employed various tactics in order to try to make the board more efficient in its operation. His philosophy for directing the society's affairs included doing substantial behind-the-scenes manipulation and lobbying. "My usual idea of a committee is a group of men who can in fact meet and will in fact, work."[22]

Throughout his term Griscom was under a constant strain in his attempt to control the activities of John Baker. His prognosis of trouble with Baker once the latter became president apparently was borne out by subsequent events, and he was continually alerting others on the NAS board to the problems of a "one man show." Soon after he took over as chairman, Griscom wrote to Emerson, who remained a director of the society.

> I am personally convinced that the operational set-up in the head office has various flaws, that they really reflect the flaws in the President because the Society is virtually a one man show. I am very very skeptical of the degree to which John Baker can be made over at the age of fifty and the degree to which he can successfully continue to run the Society assuming that an outside analyst [sic] and the Board force him to run it in certain directions contrary to his natural genius and inclination.[23]

Baker often listened to Griscom's advice, but early on Griscom recognized that there were limits to his ability to influence Baker. So instead he adopted the strategy of applying a constant but tolerable pressure on him by using other directors. In a 1945 letter to Emerson, Ludlow describes a subterfuge involving Charles C. Adams, designed in part to effect changes in Baker's behavior.

> You know that at my suggestion Adams was induced to spend several days at Audubon House, making a study of daily activities of the office staff, day by day. My professed object in asking him to do so was to give an outside and individual director a proper idea of the volume of business daily flowing through the office so that if necessity arose, he could speak with authoritative knowledge at subsequent Board Meetings, in case one director or another hatched an idea which would inevitably put an additional burden

on the staff. My tongue was definitely in my cheek however, in that I thought that he might have one or more useful reactions as to the degree to which the organization of the work in Audubon House was officially planned. Just between you and me, I now have a first draft of his report of his comments and criticism, and he finds strong grounds for unfavorable comment in this respect. He has already gotten John a little disturbed about it and, as he is a very honest, simple, and sincere gentleman, he wants to know if in my opinion some of this criticism should be suppressed. I am writing him that under no circumstances should it be suppressed and that in due course of time a properly typewritten final report will be sent to every member of the Executive Committee.[24]

Having stirred up Adams, Ludlow then had to calm Adams down. He damped the effects of Adams's anti-Baker findings in answering the question, "What happens next?"

The answer is that nothing happens next. John's services to the Society, his assets, enormously outweigh his faults. If we combed the country, we could not find anyone with so many of the special abilities so controversial and difficult a job requires. The directors never supposed they were hiring a second Jesus Christ and you cannot seriously disillusion them.

Suppose you comb the country and *do* produce a man with fewer faults and an even wider range of talents and ability to serve the Society. Then there really would be a constructive suggestion for the Exec. Com't to discuss. It may surprise you, but John Baker is the kind of man who would appear at the meeting to urge the directors to accept his resignation and hire Mr. X. Moreover, he would probably have worked out a scheme by which it could be managed with a minimum of public gossip and eye-brow lifting! Baker is "high class," and most people have to hump themselves to keep up with him. The people I know who don't like him are chiefly those who have not been able to![25]

Roger Tory Peterson, in an interview, said that John Baker was a man who knew how to handle situations, but he often rubbed people the wrong way because he was so positive, had a great deal of integrity, and tended to railroad people. Baker leaned heavily for support on Ludlow, who shared many of Baker's character traits. Notwithstanding his own sometimes brusque personality, Ludlow managed and manipulated people with great skill. He had a flair for administration and was endowed with that undefinable but indispensable quality, common sense. It was difficult to oppose Griscom, Peterson recalls, mostly because he was so often right. It is his opinion that Baker was the best president that the Audubon Society ever had, and with the help of Ludlow,

Emerson, and Roger Baldwin, the society did some of its greatest work.[26] They started projects some of which carry through to the present day. The magazine prospered, and they revitalized the junior programs, implemented a research program, and started a lecture program. Griscom was a guiding figure in all of that.

Perhaps the best summary of Ludlow's qualities as a leader was provided by Carl Buchheister, who worked with him for more than a decade.

> I was struck especially with his human traits. He had great integrity. In his judgments as Chairman of the Board of Natl. Audubon he weighed both sides of a controversial issue and gave an honest opinion, in his judgment of the work, performance of staff members, when their advancement, or their continuation or dismissal from their positions came before the Board, his views and decisions were completely unbiased, even when he was known to dislike a person, fair and with a charitable understanding, and a decision or action that would be charitable to all concerned in a person's family.
>
> Unlike any other Chairman of the Board in my long experience, Griscom was downright interesting, refreshing and humorous. With a big smile, with clipped & decisive words, he would call the meeting to order & say, "First, I want to know what of interest you have seen in the bird world." That caused everyone to laugh, to relax and tell us what they saw. Some didn't of course. Then Griscom would relate in his characteristically rapid, authoritarian manner what he had seen. His words were listened to with rapt attention, because what he told was not just what he saw but why, and their behavior.
>
> From the introduction on birds he went to the business of the agenda. He conducted a meeting quickly, thoroughly and with a combination of dignity and humor.[27]

Despite deteriorating health, beginning with the 1950 stroke from which he never fully recovered, Ludlow remained chairman of the board until 1956, when his health problems became truly debilitating. At that point the Audubon Society honored his contributions to the society by electing him an honorary president of the society. John Baker remained as president until 1959, when he handed the reigns over to Buchheister.

As director, and then as chairman of the board, Griscom provided substantial input into the direction and implementation of the organization's diverse conservation efforts. For example, in 1942 Griscom was battling other directors and conservationists outside the organization on the issue of recommendations for Wood Duck hunting prohibitions, which he thought went too far. He was very vocal about it, and ultimately got his way. "I strongly disagreed a year ago with the Society's stand on the Wood Duck and thought the leaflet, after the Federal shooting regulations for the year were an accomplished fact, was a mistake."[28]

In 1945 he wrote to David A. Aylward, president of the National Wildlife Federation, to further the mutual understanding between the two organizations. "I had deplored the foolish and unnecessary schism between the National Wildlife Federation and the Audubon Society, as my strong personal conviction has been and will continue to be that for the sake of the advance of the cause of conservation in which we are both interested, the more organizations exist which are actively endeavoring to advance, the better."[29]

In addition to pouring oil on troubled waters among the various warring conservation groups, Ludlow attempted to help out the director of the Fish and Wildlife Service, Ira Gabrielson, by endorsing the board of directors' action of passing a resolution that Gabrielson had requested. Ludlow on one occasion stated that the Fish and Wildlife Service was presumably the greatest conservation organization in the world, and hence, helping out the service was helping the cause of conservation.

He further espoused this position in a 1946 statement to the Plan and Scope Committee of the Audubon Society.

> the development of the times makes it out of the question for the Audubon Society to have the commanding position it once did. When it initiated the Era of Protection and forced it on the country almost single-handed, its leaders were the outstanding authorities in the country and in the world. It did not initiate the Era of Conservation, in which we now are. Government is supreme in conservation, its four grand divisions staffed by scientifically trained professionals. The universities and colleges supply the education and training. Selfish pressure groups and a maze of conflicting interests handicap these men in their work or prevent further constructive legislation.[30]

His policy was one of moderation, cooperation, and compromise. A blunt statement in reply to a director's memorandum read in part, "All that the Society need do to escape criticism is to keep quiet in those fields where at the moment it is unable to make any real contribution."[31]

By 1947 Ludlow's own policies of emphasis on habitat preservation were beginning to broaden the scope of the Audubon Society as it searched for a conservation base wider than the birdwatchers and ornithological community. He didn't particularly like some of the side effects but fully understood that the broadened base was essential. When *Audubon Magazine* changed its target audience, Ludlow had to soothe some ruffled feathers, as he did in a letter to Hustace Poor, a birding friend.

As regards Audubon Magazine, I have exactly the same personal reaction as you, but the trouble is that our interest in birds and conservation is safely in the bag and is a relatively high-class and expert one. The Magazine actually exists to arouse interest in natural history and conservation in people who know nothing about it whatever, as this is the cause for which funds with which to publish the Magazine were given. The Directors are now spending some capital in an endeavor greatly to increase the circulation and subscription list, and the more popular makeup of the Magazine in recent years, which leaves me cold and which you do not like, has already more than doubled the subscription list.[32]

Sometimes Ludlow strongly disagreed with Baker on a conservation issue, and let Baker know about in forceful terms. Such was the case when Baker opposed a test spraying of DDT, and Ludlow disagreed at length in a 1945 letter.

I strongly favor it and I am almost astounded to gather that you "strenuously oppose the project as fundamentally unsound." There has been much talk and some publications about the appalling degree to which D.D.T. is suspected of being lethal and devastating to many forms of wildlife, as well as the insect pests it is desired to eradicate, with the result of too seriously disturbing the balance of nature. Assuming that this would prove to be the fact, the National Audubon Society would, of course, oppose as strenuously as possible the unrestricted use of D.D.T. after the war by people no matter how well intentioned—and above all its free public sale should be sharply restricted. I happen to know that Clarence [Cottam] is only one of many sound conservationists who are very much disturbed about it.

It is, I take it, a common-sense axiom that successful opposition is, in part at least, always based on sound first-hand knowledge and experiment. I consequently commend heartily the proposed research on the part of the Bureau of Entomology, the Plant Quarantine Branch of the U. S. Department of Agriculture, for carefully controlled pest-spraying of selected small tracts and it would be highly to the advantage of the U. S. Fish and Wildlife Service to partake of these investigations so that their research department can speak in opposition in subsequent years on a basis of first-hand knowledge. I cannot see why the Audubon Society would not profit by exactly the same arguments and I feel strongly that it would be of the greatest advantage to the society if you personally—no matter whether some member of the staff is also assigned—should be present at one of the experimental sprayings.

Just how the lethal qualities to various forms of wild life of D.D.T. are to be determined without the spraying of an experimental tract, I fail to see. After all, the 5,000 acres of forest land are a minute decimal of 1 per cent of the total acreage in the United States, and this acreage will be divided into small lots among eight widely scattered states.

For the Society to strenuously oppose the proposed project would, I believe, be disastrous for its reputation among the more scientific bureaus of the Government and would be hopelessly unconstructive.[33]

Baker's letter a month later to Clarence Cottam, chief of the Division of Wildlife Research, the Fish and Wildlife Service, tells the story. "Please be advised that our Board of Directors, at a meeting February 20th, officially voted to accept the invitation extended by the Fish and Wildlife Service in your letter of January 12, 1945 to participate in the experimental projects this year through the stationing of an observer, or observers to record the results of the experiments."[34] Ludlow persevered and in a letter to Emerson describes his follow-up activities with the spraying project. "I am, of course, running into acute personnel shortage difficulties [because of World War II] as regards the DDT project in cooperation with the U. S. Fish and Wildlife Service. I have, however, persuaded one of the most distinguished living entomologists, Professor Charles T. Brues of Harvard University, to accept the appointment of general Officer-in-Chief."[35]

In 1956, when Griscom retired as the chairman of the board of directors, he was awarded the Conservation Medal by the society, for his outstanding work. Although too ill to attend the ceremonies, his response, read to the gathering by his son, Andrew, sums up his philosophy.

In spite of our great system of national parks and wildlife refuges, they are always under attack. There is the inevitable temptation to try to use them for some sort of economic reward. Eternal vigilance is always necessary to defeat these attempts. To succeed in defeating them, education is of vital importance and with a fair sized endowment this is precisely the service the National Audubon Society is well fitted to perform. Let the magazine and our published literature steadily run a flow of sound conservation messages. The government officials in authority are hard pressed and are calling loudly for help. Let us try and give it to them to the best of our ability.[36]

Massachusetts Audubon Society 14

In 1896 two Boston women, Harriet Hemenway and Minna B. Hall, met over tea to discuss the formation of a society for the protection of birds.[1] Among other things, they were outraged by the slaughter of egrets in Florida during the breeding season for the purpose of securing plumes for the millinery trade. Several meetings followed, with several prominent members of the Nuttall Ornithological Club (NOC) in attendance, at which committees for the formulation of by-laws and publications were established. William Brewster, a founder and president of both the AOU and the NOC, became the first president of the Massachusetts Audubon Society and remained in this capacity for seventeen years. Within a decade the society had a membership of more than 6,000 and was soon leading the charge for the preservation and conservation of birds. The society was the first of its kind and served as a model for other state and local organizations. It began the publication of a *Bulletin* in 1917, developed a strong education program, recruited prominent ornithologists—including Arthur Cleveland Bent and Charles W. Townsend—for its board, and had as its second president the venerable ornithologist Edward Howe Forbush. By the time Griscom moved to Cambridge, the society was an important force in conservation, both on the local and national level.

In the decade after his arrival, Ludlow Griscom had a growing influence on the development of the Massachusetts Audubon Society. His championing of sight recognition in birds and of the burgeoning sport of birdwatching and listing affected all levels at the society, from the backyard birdwatching member to the president. Many of the most active members and staff were, in effect, Griscom protégés. He reached them through personal contact in the field, either by inviting people to join his entourage for a day of birding or through accidental contact as the Griscom party crossed paths with other groups.

Perhaps his greatest effect on the membership of the society came through his publications. Beginning in 1932, Griscom sent, by request, his year list of Massachusetts birds to Francis Allen, editor of the *Bulletin.* He contributed his first feature article in 1935, and his bird-sighting records, which he had previously published most frequently in the *Auk,* began to appear in the *Bulletin* in 1936. In all he published nearly thirty features, about a dozen book reviews, and many other articles on the highlights of bird migration in Massachusetts and other synopses of seasons and years.

There exists only a limited written record of Griscom's involvement in the affairs of the Massachusetts Audubon Society. This scarcity probably resulted from his contacts being of a local nature, and hence most of his business would have been conducted in person or by telephone. Most of the extant information thus comes from testimonial statements and interviews. Such a testimonial was offered by Henry M. Parker shortly after Ludlow's death. It provides an overview and context in which his specific contributions can be assessed.

> To appreciate the true depth of this support and the quality of his friendship requires a working knowledge of at least three decades in the fields of ornithology and conservation, for a fair share of the progress of the Massachusetts Audubon Society over the past thirty years was either indirectly stimulated or directly achieved through Mr. Griscom's personal efforts.
>
> He first served the Society as an Honorary Vice-President from 1940 to 1947, then as a Director for nine years. During this period his pungent wit and razor-keen sense for the developing needs and prospects of his profession contributed immensely towards furtherence of these needs and aims by the Society as it developed into the active organization of today. To aid in surmounting the problems and difficulties encountered by all growing institutions he was never loath to throw the weight of his considerable personal and professional prestige into the balance to effect the desired end.[2]

Griscom occasionally led Massachusetts Audubon sponsored field trips, including the Cape Campout on Cape Cod, but leading large groups was not his forte, and he remarked about one trip that his style was badly cramped. While Carl Buchheister was secretary of the society, he frequently solicited articles for the *Bulletin,* and he asked Ludlow to give talks, up to an hour in length, at the annual meetings, a custom that was to be adopted by the subsequent director for more than a decade. Buchheister clearly depended heavily on Ludlow for advice and support, and he acknowledged his debt in a letter discussing his attendance at a dinner honoring Griscom: "I came because I was impelled by deep feelings of affection to do so. You will never know how much you helped me when I first came to Boston in 1936 to take over the Secretariat of the Mass. Audubon Society. I was not yet dry behind the ears and knew nothing and you encouraged, aided and instructed me. I have *not* forgotten!"[3]

Largely at Ludlow's instigation, in 1936 the Boston Society of Natural History began the publication of records of Massachusetts and New England birds, referred to at different times as the "Monthly News Service," "Monthly Bulletin of Bird News," and eventually "Records of New England Birds." It was edited originally by Juliet Richardson and later by David Garrison, Rolland Clements, Ruth Turner, and Annette and William Cottrell. In 1945 it was taken over by the society and published as a supplement to the *Bulletin,* with the Cottrells and Ruth Emery sharing editorial duties. The editors always relied on Griscom's watchful eye and judgment for any needed censorship, and the records were routinely given a final reading and approval by Ludlow before they went to press.

In 1939 Ludlow was invited to lunch with Buchheister and Robert Walcott, president of the society, to discuss candidates for the top administrative position in the society, which would become vacant when Buchheister moved to the National Audubon Society in New York. C. Russell Mason got the job of executive director and almost immediately tried to push Griscom into writing a monthly column on Massachusetts birds for the *Bulletin.* For once Ludlow declined.

I have your note of January 4th and am going to decline your proposition to write a resume of bird movements in Massachusetts each month. You will understand that it is nothing personal as between you and me, but one or more members of your Board are becoming over enthusiastic in trying to put me to work for the Audubon Society for nothing, and I think it is high time that I got enough backbone to say no at least once. It seems to me that Dave Garrison could do this job equally well, and in a few months more, if you could get out in the field sufficiently often, you could certainly do it yourself.[4]

Mason was apparently not put off completely by this refusal and later in 1940 successfully solicited Griscom's participation in the annual meeting.

After entertaining the idea for several years, in 1945 Robert Walcott finally asked Griscom to become a member of the board of directors. In the following letter Walcott gives a brief analysis of the delay, and then immediately puts Ludlow to work.

I am delighted to know that you will be willing in the New Year to assume the heavy duties of Director of the Massachusetts Audubon Society. This is a consummation devoutly to be wished, and is most appropriate because of your having given aid and comfort to the Society for so many years. I should have asked you to become a Director shortly after you arrived in Cambridge but that in those years I got the idea that you did not consider the Society of any great importance or doing any work of value, and I thought at that time your association with the Massachusetts Fish & Game Protective Association was more important for you and for the progress of conservation. If such was your opinion, I think you were very largely right, because while John Phillips was at the head of the Fish & Game Association it was ably conducted and its influence was far reaching. And, until we were able to pension off Winthrop Packard as our Secretary, nothing very startling originated in the Massachusetts Audubon Society.

On the 19th of February we plan to have a Luncheon or Dinner to commemorate the Fiftieth Anniversary of the organization meeting of the Massachusetts Audubon Society, the oldest organization in USA for protection of birds that is still in existence, and I should like very much if you would be willing to talk to us on that occasion much as you did to the National Audubon Society at its last Annual Meeting.[5]

Two years later Griscom agreed to serve on three committees of the Massachusetts Audubon Society—the budget-finance, executive, and publications, the last of which Ludlow chaired. Walcott referred to these committees as the backbone of the society, so it is clear that Griscom had assumed a position of real power and authority. Of his business philosophy, Henry Parker said:

Family background and early financial and business experience ingrained a personal demand for solvency and "pay-as-you-go" progress, and he fought consistently and forcefully for such an approach by the Society in all its works. He was a man of strong convictions. Even those who could not agree with him were forced to admire the directness of his opinion and his unswerving line of flight to whatever target he set for himself or the organization which he served.[6]

In 1948 Griscom was thanked for giving so much time, for both field trips and evening workshops, to the Natural Science Workshop, which was in its first year of operation. Three years later Ralph Lawson asked Ludlow to be on a sanctuary committee for the society's new acquisitions at Topsfield, Hamilton, and Wenham. Despite his physical disabilities, Griscom remained active in society affairs, corresponding regularly with C. Russell Mason and with Allen Morgan, who succeeded Mason as executive director in 1957, largely through Ludlow's influence.

After Griscom's death, most of the memorial statements recognized his contributions to the conservation movement. The comments of Henry Parker are typical. "With the death of Ludlow Griscom . . . the Society lost a staunch supporter and an enduring friend. . . . Many of us may not have fully realized his grave concern and tireless drive for a wider knowledge and acceptance of sound conservation methods throughout the country. This he saw as the backbone and 'raison d'etre' of the Massachusetts Audubon Society."[7] In this organization, perhaps more than in any of the others in which he served, Griscom's personality became a critical factor, the consummate showman leading the charge for an increased public awareness and appreciation of birds and the natural world.

Conservation 15

Ludlow Griscom was actively involved in conservation during virtually all of his adult life. His interest dates back at least to his days at the American Museum of Natural History, and later efforts in this field are inextricably interwoven with his work both at the Museum of Comparative Zoology and for the National and Massachusetts Audubon Societies. He was an activist, and in an arena where polar positions were prevalent, his moderate and eminently practical course often drew criticism from both fringes.

Early on, he explained changes in birdlife in terms of human population growth, excessive hunting, and habitat alteration, and described the hazards to native birds from the introduction of foreign ones. In his *Birds of the New York City Region* (1923), he clearly describes these elements.

The rapid growth of the city, and the development of the suburbs, led to the draining of marshes and the clearing of land still suitable for many kinds of birds. The rapid increase of a low-class foreign population, for whom everything with feathers was game, greatly affected many common species which had become adapted to the vicinity of man. The successful introduction of the English Sparrow began during this period seriously to harm those species which were unable to compete with it. These factors still persist at the present time and will undoubtedly continue. The introduction of the

Starling in addition promises to work even greater havoc with native species than the English Sparrow.[1]

In 1923 there was a suggestion that pheasants should be introduced to Martha's Vineyard for hunters, and Griscom opposed this on the grounds that it would lead to the extinction of the remaining Heath Hen population. In a letter to William C. Adams, director of the Division of Fisheries and Game, Department of Conservation, we see a hint of Ludlow's commitment to practical tactics in conservation. He suggests that newspaper publicity would probably arouse public interest, as has the previous extinction of North American bird species. Then he defends protection of the Heath Hen. "I am only too glad to go on record as strongly urging the continued protection of the heath-hen in every possible way on purely sentimental grounds. I cannot believe that the extinction of any form of animal life which it has taken the operation of great laws over vast ages of time to evolve can possibly be expressed in terms of dollars and cents or can be decided on a purely economic basis."[2]

Griscom's writings are replete with comments about local habitat destruction and the reduction of a bird's temptation to alight and rest because of the destruction of woods and fields.[3] His journals, including those that describe his expeditions in tropical America, often comment on habitat destruction.[4] When observing an ecological disaster, such as one caused by an oil spill, he would carefully document counts of oiled birds and thus provide documentation as ammunition for future conservation fights.

He actively participated in organizations where he could administer some clout. For example, in 1931 he was the Boston Museum of Natural History's representative on the Advisory Council of the state's Division of Fisheries and Game. In 1948 he was appointed chairman of the board of that division by his good friend Governor Bradford.

Duck hunting had always been Ludlow's second favorite sport (after birdwatching), and as a result he bridged the gap between the hunter and conservationist contingents, who were often at polar ends of the spectrum on conservation issues. That his philosophy was always a practical one, aimed at reasonable compromise, is illustrated by his response to Margaret M. Nice, an eminent ornithologist:

I am acquainted with Ralph King's "Ruffed Grouse Management," and thoroughly agree that his statement of policy on what constitutes a game bird is biologically ideal and sound. On the other hand, we live in a practical world and have to deal with people who want to shoot certain birds regarded as game birds for sport. Were King's definition [that only demonstrated surplus populations should be hunted] strictly applied, it is doubtful if any bird in

North America could ever legally be shot right down to the present moment! If the Fish and Wildlife Service should suddenly try to put this principle into practice they would surely deserve just what would happen to them. They would be torn limb from limb, the migratory treaty would be repealed, and the Fish and Wildlife Service abolished by the infuriated taxpayers, and you and I most certainly could not prevent it.[5]

Griscom was considered a prominent conservationist by most of those who knew him. He felt that his efforts in stimulating the sport of birding had important conservation implications. Further, he thought that a primary means of effecting conservation was through education, both in the classroom and in the field. Juliet Richardson French, one of his protégés, stated that all her conservation work started with Griscom's Harvard summer school course in ornithology—a comment typical of those who learned from him.[6] Cora Wellman, another birding companion of Griscom's, recalled his observation at a time when "housing developments were demolishing one after another of the woods and thickets which had once trapped so many migrating birds. This led him to say that people become sentimental if they happen to see a shrike take a bird but do not so readily recognize real threats to birds when habitats are destroyed."[7]

Griscom's correspondence provides some insight into his philosophy of conservation and the political problems that the conservation movement faced. In 1944 he wrote to Robert F. Griggs, chairman of the Division of Biology and Agriculture of the National Research Council, suggesting that a proposed Council of the Federated Conservation Agencies become a committee in Griggs's division. An exchange of letters followed in which Griscom outlined some of his thoughts on the state of conservation in general, an analysis of several major organizations, and some suggestions on tactics and organizational structure.

I venture to submit as concise a picture of the "human" problems concerned as far as my knowledge makes possible.

Conservation is a branch of biological and agricultural research, a scientific profession, now requiring advanced and special studies, but as a science it is still in its infancy. Unfortunately, the country is faced with innumerable "conservation" problems in every direction, and action cannot be deferred until research is concluded and all possible facts are in. Moreover, most of these problems impinge so greatly on human interests and passions that they cannot possibly be solved on a pure scientific research basis alone; too many men whose interests are unfavorably affected will not stand for it. This is why the field is as controversial, and why political or legislative action is usually a compromise.[8]

Griscom goes on to analyze the history and status of the National Audubon Society, the Wildlife Institute, the National Wildlife Federation, Ducks Unlimited, and the Izaak Walton League. He then states:

> My summary, also must be the recognition of the existence of jealousy, rivalry, and ill-[w]ill. Most of it is childish and second class, and all of it is beside the point. As far as the advance of the cause of conservation is concerned, the more groups the better. I agree on this heartily with [Ira] Gabrielson. In good times, he cares mighty little what they all think, do, or recommend, but in a jam with Congress, he calls for help, and then wants a flood of telegrams from ten organizations with ten different membership lists. . . .
> On the other side are the purely scientific societies, interested in research, and mighty cautious about getting involved in controversial matters. Of those in my field of knowledge, the Wilson Ornithological Club is the only one making a genuine effort to have a live wire conservation committee.[9]

He concludes that there needs to be three "councils": one for expert scientific knowledge, a second for uniting action groups, and a third that merges action and scientific groups with broad interests.

Ludlow recognized that political action was an exercise in compromise, but for him that was no reason not to support it. On the contrary, in a 1947 letter, he expressed his basic faith in the democratic structure.

> I also am one who has always strongly felt that both Federal and State legislatures are on the whole trying to do the right thing, and I have little but amused contempt for those conservationists who think that all legislative action is based on politics and that all of them are intrinsically dishonest bums. Moreover, this attitude is easily discovered on the part of these officials and does not tend to make conservation popular with them. One of the greatest questions of the times is whether the needed work can best be done by a large number of small units or a cooperative super organization. At the moment, in the various scientific fields, the latter system has proved overwhelmingly superior.[10]

A more serious obstacle to effective action lay elsewhere. Throughout his career, Griscom saw a persistent weakness in the conservation movement in the bickering and fighting among conservation groups, or conflict between different aspects of the work.

> It is the tragedy of modern conservation that the great majority of these conservationists are nature lovers rather than naturalists. While the wild life is decreasing they are quarreling and fighting with each other as to the ideal methods to stop the decrease of wild life, slinging mud at each other and disgusting the general public. The real reason from the point of view of the trained ornithologist and the experienced field man like myself that these various organizations and people are quarreling as to the ideal method of saving wild life is that they are inadequately informed as to their exact existing numbers and as to the reason why any one of them is actually decreasing.
>
> The sportsmen, on the other hand, are equally at fault. Dr. Hornaday, for instance, listed the Wood Duck as one of the next North American birds to become extinct at a time when, thanks to protection, it was patently and rapidly increasing throughout the United States, and the sportsmen tell preposterous and fabulous stories about the abundance of ducks in an effort to prevent further drastic restrictions on the shooting season. What the conservationists like Mrs. Edge cannot realize is that while the sportsmen are patently wrong and prejudiced, from the point of view of the scientific the conservationists are equally wrong and prejudiced in the opposite direction and until they live down this reputation with the scientists and the general public they will never receive adequate support.[11]

In "Fifty Years of Conservation" (1946), Griscom assessed the past efforts of conservationists, discussed the current situation, and clearly stated the fundamental importance of habitat preservation and education to the conservation movement. He traced the "era of protection," which he considered successfully concluded because of the implementation of broad protectionist legislation, and the "era of conservation," which he felt was just beginning. Griscom thought that bird species which had not recovered under protection posed ecological questions. Habitat preservation was a major concern:

> No bird can exist in greater numbers than can find suitable breeding territory. If civilization has destroyed 50 per cent of the Redhead Duck's former breeding range, an indefinitely closed season will not raise its total population much above 50 per cent of a former 100. . . .
>
> The carrying capacity of the remaining winter range is just as important. Of what avail is it to raise a large crop of young on the breeding grounds if the winter range will at best support two thirds of them only?[12]

He goes on to point out that many shorebirds which have not recovered former abundances winter in the Argentine pampas, where "civilization has developed by leaps and bounds in recent years."

Perhaps Ludlow best summed up his own feelings about conservation in a 1949 letter discussing Aldo Leopold's *Sand County Almanac.*

> Delighted with the book by Leopold. Everyone interested in conservation and nature should not only read it but reflect on its basic philosophy. Conservation today suffers from two extremes. On the one hand extreme sentimentalism. On the other hand an effort to sell it by putting it on an economic basis, one of purely material advantage. Leopold points out that there are other reasons for enjoying and preserving the world of nature. Ethics and sound biology are combined.[13]

Considerations of national policy and philosophy often had specific, local applications. By 1938 Monomoy—which was then a peninsula on the south side of Cape Cod, rather than two islands the way it is now—was showing signs of human pollution, with squatter's shacks cropping up and heavy summer beach traffic. Monomoy was Ludlow's favorite spot on the cape, largely because it was such a marvelous trap for migrating birds, especially shorebirds. Hence when rumblings out of Washington began, suggesting the possibility that the area might be taken over as a federal property, Ludlow offered his support. He articulates his position in a June 1938 letter to Robert Walcott, president of the Massachusetts Audubon Society, whose endorsement was important since the society owned part of Monomoy.

> I heartily agree that as a national project there is scarcely anything better worth having in New England, and I am concerned at the degree to which cottages and summer camps are being built. . . . I very greatly doubt if developing it as a national park or some sort of public benefit would seriously harm it as a bird paradise. . . . My chief fear is that the National Park Service would reject the whole proposition because of the grave risk that Monomoy might become an island once more at any time and the motor highway approach south of Chatham would be carried away by the Ocean.[14]

By October, Griscom was suggesting that he would rather see the U. S. Biological Survey (later the U. S. Fish and Wildlife Service) acquire the property, and he wrote to Clark Salyer II, chief of the Division of Wildlife Refuges, outlining the significant ornithological features of Monomoy and recommending it for a National Wildlife Refuge.

> You, of course, know that Monomoy is one of the most famous migratory highways for water birds of all kinds, and also for land birds. The shoals off

the Point and the Stone Horse Reef are one of the greatest concentration areas for wintering waterfowl in the northeast and support, among other things, at least half the existing population of American Eiders. . . . I view with concern the increasing traffic down the beach and the encroachment of the moors by squatters' camps and hunting lodges, driving away the Curlew and Golden Plover that occur there in some numbers every year. Unless, therefore a large supply of breeding ducks is a prerequisite for a Wildlife Refuge, I can state from long years of personal field experience that there is no better place on the northeastern Atlantic seaboard for a Wildlife Refuge than Monomoy Island.[15]

In December, Griscom received a letter from A. C. Elmer, acting chief of the Division of Wildlife Refuges, asking Ludlow to evaluate Crane Mill Pond and Parker River as possible migratory waterfowl refuges and to assess their merits relative to Monomoy. Ludlow, apparently acting on the assumption that you must take one step at a time, downplays the merits of Plum Island as a refuge possibility in a March 1940 letter to Clarence Cottam of the Biological Survey.

Regarding the question of Plum Island and Monomoy as potentially valuable for waterfowl and other forms of wildlife. . . . I have also had several long discussions with Gabrielson about the same matter. I don't think that Plum Island is worth a damn, and while you might be able to develop a good refuge in the Parker River section. . . . I would say that both in number and variety of species the odds are 10-1 in favor of Monomoy.[16]

Local opposition to the Monomoy project was developing, and Griscom comments on it and his conversation with Ira Gabrielson in a letter to Robert Walcott. Gabrielson was chief of the Biological Survey at the time. When Ludlow lobbied, he liked to lobby at the top.

My comment on this whole rumpus, about which I have already heard a good deal, is that the opposition always misses the point. On the outer Cape it is taken for granted that if Monomoy becomes a Wildlife Sanctuary all use and enjoyment of it by the townspeople of Chatham will cease. This, of course, is a pure fallacy. . . . I had a long talk with Gabrielson, Chief of the Survey, after he had been down to Monomoy to look it over, and I understand that he has every intention in the course of time of acquiring it as a wildlife refuge. It, of course, makes no difference in the long run to the Federal Government how much local opposition there is to such an affair, as they have the absolute right of taking it by eminent domain anyhow. Experience with all these wildlife refuges has invariably been that the local community concerned is 100% against it at the start and after it has been a going concern for two or three years they discover that it turns out to be a pretty good thing, or at least not a bad thing in the long run.[17]

When Oliver Austin, Jr., joined the opposition, Ludlow duly reported the problem, and some of the opposition tactics, to Gabrielson:

I am taking the liberty to write you about the Monomoy question as more trouble seems to be brewing about it in this state. While you may know all about these facts yourself, there can be no harm in my writing you about them on the chance that one or more of them you might not have heard.

Young Oliver Austin, now a resident of Wellfleet, on the outer Cape, and with a private grudge against the Survey, as you well know, has put his finger in the pie and has become one of the leaders of the local opposition. . . . I had a talk the other day with Judge Robert Walcott, President of the Massachusetts Audubon Society, who is an ardent advocate of Monomoy becoming a wildlife refuge. He is disturbed about the situation because there is plenty of publicity in this State now in opposition and there is no publicity by the Survey or its local representatives in favor of the idea or to deny the alarming reports about the loss of fishing rights, etc. He informs me that there is a statute in this Commonwealth permitting the United States to take over land in the Commonwealth by eminent domain for wildlife refuges. The opposition to Monomoy as a wildlife refuge is now taking the form of introducing a bill into the Legislature to have this law revoked, which would mean technically that only the Army and the Navy would have the right to take land by eminent domain against the possible wishes of the citizens of the State.[18]

In March 1942 S. B. Locke, regional director of the Fish and Wildlife Service, invited Ludlow to participate in a meeting between "representative people" and Washington officials about the establishment of a federal waterfowl sanctuary in the Cape Cod area. Finally, in June 1944, Monomoy was established as National Wildlife Refuge, under the U. S. Fish and Wildlife Service, and in 1970 most of it was designated a Wilderness Area.

During the better part of the 1940s, a controversy raged over the establishment of what would become the Parker River National Wildlife Refuge. By 1940 the Fish and Wildlife Service (then the Biological Survey) had shown an interest in acquiring a portion of Plum Island and the adjacent saltmarsh through which the Parker River flows, as well as considerable land to the interior in the Newburyport area. The initial surveys and other local work by service employees was apparently poorly done from a public relations standpoint. For example, they cut a 100-foot-wide survey line through forty-year-old pines, which outraged the local citizenry. They also made some poor biological decisions on the proposed management of the system, particularly regarding the construction of water impoundments on Plum Island. One of the men whom the service people ignored and infuriated was Joseph A. Hagar, an extremely competent biologist in the area of Black Duck biology and at the time state ornithologist for Massachusetts. He joined the local people and the sportsmen who feared curtailment of the hunting privileges, forming an opposition of considerable force. The Massachusetts Audubon Society, partly because they owned land on Plum Island that they could not afford to develop for wildlife the way the Fish and Wildlife Service could, joined with Griscom as the chief supporters of the proposed federal refuge. The whole issue was muted during World War II, but in 1945 it surfaced again and local passions became inflamed, spilled over into a long series of letters in the local newspaper, and produced virtual hysteria over such assertions as that the impoundments would cause outbreaks of malaria. The fight became intense and apparently led to the introduction of a legislative bill to abolish the office of state ornithologist, which some say Griscom supported, thus eliminating Hagar's job. (The bill did not pass.)

In February 1940, Clarence Cottam of the Biological Survey wrote to Griscom asking for recommendations and comments about Plum Island as potentially valuable for waterfowl, commenting that Griscom should keep this quiet since federal interest in an area often drives up land prices. Cottam mentioned that he thought that they could develop a good refuge in the Parker River section if they could get part of Plum Island as well.[19]

It was not until 1944 that Ludlow turned his full attention from Monomoy to Parker River, which had been partly under federal control since 1942 but needed development. He defended it as a good potential refuge.

The Parker River and Plum Island meadows l[a]y squarely on the great Atlantic Coast flyway. Ninety percent of the Canada geese that use this flyway pass over and rest on this great stretch of meadows. The same is true of the black duck, though here the percentage of the total number is very much less. . . . Over 300 species of birds have been found in a period of ten years in the dunes on Plum Island and every duck, every tern, every gull and every shore bird ever reported from New England in the last hundred years has been found in this area in the last ten years. . . . The locality consequently comes as near being unique ornithologically as any in the entire

Atlantic seaboard region of the northern half of the United States and no
area in eastern Canada can touch it. The claim, therefore, that the proposed
Wild Life Refuge is not a normal migration route is a most utter and incompetent nonsense.[20]

In 1945 Hagar published a nineteen-page booklet, *Parker River National
Wildlife Refuge: The Case for Revision of Plans,* in which he outlined his objections
to the whole project.[21] In brief, he stated that the project was not a workable
plan for increasing waterfowl, with disadvantages outweighing proposed advantages. He argued that revision was necessary to overcome the hostility from
local people and that the proposed refuge was too large for a heavily populated
area like Massachusetts. Parts of the proposed refuge would conflict with maximum local usage for recreation, fishing, and clamming. He asserted that the
only area that would make a good refuge was part of Plum Island, a section
that was perhaps too small for the federal government to worry about, and that
might best be administered by the state. Hagar quite correctly challenged both
the application of experience with other federal refuges to this portion of Massachusetts and the adequacy of the preliminary studies. He also questioned the
idea that Massachusetts is an essential part of the Atlantic Flyway for migrating waterfowl.

While the local politics and uproar proceeded, Griscom attacked the problem at a higher level. In a letter to Harold J. Ickes, the secretary of the interior,
he strongly defended the proposed refuge but pointed out the antagonisms
that the Fish and Wildlife Service had brought upon itself.

My warm friend and greatly esteemed colleague Dr. Ira N. Gabrielson, the
chief of the U. S. Fish and Wildlife Service, has asked me to write you a full
letter on the ornithological merits of the Parker River Wildlife Refuge in
Essex County, Massachusetts. To date, this whole proposition has resulted
in one unfortunate row after another. . . .

Dr. Gabrielson's selection of the Plum Island and Parker River marshes as
the basis of one of his proposed refuges in Massachusetts was in part due
to my favorable and enthusiastic endorsement of the project some five years
or more ago when the matter first came up for consideration. . . . I now
gather that the whole area has been attacked as 1) no good and 2) it is
alleged that there are no possibilities for improvement.

Both claims are arrant nonsense as I shall show later, but I am now
gravely concerned that the fundamental soundness of the proposition is
jeopardized due to the fact that the errors and incompetence of U. S. Fish
and Wildlife employees have either aroused unnecessary antagonism and

opposition, or are obviously open to attack [he then documents the "atrocious" public relations]. . . .

The only opposition which seems to me worthy of serious consideration and which cannot immediately be dismissed with contempt is 1) the unfavorable report of the State Ornithologist J. A. Hagar and 2) the unfavorable report of the Committee for the Preservation of Duck Hunting in Essex County, Massachusetts, written and published by Charles D. Mahoney in 1943. As a matter of fact, the second item leaned heavily on the reports and statements of the State Ornithologist.

I happen to know Hagar very well and was one of the people who helped get him his position years ago. He was an excellent amateur field ornithologist, but lacked any real experience elsewhere, and never had the opportunity of knowing the bird-life of any area subsequently taken over as a wild life refuge, so as to see at first hand the startling changes which always take place. He reversed an originally favorable report, after completing a brilliant study of the food of the Black Duck in Essex County. He was infuriated and stunned by the know-it-all and supercilious attitude of minor survey officials, who ignored his evidence, and scouted his knowledge and experience, and refused to pay any attention to his recommendations that proposed methods of development useful further south would not work in an area with a 14 ft. tide fall and a bitter northern winter. He now regards the Service as a bunch of crooks, who are misappropriating public funds with false claims. . . .

Therefore, I heartily endorse the judgment of my friend Dr. Gabrielson and the overall correctness of his decision. He has my hearty sympathy in finding himself stuck with certain lands in the interior which cannot be successfully defended as ideal for wildlife, and it is his hard luck that the bitter opposition and unfair criticism that has arisen against the project in Essex County should in part have been aroused by the tactless public relations and the superiority complexes of his local representatives. . . .

The opposition of local sportsmen on the ground that their local duck hunting will be destroyed is the usual provincial delusion. . . . The Committee of Essex County sportsmen would have been well advised to spend their money sending an investigator to study the improvement to hunting at other Atlantic refuges, instead of printing a phoney ornithological analysis.[22]

In 1946 Ludlow advised Clarence Cottam on his defense of the proposed project and pointed out that Hagar was right about the enormous tides in Essex County constituting a local problem that does not exist in other Atlantic Coast refuges to the south. Further, there was an error in the assumption that the

Black Ducks feed on animal food in the winter because of the lack of vegetable food.[23] In 1947 he prepared a statement for the Massachusetts Conservation Council, in which he affirmed his authority to make such a report, defended the refuge proposal, and pointed out that compromise offered the best solution.

A developed Parker River National Wildlife Refuge became reality in the early 1950s, with a total acreage of about half that originally planned. Still the battle was not over. In 1953 Griscom and others had to fight a movement to have the federal government give back to the state the Plum Island Refuge and Monomoy as well, which according to Ludlow would "indeed be disastrous and unfortunate if any such thing should happen."[24] In the end, the refuges remained under federal control.

In addition to his conservation efforts related to his major professional associations, and the occasional ad hoc brawl such as over Parker River, Ludlow was involved in much other conservation work to a lesser extent. For example, in 1938 he wrote to James F. Mahoney asking him to vote against a Senate bill that would remove protection from some hawks and owls, stating, "I consider it a very bad and wholly unnecessary measure."[25] In 1939, when the state Conservation Department was reorganized with Parks and Recreation, he was asked to serve as a consultant. In 1941 he was invited to give a paper at the New England Game Conference but was forced to decline because of his war work with Harvard Defence Group and Naval Intelligence monitoring foreign language newspapers and radio broadcasts. That year Griscom became a member of the Wilson Ornithological Society Conservation Committee, and in 1943 he was elected to the Advisory Board of the American Committee for International Wildlife Protection.

Another group in which Griscom showed an interest was the Ecological Society of America. In 1944 he wrote to Victor E. Shelford, perhaps the foremost animal ecologist of the first half of the twentieth century, to suggest a course of action for the society.

> I think it a great pity that the Ecological Society which could easily get into a position of commanding influence and authority, takes no action and appears to have no long-range policy in matters of conservation. . . .
>
> Through my connection with the National Audubon Society, I have been much interested in and have visited the famous Singer Tract in northern Louisiana, which is now rapidly being lumbered to the ground. I am by no means so narrow minded that my interest in this tract is based entirely on

Ludlow Griscom. Photograph originally published in *Ludlow Griscom, Virtuoso of Field Identification* (1945), a picture story by Edwin Way Teale, *Audubon* 47:349–358. Courtesy of the National Audubon Society.

Ludlow Griscom at work on his field journals at his desk in his home on Fayerweather Street, Cambridge, Massachusetts. These journals are now housed at the Library of the Peabody Museum of Salem. Photograph by Edwin Way Teale, 1945. Courtesy of the National Audubon Society and Edith Griscom.

Ludlow Griscom with his huge spotting scope, a trademark of Griscom's field trips. Photograph originally published in *Ludlow Griscom, Virtuoso of Field Identification* (1945), a picture story by Edwin Way Teale, *Audubon* 47:349–358. Courtesy of the National Audubon Society.

Ludlow Griscom (with telescope) with his entourage on a birding trip. Rosario Mazzeo is directly behind Griscom. Ruth Emery standing with white cap. Frances Burnett is at the extreme right. Photograph courtesy of Ruth Emery.

Photograph of the O.C.B.C.—Outer Circle Bird Club or Old Colony Bird Club—when the club's bird list was published. Griscom referred to it as the "Old Cluck's Bird Club." *From left to right, front row:* Ludlow Griscom, Margaret Argue, Frances Burnett, Arthur Argue, Cora Wellman, Miss Caldwell; *rear,* Ruth Emery, C. Russell Mason, Rosario Mazzeo, Maurice Emery, unknown. Photograph courtesy of Ruth Emery.

Laying of the cornerstone of the East Wing of Boston's Museum of Science, December 14, 1949. *Left to right:* Bradford Washburn (director of the museum), Major General William H. Harrison (representing Governor Paul A. Dever), William T. Morrissey (commissioner, Metropolitan District Commission, Commonwealth of Massachusetts, on whose land the museum was being constructed, Science Park on the Boston Esplanade), J. C. Richdale (president of the New England Council), Ludlow Griscom (president of the museum's Board of Trustees), Mattias A. Sundberg (building construction foreman), Angelo V. Berlandi (House of Representatives), Monsignor Cornelius T. H. Sherlock (supervisor of parochial schools, archdiocese of Boston). Photograph courtesy of the Museum of Science.

Roger Tory Peterson *(left)* and Ludlow Griscom. Courtesy Smithsonian Institution Archives, Record Unit 7150, American Ornithologists' Union Collection 1883–1977.

Ludlow Griscom standing in front of the beach buggy "Sandpiper's Rest." Photograph with courtesy, from the files of the Massachusetts Audubon Society.

The dedication marker near Hellcat Swamp, on Plum Island National Wildlife Refuge. Photograph by Ruth Emery, with courtesy, from the files of the Massachusetts Audubon Society.

Nuttall Ornithological Club meeting at the home of Charles F. Batchelder, 5 January 1948. *Left to right, seated:* Charles F. Batchelder, Wendell Taber, James Lee Peters, Joseph A. Hagar, Charles H. Blake; *standing:* Arthur Argue, Maurice Emery, Dr. Morton Cummings. Until the early 1950s, this "Victorian men's club" met in private homes. Photograph courtesy of the Nuttall Ornithological Club.

Ludlow Griscom examining bird skins at Boston's Museum of Science. Photograph courtesy of the Museum of Science.

Left to right: Andrew, Joan, and Edith Griscom on roof of Sears Point house (summer 1949), Chatham, Massachusetts. Photograph courtesy of Andrew Griscom.

Edith and Ludlow Griscom in front of their Sears Point summer home in Chatham, Massachusetts. Photograph courtesy of Edith S. Griscom.

the Ivory-billed Woodpecker, but I regard it as a thousand pities that some part at least of this magnificent Mississippi bottom land of primeval forest could not be preserved for posterity. One would suppose that the Ecological Society would be as interested in preserving a sample of this particular association as any organization in the United States.[26]

In 1946 Griscom he was asked to address the New York State Conservation Council, and the following year he critiqued a manuscript for Rachel L. Carson, then an information specialist with the U. S. Department of the Interior. In a 1947 letter to S. Prescott Fay, chairman of the Massachusetts State Committee of Ducks Unlimited, Griscom argued the merits and necessity for closed seasons on some ducks.

Every time a closed season has been put on one or another of our North American wildfowl, it has been a conspicuous and gratifying success. For example, the Wood Duck, the Eider, the Snow geese, and the Whistling Swan. It consequently follows that the opposition of sportsmen to a closed season is most human and natural, but biologically unrealistic. It is the only absolutely sure way of bringing back the numbers of any animal on earth, but sportsmen cannot bear to sacrifice the pleasure, sport, and recreation for long-range permanent gains. I must admit that intrigues me and I do not quite understand the reason. Even the more ignorant class of dirt farmers are adopting soil conservation measures; lumber companies of the better class have adopted sound forestry practices throughout the civilized world for decades; ardent trout fisherman accept the closing of a certain stream so that it may be restocked with trout; but the majority of duck shooters in the United States have always opposed not only a closed season, but any reduction in the bag limit or the length of the open season.[27]

Even after his first major stroke, Ludlow continued to work on conservation projects.

In 1953 he wrote to Secretary of the Interior Douglas McKay, lobbying for a closed season on duck shooting in the Sacramento Waterfowl Refuge in California, and inviting him to Cape Cod so that "I could take you down to the world famous Monomoy and perhaps have a chance to tell you a little of the local dope."[28] Nor did his poor health inhibit his brusque approach to rejecting what he considered an extremist position: "I do not admit that bird protection in 1953 is more urgent than in 1888 in fact I regard the statement as patently ridiculous."[29] In 1955 he was requested by the National Wildlife Federation to do species accounts for birds in their Wildlife Week educational brochures, and in 1956 he was invited to participate in a Whooping Crane Conference in

Washington, D. C. Right to the very end of his working life, Ludlow was interested in a broad spectrum of conservation affairs.

Ludlow Griscom's contributions to conservation were, perhaps, best expressed by his close friend G. William Cottrell in a letter to Edith. "In the death of Ludlow Griscom . . . the entire conservation movement have suffered an irreparable loss. His contribution was unique in the same way that he himself was unique; neither can be duplicated."[30]

Part Five

THE FINAL YEARS

The Last Decade 16

From 1950 to 1959 Ludlow Griscom's life was marred by ill health. Circulatory problems resulted in a series of major and minor strokes, which left Ludlow impaired. He seemed to ride a roller coaster between severe disability and nearly complete recovery. This pattern, with its constant uncertainty, made his working life difficult and he gradually withdrew from professional commitments. His spirit was indomitable, however, and with only occasional lapses into despair, he charted a course marked by a cautious optimism and never lost that sense of wonder, enjoyment, and enthusiasm that he derived from even the commonest of birds in his garden.

It was this last decade that most of his contemporaries remember. People who did not like him began to exploit his weakening abilities, but his friends remember his increased personal warmth. It was during this time that he received his greatest honors, the fruits of a lifetime of achievement. But the glory was tempered by his physical infirmities.

Indications that health problems were developing are found as early as 1938, when he was urged by his doctor to give up coffee, tea, and tobacco. In 1943 Griscom complained, "My weight dropped from 170 to 159 pounds which is considerably less than I weighed when I entered college."[1] Elsewhere he wrote that "on the Doctor's advice I am unloading several of my present chores."[2] By 1945 Griscom was complaining about a long bout of illness. Tooth problems were to plague him for years, and he was still complaining of them in 1949.

The major health difficulties, however, were related to circulation problems that restricted his physical activities. He outlined the effect of his circulation problems in a March 1947 letter to Guy Emerson.

It seems to be definite that I have lost 50% of my normal circulation in my right leg and at least 80% in my left, where two rather severe arterial occlusions have been located. I must consequently never again get that particular leg wet or cold. I must never force exhausted and under-nourished muscles to perform work for which they are unfit, and that limits me to one flight of stairs at best or 50 yards on the level without pausing for rest. If I am very good and spend two or three hours a day on certain excercises, the 50 yards might be raised to 100.

My personal judgment, consequently, is that the best thing to do is to accept it and to adopt the philosophy which you so wisely hint at in your good letter. Let the period of intensly active field work be declared over and let me now actively begin the writing up of the results of the interesting and extensive field experiences I actually have had. Now that I have had a couple of weeks to think it over, I don't seem to mind particularly.[3]

Ludlow was perhaps grandstanding a bit and being overly brave in the face of a somewhat overstated adversity, but his attitude is nonetheless positive, and he maintained to another friend, "I am in fine shape, as sound as a bell, and ready to lick my weight in wildcats and defy all my enemies."[4]

The strain of professional commitments, especially relating to the Boston Museum of Science, were weighing heavily on Ludlow. His circulation problems, exacerbated by heavy smoking (perhaps 2½ packs a day) were pushing him to the brink. In an August 1949 letter to John Baker, he gives some of the particulars of his situation.

I find myself increasingly overworked and overextended in too many different directions. I have publishers' contracts with deadlines for three different books. One of them is October 1, 1950 and the first volume of another proposed work must be in the hands of a different publisher on January 15, 1950. I have my job here at Harvard and commitments with the National Audubon Society and the Boston Museum of Science and two other boards. Some means of simplifying my life must be found.[5]

Unfortunately, that means surfaced in the middle of July 1950, when at age sixty Ludlow Griscom had a major stroke. Within a few days the letters of encouragement and advice began to pour in. Thornton W. Burgess wrote:

I suspect that already the unanimous chorus of "Take it easy," and "Don't do this," and "Don't do that" has begun. You will get used to it. Between you and me, though I hate to admit it, it is sound advice. . . .

My sincere wishes for your speedy recovery, and that in everything else you will move slowly that the recovery may be complete and lasting.[6]

In September Ludlow received a letter from Ira Gabrielson.

"You certainly must hurry up and get well in time for American Ornithologists' Union meeting. If you don't make it, who the h— am I going to take a drink with when the proceedings of the business meetings are otherwise too boring? I know of no other man who gets bored so completely by the same things as I, and I will be a completely lost soul at the meeting."[7]

He never fully recuperated from this stroke. Edith Griscom recalled that "Ludlow recovered almost completely after his first stroke, but was an 'ordinary man' after that. Before that he was a genius, an acknowledged genius. He never stated anything definitely towards the end— always a case of 'I think.'"[8] Roger Tory Peterson in an interview related that Griscom "changed very much in later years, in the last ten years of his life—a very different man. A lot of that went out of him after he'd had a stroke or two. He was a much more human person."[9]

Given the severity of his stroke, Ludlow's recovery was nevertheless quite remarkable. By September he was writing to Chandler S. Robbins in regard to the "Changing Seasons" section of *Audubon Field Notes*. "So far as I can see, I am improving very rapidly indeed and there is every reason to believe that I can continue to prepare the summary for the next section provided that John Aldrich sees fit for me to try and attempt it. There would appear to be little of unusual ornithological note hereabout and so far the fall migration of the small land birds has not really yet got under way."[10]

Despite his comments to the contrary, Griscom was not following the doctor's orders, and he stubbornly continued to smoke and in other ways continued to contribute to the circulatory problems that plagued him. He certainly had not lost his indomitable will nor the twinkle in his eye, as an interview with Sibley Higginbotham suggests.

I visited him a few times at home after his first stroke. He had on his big red bathrobe, and he would be sitting in there [in bed], and he'd yell "Mouse" [Ludlow's affectionate name for his wife Edith] . . . and when she came in he says "time for what the doctor ordered," and she turned and said "He's talking about the double martini he talked the doctor into. He said that the doctor said that it was two double martinis, but my recollection is that it was one." So they had a little argument and she went out. But what the doctor did say was absolutely no smoking, so she left and he looked around and said "Sibley! Is she on the other side of the house?" and I said "Yes." He reached into this big red robe and pulled out a pack of cigarettes and lit one and said "If you hear her coming let me know." He had a big fireplace, and when she came back, swish goes the cigarette into the fire! She must have been able to smell it, but I don't know. He wasn't going to give up his cigarettes.[11]

Dr. Charles Walcott stated that from a doctor's standpoint Ludlow was not an easy person to handle.

You'd tell him he shouldn't smoke, and he'd defy you by lighting up and puffing away. A gallant thing to do, but not very wise—and he certainly paid the penalty. It was pretty well documented that you can shrink the blood vessels that way, and he surely did it in a defiant manner, as if to say "well, take that you bastard." That was his way, you know, he had that quality to him. All very able, very bright, very talented, and I guess, sometimes people are that way. He was more so than most. I've usually been able to handle people. . . . [He was] a very defiant person.[12]

To the great surprise of everyone, Griscom announced in March 1951 that he was about to depart on a trip. On 23 March, Ludlow and Edith sailed on the *S.S. Esparta* for Puerto Barrios, Guatemala, arriving there five days later. They then sailed to Puerto Cortes, Honduras, where they changed their mode of transportation to the railways. They were the guests of Governor W. Cameron Forbes and took "various excursions." They sailed on 13 April aboard the *S.S. Ulna,* and arrived in New Orleans on 16 April.[13] The ornithological record of this trip is skimpy.

Despite his disabilities, Ludlow began to assume again certain of his responsibilities. He decided to continue as chairman of the board for the National Audubon Society and went to the meeting in New York. In addition, in November 1951 he became a member of the Publications Committee of the AOU.

Griscom traveled with Edith to New Orleans for the AOU meeting in October 1952 and took the field trip across marshes to Grande Isle. In September he had tested his endurance with a fall "Big Day."

Griscom's correspondence suggests that he was feeling his age, and even getting depressed at times, although he did manage to make an extensive western trip with Edith in the fall of 1953 to the AOU meeting in Los Angeles. They got some birding in with Arnold Small at Playa del Rey. Next they took a bus trip to the San Gabriel Mountains, Yosemite Valley, and then around through Tucson, Arizona, to Madera Canyon in the Santa Rita Mountains, and finished with a drive to the top of Mount Lemmon, more than 9,000 feet in elevation.

Despite passing this endurance test, a 1953 letter suggests that Griscom was considering some measure of withdrawal from his commitments.

> Thank you so much for your kind, friendly and delightful letter. I found myself unable to retire this spring and thanks to the kindness of many friends have managed to have a most respectable season. But I still have a psychological problem which bothers me, on which I would appreciate your helpful suggestions. I hate the idea of being like some opera singer who with declining voice goes squalling on from concert to concert. The time is bound to come when physical energy, eyesight and keenness of hearing will fail and I dislike the idea of people saying:— "Poor old Griscom, how pathetically he has run downhill." The only way to avoid this is to retire before your powers are too seriously impaired.[14]

His circumspection did not prevent him from attending the Wilson Ornithological Society meeting at Cape May, New Jersey, in June, and the AOU meeting in September in Wisconsin.

Dr. Norman Hill, who frequently went birding with Ludlow during this period, stated in an interview that the peripheral hardening of the arteries in his legs left Ludlow unsteady, and subject to falls. He recalled that once during the mid-1950s Ludlow stumbled and fell from a catwalk into the water. Hill always carried an emergency kit when on a trip with Ludlow during these later years.[15]

Still, Griscom had a productive year in 1954, as an October letter, presumably an annual report of sorts, to Alfred Romer, Director of the MCZ, attests.

> As my colleagues were still far behind on the Mexican Checklist, there was little or no activity to report during the past year. Active work was therefore continued on my various local fauna studies in New England; further progress was made on the introduction to Cape Cod bird life. The history, introduction and complete systematic list of the birds of the island of Martha's Vineyard was completed, and this list is now being finally brought up to date by Guy Emerson, with whom I am in constant touch. The introduction and complete systematic list of the Elizabeth Islands was also completed with the kind assistance of W. Cameron Forbes and other members of the Forbes family. Moreover, at the request of the U. S. Fish and Wildlife Service, I took time to write the ornithological history and complete systematic list of the birds recorded from Plum Island. . . . It is hoped that this will be promptly and separately published.
>
> I continued my activities as an official of the American Ornithologists' Union and the National Audubon Society, as well as many other local organizations.[16]

The normal deterioration that accompanies old age began to afflict him. His extraordinary hearing was beginning to go. Higginbotham recalls the frustration with which Ludlow greeted the discovery of a hearing problem.

> All four windows were down in his big Nash and you were supposed to call out a bird that you heard, so I called out very casually "Blackpoll Warbler." He went another 50 yards and said "What did you say Sibley?" I said "Blackpoll Warbler." He slammed on the brakes, and he backed up and said "Tell me when it sings," and I said "There it is." He looked at me, threw it into low, and off we go in a cloud of dust with the tires screaming. Then he said, "Another Goddamn bird bites the dust. Last year it was the kinglet, now it's the blackpoll."[17]

All in all, 1955 was not a good year for Ludlow. His ornithological diary for 1955 has but a single entry, "Go nowhere!" A letter from Nathan Pusey, president of Harvard University, spelled out the end of a long career at Harvard, and the probably bitter pill that he would not receive an Emeritus title, since that was restricted to professors.

Edith Griscom recalled that when the retirement occurred Alfred Romer, Joan Griscom, and she all pitched in to transfer Ludlow's files from the MCZ to their home on Fayerweather Street. Ludlow was too frail to help. She said that Romer, whom Edith considered a good friend of Ludlow's, showed up on the appointed Sunday with clean chino pants that were black by the time the move was completed.

In an early December 1956 letter to M. Ellis of the Division of Fisheries and Game, Ludlow turned in his collecting permit.

> I herewith return the scientific collecting permit you so kindly issued to me on February 8, 1955, with a report as required that I collected no birds, nests, or eggs during the current year.
>
> Due to age and increasing infirmity, I see no reason why it should be renewed, and wish to express my warm thanks to the Division for courtesies extended since 1922.[18]

It was during this period that Griscom's last major publications appeared. His precise editorial skills were clearly slipping, and this was reflected in criticism in many of the reviews. *The Birds of Massachusetts,* coauthored in 1955 with Dorothy Snyder, fared better than *The Birds of Concord.* In general, the tough standards set by Griscom for an acceptable state record drew a friendly response. Eugene Eisenmann in a review in *Auk* states, "The senior author's vast experience and pre-eminence in field identification give interest and great weight to comments as to changes of status, discrimination of related birds, and the standards needed for screening sight reports. The comments are pungently expressed and stimulating even to readers not concerned with Massachusetts status."[19]

Roger Tory Peterson gave the book a highly positive review in the *Bulletin of the Massachusetts Audubon Society:*

> Discarding the wheat from the chaff with scholarly and critical thorough-ness, Ludlow Griscom, dean of field ornithologists, and his skilled lieuten-ant, Dorothy Snyder of the Peabody Museum of Salem, have brought Massa-chusetts field ornithology up to the minute—or at least up to the year 1955. . . .
>
> This little book, formal in aspect though it may seem, is nevertheless one of the most fascinating regional works I have ever read, a digest of the experiences of thousands of bird watchers over the span of a century.[20]

Aaron M. Bagg in the *Wilson Bulletin* emphasized the criteria needed for an acceptable bird record in Massachusetts.

> As a consequence of Mr. Griscom's residence in Massachusetts since 1927, the science and the sport of recording birds in that state have achieved peaks of popularity and brilliant technique equaled in few similar areas. This has produced a great increase, quantitative and qualitative, in information about Massachusetts birds. . . .
>
> The student of avian faunistics who is concerned with the problem of what constitutes a valid record will find the case for the "severe school" presented ably (and at emphatic length) in this book. . . .
>
> It is difficult to fault this book in any serious respect.[21]

There was a long errata sheet with the book, which more careful editing could have prevented. However, it was generally well received by both the Mas-sachusetts and general ornithological community.

The Warblers of America (1957), edited by Griscom and Alexander Sprunt, Jr., with contributions by others, received more severe treatment in most pub-lished reviews. William H. Drury, Jr., in a *Bulletin of the Massachusetts Audubon Society* review, made a number of critical comments including:

> After all the advertising by the publisher, this is a very disappointing book, perhaps because the authors on the extended list did not play a more im-portant part in the main text. . . .
>
> This book is not deserving of Mr. Griscom's general knowledge nor edit-ing abilities. . . .

Ludlow Griscom's discussion of classification is good, but perhaps over-technical for such an overpopular book.[22]

George Miksch Sutton, in a review in the *Auk,* points out that the book purports to be a major reference work but barely mentions juvenal plumage, and concludes: "There appears to me to have been over-hastiness in getting certain parts of the book together."[23] A review in *Ibis* states, "Most of the species accounts are accurate but unimaginative and rather wasteful of words."[24] One in the *Wilson Bulletin* was largely negative in tone, emphasizing the lack of careful and uniform editing, and it concluded: "In striving to be both popular and technical, the book falls short of its true potential in either category. If I seem unduly critical, it is because I thought this long-awaited book would be the new definitive warbler work. Instead, it has its place along with Chapman and Bent in my library and contributes much which they do not offer, but it does not supercede them."[25] It appears that by 1957, Griscom may not have been able to handle a project this large and cumbersome, involving, as it did, a number of authors.

Griscom's last book, *Birds of Martha's Vineyard,* written with Guy Emerson, was published in 1959. It was given largely friendly critiques, although the reviewers for both the *Wilson Bulletin*[26] and the *Bulletin of the Massachusetts Audubon Society*[27] found fault with the section on where to find birds. Clearly, this book was completed at a time when Griscom was no longer able to substantially influence the book editorially or implement any major revisions.

The year 1956 seemed to begin well, with Ludlow thinking of trips. In a February letter to George Sutton, he outlines some travel plans.

> If I have money enough left after paying my income taxes, I am flirting with the possibility of running out to the Wilson Club meeting, unless you think that I might be in the way. I should of course see your new layout, and I am rather anxious, if humanly possible, to go sufficiently far west so as to see, and above all hear, the Lesser Prairie Chicken on its booming grounds, as this would round out my experience with the species including the Heath Hen. I would then want to turn South to try and get the Edward's Plateau specialties, such as the Black-capped Vireo and Golden-cheeked Warbler. You will bear in mind that I am now quite elderly, very weak in the legs, and do not wish to cramp the style of a younger guide. But the question arises, can I be directed to a definite or sure locality.[28]

Considering the obvious difficulties that Ludlow was having, it may have surprised most people when, in April 1956, Ludlow and Edith left for a trip to

Mexico, where they were joined by Dorothy Snyder. In an interview Edith said, "He wanted to die with his boots on and I was willing to accommodate him."[29]

Dorothy Snyder's detailed journal of their trip, indicates that Ludlow was struggling to have a marvelous time, and succeeding at times, but was weighed down by his afflictions. Finally, the trip came to an unscheduled and sudden end when Ludlow suffered another major stroke. He came very close to getting his wish.

Edith took complete charge of the situation and demanded the best doctor available rather than the board of health man that had been called to attend Ludlow. The doctor came and agreed with the board of health man that the prognosis was poor, unless the patient was returned to sea level in a hurry. The major commercial airlines were all booked up so Edith hired seats on a Mexican-owned single engine six-seater with bucket seats, and the following morning they flew from Mexico City straight across to Miami. There were only two other passengers on board. This was Griscom's first airplane flight. Edith later reported that "if the plane crashed, C'est la vie. My children were all grown, and Ludlow would die anyway if we didn't get him back."[30] In Miami, Ludlow began to recover, regaining his ability to talk as well as to eat and drink. After a three-hour layover they boarded a flight to New York City, where the pilot pushed Ludlow in a wheelchair into the terminal. The following day they took the train back to Boston. The trip had involved a calculated risk, and Ludlow had almost lost his life in the gamble.

Things went from bad to worse in early May. A series of strokes reduced Ludlow's health to another low, and he recorded these events in his field jour-

> Have had second and third stroke on Saturday. Unable to do much birding cannot use field-glasses; a very cold and backward Spring - The first wave on May 12th - Seen in Garden during May -

nal.[31] These physical setbacks essentially ended his professional life. He no longer could contribute in the same substantial way he had for so many decades. And as he stepped down, honors began to be bestowed upon him.

The greatest of these accolades was the presidency of the American Ornithologists' Union. His election required extensive negotiations, since it was clear to everyone, Ludlow included, that he was simply not physically capable of undertaking that responsibility. The negotiations began with an August, 1956 letter to Edith from Josselyn Van Tyne.

May I, as one of Ludlow's most devoted friends, ask your advice? First, please understand that this is a purely personal note stimulated by my deep interest in Ludlow. . . .

As you know, Miller is completing the traditional three-years as President of the A.O.U., and Ludlow would normally be elected President in Denver. But there are two things involved: 1) the honor and recognition involved, and 2) the duties of a quite strenuous executive job as the head of the world's largest organization of scientific ornithologists. We judge that Ludlow would not be in condition to carry on the executive work during this coming year. So what would you and he want us to do?

His friends will hesitate to put him in a position that may embarrass him and perhaps even tempt him to try the impossible. A great many of us want very much to give Ludlow that honor now. Is there some way we can do it without risking injury to either Ludlow or the A.O.U.?

Perhaps Ludlow has already sent word to Miller or someone. If so, please forgive my bothering you, but a very recent letter of Miller's implies that he has not had any word.

This has been a hard letter to write, but I am confident that you will accept it as meant in the most friendly way.[32]

Edith responded, apparently after discussing the matter with Ludlow.

It would be difficult for Ludlow to undertake this work this year, though he is vastly improved. His mind is crystal clear and he can talk easily though his vocal chords tire. It is a bitter cross to him not to have the honor of being president and permanently be on the council but feels it might not be fair to the A.O.U. as he is partially paralyzed and cannot be sure how rapidly he will improve. He almost could do it but the strain might not be good. Please give this message to his friends in Denver and also his best wishes. For your personal information he has resigned as Chairman of the Board of the Nat. Audubon after 13 years on the ground of ill health & has just been awarded the Audubon Conservation medal. Should Ludlow be elected by his friends he would of course resign almost at once also on the grounds of ill health.[33]

At the AOU Council meeting, this suggestion was followed and Ludlow was duly elected president. Edith recalled that Van Tyne called the Griscoms at Chatham to give them the good news and that Ludlow was too sick to come to the phone. Van Tyne told Edith, "We have given Ludlow the greatest honor that we could."[34] Ludlow immediately sent a letter of resignation to Harold Mayfield, secretary of the AOU.

Two days later, Griscom sent his congratulations to Ernst Mayr, who became president upon Ludlow's resignation.

I have received several pleasant letters and phone messages from you which I hereby acknowledge with thanks.

We have been in constant touch with Denver and greatly appreciate the action taken there in electing me President and permanent member of the Council. I have heard enough of the dope to understand as soon as my resignation is received on the grounds of ill-health that you will become President.

I have just written Mayfield my resignation, and I wish to send you my congratulations and best wishes, as you are far more competent to discharge the duties of the office than I am.

Edith joins me in kind regards to Gretel and warm affection and thanks to you for your possible help in the affairs at Denver.[35]

From time to time Griscom gives some indication of his current health status, as in a letter to his close friend Richard Eaton. "My nice nurse, Mrs. Farmer, makes a pleasant companion, but her eyes are extraordinary poor. As a matter of fact, dear old fella, I am coming along in good style and ready to lick my weight in wildcats. The only thing the matter with me is that I am paralyzed."[36] Mrs. Farmer, a full-time nurse, now accompanied him on ornithological outings and on occasion wrote up his dictated field notes. In a letter starting "Dictated December 19, 1956," we find that Ludlow plans to take part in a Christmas count.

I am still able to get out occasionally in the field, thanks to the kindness of several of my friends, and when last at Cape Ann had the good luck to see an adult Puffin offshore. You have probably heard from Ruth of the flight of Arctic Three-toed Woodpeckers into southern New England for the first time in thirty years. I was so fortunate as to add this bird to my Massachusetts list about a week ago.

I shall be allowed to take part in the Essex County census next Sunday, but I am absolutely forbidden to go to Cape Cod, much to my disappointment. Edith and I are planning a trip to Florida beginning about February 1, and the doctor wants me to do everything possible to avoid any infection before that.[37]

John Baker describes the success of the Christmas count. "Late in December 1956, when I called on the Griscoms in Cambridge, Edith said, 'Ludlow is so foolish. What do you think he has been doing?' I said, 'I can't imagine.' She said, 'He has been out eight straight hours in a car with a chauffeur and a trained nurse taking a Christmas Count.' Ludlow looked at me, and beaming all over like a little boy caught stealing ice cream from the refrigerator, said '*And in a northeast storm too!*'" [38] The following year's Christmas count was to be his last.

Remarkably, in February 1958 Ludlow, Edith, and nurse Josephine Heffron departed on an extensive cruise. They arranged for cars and chauffeur at most of the ports of call and had contacted birders for a few select locations. They had a wheelchair with them for their visits ashore. According to Edith, Ludlow was at this time quite paralyzed, and the nurse came to their cabin each morning to help Ludlow get dressed and down for breakfast. He had to be fed by hand and couldn't talk at the table without choking. His mind, however, was quite clear. Ludlow could walk fifteen or twenty feet with help, and since they had a cabin by the elevator entrance and had reserved deck chairs close to the elevator exit, he didn't need the wheelchair while on shipboard.

They started from New York on 6 February aboard the *M.S. Oslofjord,* a cruise ship (usually they had traveled by freighter), and the first stop was Port of Spain, Trinidad. On 15 February they arrived at Pinheiro Point, and then sailed to Recife in northeastern Brazil. At one port they were unable to hire a car and driver, so one of their contacts asked at a bridge party whether someone would like to show a famous man around, and a woman volunteered her chauffeured car, which took the Griscoms birding in the countryside and then shopping.

They then sailed to Jamestown, South Africa, and St. Helena Island. The next stop was Cape Town, where they had nine days for exploration. They had written ahead to arrange for Richard Liversidge (who with G. R. McLachlan revised *Roberts Birds of South Africa*)[39] to accompany them and show Ludlow some of the African birds. He was unavailable, however, and asked Peter Steyn, an ornithologist in his early twenties, to accompany the Griscoms. Steyn recalled that when they were watching flamingos Ludlow insisted on going closer, and when Edith fussed over him, Ludlow replied, "Goddam it woman, leave me alone, I'm gonna die with my boots on."'[40]

Edith also recalled the flamingo scene. Ludlow had a simple canvas fold-up stool with no back, and he walked out among the flamingos, perhaps 200 feet: "A good distance for a man as crippled as he was, by himself—got way out in the middle of them, put his chair down and sat on it because he was tired. Most adventurous thing he did, minus any help, on the whole trip. It shows his recklessness. His friends over here couldn't get used to the fact that he didn't give in, until brute strength made him give in."[41]

At one point they visited an ostrich farm and Ludlow took a picture of nurse Heffron sitting on an ostrich. The South African adventures were certainly the high point of the trip, and afterward Ludlow began to tire. The difficulties with drivers who couldn't speak English and the lack of fellow birders to take him around bothered him. Nonetheless, they managed to visit some exotic places, as the ship steamed to Luanda in Angola, Pointe Noire in Congo, Abidjan in Ivory Coast, Conakry in Guinea, Dakar in Senegal, Funchal in the Madeira Islands, and Casablanca in Morocco. They landed in Cadiz, Spain, where they drove inland to Seville. Their final port of call was Lisbon, from which they sailed for New York, arriving on 7 April.

It had been a daring trip, and Edith remembered it with mixed emotions. On their return Joan said to Edith, "It must have been a wonderful trip," to which Edith responded, "It was a perfectly terrible trip, but Ludlow had a wonderful time, a marvelous time, and that is all that matters."[42] An entry that Edith made in Ludlow's ornithological diary about the trip reads, "All in a wheel chair or private car. Paralyzed & would not give in."[43]

The honors that a lifetime of achievement had earned continued to pour in. In November 1958 the Massachusetts Audubon Society named the research facility associated with the Wellfleet Bay Wildlife Sanctuary the Ludlow Griscom Research Station. The formal declaration outlined Griscom's many achievements and gave a synopsis of the reasons why his friends held him in such high regard. The research station never fulfilled the expectations of its founders, largely for financial reasons, but it was, nonetheless, a testimony to the strong feelings of affection and support that Ludlow received from his admirers during his declining years.

Ludlow's mother died in 1958, releasing to him the large estate that he was now far too sick ever to enjoy. His uncle, Lloyd P. Griscom, who was at that time an investment counselor, offered to help Ludlow manage these new funds and implied that the inheritance was substantial.

As his illness had progressed and receded over the preceding decade, Ludlow spent more and more time at Chatham, on the porch, a private place where he could see an occasional bird. After the strokes had left him severely limited in his mobility, Edith began to protect him from the outside world. For example, at the AOU meetings, to which Edith faithfully accompanied him, Ludlow would be unable to leave the hotel room for long periods of time, and when someone inquired about him Edith would reply, "He is in conference."[44] At one point Julian Huxley was brought to the Griscom home, only to find that Ludlow was asleep and that Edith was unwilling to wake him. As Ludlow's health failed, Edith made sure that he was protected from situations where he might tarnish his reputation or give signs of failing abilities.

Joan Griscom recalled seeing her father sitting at the piano with his one workable hand trying to play a few notes. "I can remember really hurting for him."[45] Even toward the end of his life, however, Ludlow continued to persevere and to gain enormous satisfaction from his birds. According to Edith, he would sit by the window at 11:00 at night, watching bird after bird going across the moon. Annette Cottrell remembered that "his enthusiasm and his appreciation for birds and nature was as fresh as it had been fifty years before—a sense of wonder and excitement never left him. It was one of his most remarkable qualities. He would stand on the porch, seeing which way the wind was blowing, and what it meant to him, where the birds were coming from, never getting tired of looking at a Magnolia Warbler."[46]

He could speak only with great difficulty and became an invalid during the final six months or so of his life, but he never gave up. We see testimony to tenacity and courage in the dictated entries to his field diary.

Oct 2 (Thurs) Edith kindly takes me for an hour to Mt Auburn Cemetery. Do very well around Willow Pond. . . . [twelve species including a Rusty Blackbird]

Nov 27 (Thanksgiving) Bitterly cold 28° in early a.m.

1 *Arctic Three-toed Woodpecker.* 1 imm male feeding on a dead Elm on the corner of Brattle and Brown Street. Here since last Sunday. Second record for Cambridge Region, the last in 1882. Drive around Fresh Pond find only 4 Scaup, the Canvas-back having gone.

Dec 20 (Sat) Allen Morgan kindly takes me & Edith out to Concord Mass and shows me

256. [year list] 1** *Hawk Owl* 1 Here for a week on corner of Lowell Road and the next side street. It has been living near a lumber yard where it gets plenty of mice and is obviously well fed. It was seen today by a large crowd of birders and photographed in color with movies. It was last seen on Christmas afternoon. Its long tail was broken and frayed and when it flew it reminded me of a Sharp-shinned Hawk, always flying very low and rising to a conspicuous look out perch. It has been seen to catch mice several times. Last seen in Concord in 1907. And last reported in the States in 1927. I now believe that I have glimpsed it twice in Essex Co but I'm glad I waited for a really good view." [This was Ludlow's last life bird.]

May 12 (Tues) Ideal conditions, very warm & muggy night. Poured rain at 11 PM. A lull around 3 a. m. Hear thrushes pouring over at the rate of several 100 per minute and this keeps up for half hour. Veeries and a few

Olive-backed Thrushes. Then pours again at 4:30 am, putting all the migrants down. As a result Cambridge Gardens deluge with many birds and the Cottrells have sensational results having breakfast in their yard . . . then go to Mt A[uburn] and get fabulous results. Later I heard the same thing is true everywhere. This is the *second big wave* of the year. I wake up at 6 a. m. and lean out the window and do very well . . . with a visit from Mrs Cottrell I sit out on a chair in the lawn all morning.[47]

In this last entry, Ludlow recorded 15 species seen, bringing his year list to 185. The following day Ludlow added 10 more birds to his year list while sitting in his garden, and he ended his diary entry, "This is my all time record in 30 yrs!" The journal entry for the following day was his last:

May 14 (Thurs) Showers all Pm. and all night break the record heat wave and Thursday a. m. is cool and pleasant. Great wave moves on. Seen in Garden

1 Wood Thrush lovely chorus all a.m.

2 Magnolia Warbler only 1 seen. sev[eral] other warblers unidentified

3 Oriole sev

4 Catbird "

5 Tanager at least 2.[48]

On 28 May 1959 Ludlow Griscom died.

Knowing that the end was near, Ludlow's friends had prepared obituaries for release to the major newspapers throughout America. The news spread quickly; the *New York Herald Tribune* phoned the Griscom home less than two hours after Ludlow's death. The next morning saw eulogies published throughout the land.

In Cambridge the funeral drew a long list of friends and ornithological notables. Services were held at Christ Church, and the procession then moved to Mount Auburn Cemetery. The burial was held there because "it was his church in a sense, I used to go there with him and the children, always went for the flowers. . . . Mt. Auburn was a part of us, it was a part of Ludlow."[49] She chose the pallbearers for their closeness to Ludlow. There were some touching moments as, for example, when Ludlow's wayward brother, Acton, knelt before the coffin.

The day was sunny and beautiful, and the migrant birds were flying overhead. At the end of the funeral Henry Parker leaned over and whispered to Edith Griscom, "Ludlow has gone with the birds."[50]

Epilogue

In time, eulogies appeared in the appropriate journals, reviewing Griscom's various accomplishments, and a series of posthumous awards were made to him. Joy Buba prepared a bronze bust of Ludlow for the Massachusetts Audubon Society. The dedication message by Allen Morgan was typical of the tributes:

> It was our privilege here in Massachusetts to have with us for many years one of the great ornithologists this country has ever produced.
>
> He was my close personal friend—he was this Society's close personal friend, and last year we attempted at our annual meeting to pay tribute to him in some small measure—to express our feeling for him. The Ludlow Griscom Research Station at Wellfleet Bay is dedicated in his name to continue his work on the Cape Cod he loved so well.
>
> Mr. Griscom left us on May 28, but his influence on the Society and his many friends will be long-standing.

At Plum Island, to this day, a bronze plaque on a five-ton granite boulder near Hell Cat Swamp reads:

> LUDLOW GRISCOM 1890–1959 This marker is dedicated to the memory of his great influence on the people and events of his time as they related to ornithology and wildlife conservation, including the preservation of Plum

Island as a place of great natural beauty within the Parker River National Wildlife Sanctuary.

But though the plaques and monuments stand as a testimony to his enduring accomplishments, perhaps more important are the memories that his friends and contemporaries carry with them. This is exemplified by a statement made ten years after Griscom's death by one of his birding companions. "In many ways, I have been conditioned by my association with Ludlow. Old birding spots are pale without him—and pale, period. Memories of the drive, wonder, and excitement of those other times must suffice, around here. Companionship in such a purpose had a special quality, didn't it? Weren't we fortunate!"[1]

More recently, the Griscom legacy resurfaced with the establishment by the American Birding Association of the Ludlow Griscom Award, the dedication of which reads, "For outstanding contributions to excellence in field birding." The first award, presented in 1980, was appropriately given to Roger Tory Peterson.

Ludlow Griscom's memory will survive through his published works and the published works about him. Articles about Ludlow are still appearing three decades later.[2] His personality has been indelibly stamped on the collective mind of birdwatchers everywhere, and although his contributions to scientific ornithology have carved for him a niche in the history of that science, this multifaceted man will probably be best remembered as "Dean of the Birdwatchers."

Notes

Abbreviations

AMNH	American Museum of Natural History
CUL	Rare and Manuscript Collections, Cornell University Library, No. 2701
Jour, PMS	Griscom field journals, Peabody Museum of Salem Library, Manuscript Collection NH 1
LG	Ludlow Griscom
MCZ	Museum of Comparative Zoology
NOC	Nuttall Ornithological Club
OD	Griscom's ornithological diary, Griscom family.
WED/	Author's interview with

1. Background and Family

1. Edward Carpenter and General Louis Henry Carpenter, *Samuel Carpenter and His Descendants* (Philadelphia: J. B. Lippincott, 1912).

2. Edith Griscom, undated note to author.

3. LG, OD, pp. 1–2.

4. Andrew Griscom, quoting his mother, to author, 29 May 1989.

5. LG to Frederick R. Goff, 20 February 1952, CUL.

6. LG to Roger Tory Peterson, 12 November 1947, CUL.

7. LG, OD, pp. 31–35.

8. LG to F. W. Loetscher, Jr., 8 December 1934, CUL.

2. The Linnaean Society and a Career Chosen

1. The title probably refers to Chester A. Reed, *Bird Guide—land Birds East of the Rockies,* (Worcester, Mass.: Chas. K. Reed, 1906).

2. LG, OD, p. 4.

3. LG testimonial dinner speech, 28 November 1952.

4. See Keir Stirling, *The Last Naturalist: The Career of C. Hart Merriam* (New York: Arno Press, 1974).

5. Mark V. Barrow, "Birds and Boundaries: Community, Practice, and Conservation in North American Ornithology, 1865–1935" (Ph.D. diss., Harvard University, 1992).

6. Ibid.

7. Ibid. See also Frank Graham, Jr., *The Audubon Ark: A History of the National Audubon Society* (New York: Alfred A. Knopf, 1990).

8. LG, 23 October 1907, Jour, PMS.

9. LG, OD, p. 4.

10. Ibid.

11. LG, 31 October 1909, Jour, PMS.

12. LG, 7 April 1911, Jour, PMS.

13. Ludlow Griscom, *Birds of the New York City Region.* AMNH Handbook Series, no. 9 (New York: AMNH, 1923), p. 10.

14. LG testimonial dinner speech, 28 November 1952.

15. LG to William Cottrell, 30 March 1944, CUL.

16. Arthur A. Allen, "Cornell's Laboratory of Ornithology," *Living Bird,* First Annual (1962):7–36.

17. LG to Dr. Charles G. Maphis, 7 March 1922, CUL.

18. Luis Agassiz Fuertes to LG, 24 April 1923, CUL. Illustration courtesy of Division of Rare and Manuscript Collections, Carl A. Kroch Library, Cornell University.

19. LG to Frank Chapman, 31 January 1915, Historic Correspondence File, Department of Ornithology, AMNH.

20. LG to Frank Chapman, 3 March 1915, Historic Correspondence File, Department of Ornithology, AMNH.

3. Marriage and Private Life

1. WED/Edith Griscom, 24 July 1980.

2. All quotes relating to LG courtship of Edith are from WED/Edith Griscom, 25 September 1980.

3. LG to James R. Barber, 30 March 1926, CUL.

4. LG to Professor Fernald, 8 July 1926, Gray Herbarium Archives, Harvard University.

5. LG, 15, 16 September 1926, Jour, PMS.

6. WED/Edith Griscom, 20 May 1981.

7. WED/Andrew Griscom, 18 August 1981.

8. WED/Joan Griscom, 20 February 1981.

9. LG to Mrs. Lloyd C. Griscom, 3 November 1939, CUL.

10. WED/Andrew Griscom, 18 August 1981.

11. WED/Annette Cottrell, 11 March 1982.

12. WED/Annette Cottrell, 28 December 1980.

13. WED/Andrew Griscom, 14 August 1980.

14. Carl W. Buchheister to author, 23 August 1986.

15. Ludlow Griscom, *The Birds of Concord* (Cambridge: Harvard University Press, 1949), p. 70.

16. LG to Lieut. Hamilton Thornquist, U.S.N.R., 29 September 1941, CUL.

17. WED/Andrew Griscom, 18 August 1981.
18. WED/Allen Morgan, 8 July 1980.
19. LG to Professor A. E. Monroe, 25 November 1933, CUL.
20. Richard Eaton to Oliver Austin, Jr., 25 March 1973, Archives, NOC, MCZ.

4. American Museum of Natural History

1. J. T. Nichols and L. Griscom. "Fresh-water Fishes of the Congo Basin Obtained by the American Museum Congo Expedition, 1909–1915," *Bulletin of the American Museum of Natural History* 37 (1917):653–756.
2. LG, 24 November 1917, Jour, PMS.
3. LG, 23, 30 December 1917, Jour, PMS.
4. LG, 18 May 1918, Jour, PMS.
5. LG to Jack (John Treadwell Nichols ?), 6 December 1918, Historic Correspondence File, Department of Ornithology, AMNH.
6. Ibid.
7. LG to Winthrop Packard, 12 April 1935, CUL.
8. Unsigned review. "Griscom on New York Birds," *Ibis* (1924):174–175.
9. Witmer Stone, "Griscom's 'Birds of the New York City Region.'" *Auk* 41 (1924):172–174.
10. Unsigned review. Notes on the summer birds of the West Coast of Newfoundland. *Auk* 44 (1927):145.
11. Jonathan Dwight to LG, 2 June 1928, CUL.
12. LG to James Bond, 14 November 1936, CUL.
13. Henry Fairfield Osborn to LG, 8 November 1927, CUL.
14. LG to Henry Fairfield Osborn, 23 November 1927, CUL.
15. LG to Thomas R. Howell, 28 January 1952, CUL.

5. Pattern of Change: Museum of Comparative Zoology

1. WED/Bradford Washburn, 22 January 1981.
2. LG to Gegory Mason, 30 December 1927, CUL.
3. Jonathan Dwight to LG, 22 January 1928, CUL.
4. David Garrison, journal, 1 November 1935.
5. LG to the Philadelphia Book Company, 10 August 1932, CUL.
6. F. E. Hennessey to LG, 16 August 1932, CUL.
7. WED/Andrew Griscom, 18 August 1981.
8. LG to Robert Payne Bigelow, 9 September 1931, CUL.
9. LG to Josselyn Van Tyne, 26 February 1940, CUL.
10. Parts 1–3, by William Brewster, were published in the *Bulletin* of the MCZ in 1924, 1925, and 1937.
11. LG to Samuel Henshaw, 13 November 1931, CUL.
12. LG to H. Wedel, 8 October 1928, CUL.
13. LG to H. Wedel, 10 November 1928, CUL.
14. LG to H. Wedel, 5 December 1930, CUL.
15. LG to Herbert Friedmann, 12 December 1930, CUL.
16. LG to Harvard University Bursar, 31 March 1931, CUL.
17. LG to Mrs. George F. Plimpton, 13 January 1939, CUL.
18. LG to Mrs. Bertha Pierce, 20 January 1939, CUL.
19. LG to Henry O. Havemeyer, 20 May 1932, CUL.
20. LG to Ernst [Erwin] Stresemann, 28 January 1933, CUL.
21. LG to Alexander Wetmore, 15 April 1935, CUL.

22. LG to Herbert Friedmann, 10 February 1933, CUL.
23. LG to John W. Aldrich, 13 April 1936, CUL.
24. LG to Joseph J. Hickey, 27 October 1939, CUL.
25. LG to Allan D. Cruickshank, 7 June 1940, CUL.
26. George Miksch Sutton, *Mexican Birds: First Impressions.* (Norman: University of Oklahoma Press, 1951).
27. George Miksch Sutton to LG, 31 January 1952, CUL.
28. E.A.W. to LG, 24 June 1935, CUL.
29. WED/Herbert Friedmann, 27 September 1983.
30. Richard Eaton to Oliver Austin, Jr., 25 March 1973, NOC archives.
31. WED/Roger Tory Peterson, 21 December 1982.
32. LG to Witmer Stone, 14 June 1935, CUL.
33. LG to J. R. Schramm, 18 March 1932, CUL.
34. LG to A. J. van Rossem, 13 May 1932, CUL.
35. Griscom's annual report to MCZ, CUL.
36. LG to F. H. Hamerstrom, Jr., 16 March 1943, CUL.
37. LG to Ernst Mayr, 22 July 1943, CUL.
38. T.C.S., "The Distribution of Bird-life in Guatemala" (review), *Wilson Bulletin* 44 (1932):244.
39. Unsigned review, "Griscom on Guatemalan Birds," *Ibis* (1932):698–699.
40. Witmer Stone, "Griscom's 'Distribution of Bird-Life in Guatemala,'" *Auk* 49 (1932):374–375.
41. T.C.S., "The Birds of Dutchess County, New York, from the Records Compiled by Maunsell S. Crosby" (review), *Wilson Bulletin* 46 (1934):129.
42. Witmer Stone, "Griscom's 'Birds of Dutchess County, New York,'" *Auk* 51 (1934):266.
43. Unsigned review, "Griscom on Panama Birds," *Ibis* ser. 13, 5 (1935):897–898.
44. Witmer Stone, Griscom on Problems of Field Identification," *Auk* 53 (1936):238–240.
45. A. W. Lindsey, "A Monographic Study of the Red Crossbill" (review), *Wilson Bulletin* 50 (1938):149.
46. Unsigned review, "Griscom's Revision of the Crossbills," *Ibis* (1937):426–429.
47. Part 1 was published in 1924, part 2 in 1925, and part 3 in 1937, all in the *Bulletin* of the MCZ.
48. G. M. Allen, "Griscom and Brewster on 'Birds of the Lake Umbagog Region,'" *Auk* 55 (1938):566–567.
49. G. M. Allen, "Griscom and Greenway's 'Birds of Lower Amazonia,'" *Auk* 59 (1942):126–127.
50. T. Barbour, "Modern Bird Study" (review), *Wilson Bulletin* 57 (1945):137.
51. Francis H. Allen, "Modern Bird Study" (review), *Bulletin of the Massachusetts Audubon Society* 29 (1945):193.
52. J. T. Zimmer, "Modern Bird Study" (review), *Auk* 62 (1945):643.
53. Herbert Friedmann, "Modern Bird Study" (review), *Bird-Banding* 16 (1945):154–156.
54. Frank A. Pitelka, "Modern Bird Study" (review), *Condor* 47 (1945):175–176.
55. Winsor M. Tyler, "The Birds of Nantucket" (review), *Bulletin of the Massachusetts Audubon Society* 32 (1948):195.
56. John W. Aldrich, "The Birds of Nantucket" (review), *Bird-Banding* 20 (1949):122–123.
57. Frederick C. Lincoln, "The Birds of Nantucket" (review), *Wilson Bulletin* 60 (1948):194.
58. Ralph S. Palmer, "The Birds of Concord" (review), *Bird-Banding* 21 (1950):42–43.
59. Francis H. Allen, "The Birds of Concord" (review), *Bulletin Mass. Audubon Soc.* 33 (1949):258–259.
60. H. I. Fisher, "The Birds of Concord" (review), *Auk* 67 (1950):259–260.
61. David E. Davis, "The Birds of Concord" (review), *Wilson Bulletin* 61 (1949):239–240.
62. D.W.S., "'Birds of Concord,'" *Ibis* 92 (1950):154–155.
63. LG to Guy Emerson, 24 July 1946, CUL.

64. LG to Mrs. Thomas Barbour, 14 January 1946, CUL.

6. Ornithological and Birding Expeditions

1. Mark V. Barrow, "Birds and Boundaries, Community, Practice, and Conservation in North American Ornithology, 1865–1935," (Ph.D. diss., Harvard University, 1992). This study provides excellent coverage of the early years of the AOU and the trinomial controversy.

2. LG to Frank M. Chapman, 14 May 1932, Historic Correspondence File, Department of Ornithology, AMNH.

3. Ludlow Griscom, "The Distribution of Bird-life in Guatemala," *Bulletin of the American Museum of Natural History* 64 (1932):1–439.

4. Frank M. Chapman to George H. Sherwood, 27 October 1927, Historic Correspondence File, Department of Ornithology, AMNH.

5. W. deW. Miller, Nicaragua draft report (transcribed by Thomas R. Howell), 1917, Archives, Department of Ornithology, AMNH, p. 17.

6. W. DeW. Miller, field journal no. 1, 1917, Archives, Department of Ornithology, AMNH, p. 78.

7. W. DeW. Miller, Nicaragua draft report (transcribed by Thomas R. Howell), 1917, Archives, Department of Ornithology, AMNH, p. 14.

8. W. DeW. Miller, field journal no. 1, 1917, Archives, Department of Ornithology, AMNH, pp. 133, 159–160.

9. Ibid. p. 129.

10. W. DeW. Miller, field journal no. 2, 1917, Archives, Department of Ornithology, AMNH, p. 3.

11. James Lee Peters, *Check-list of Birds of the World* (Cambridge: Harvard University Press and the MCZ, 1931–1987).

12. LG to Thomas R. Howell, 18 January 1952.

13. Ludlow Griscom, "Bird Hunting among the Wild Indians of Western Panama," *Natural History* 24 (1924):509–519.

14. David Garrison, journal, 3 October 1937.

15. Peters, *Check-list* 14 (1968):71–72; Charles G. Sibley and Burt L. Monroe, Jr., *Distribution and Taxonomy of Birds of the World* (New Haven: Yale University Press, 1990).

16. Gregory Mason, *Silver Cities of Yucatan* (New York: G. P. Putnam's Sons, 1927).

17. Peters, *Check-list* 8 (1979):27.

18. Edith Griscom, "Cruising in Little Known Tropical Waters" (draft manuscript), 1927, Griscom family.

19. WED/Edith Griscom, 1 June 1981.

20. WED/Edith Griscom, 15 February 1983.

21. Peters, *Check-list.*

22. LG, OD, p. 14.

23. LG, 4, 11, 12 March 1936, Jour, PMS.

24. LG, 26 March–2 April 1937, Jour, PMS.

25. WED/David Garrison, 17 January 1981.

26. WED/Annette Cottrell, 28 December 1980.

27. LG, OD, p. 22.

7. American Ornithologists' Union

1. LG to Joseph Grinnell, 28 May 1930, CUL.

2. LG to Witmer Stone, 7 September 1932, CUL.

3. L. L. Snyder to LG, 21 September 1935, CUL.
4. LG to A. C. Bent, 16 October 1936, CUL.
5. Ernst Mayr to LG, 31 October 1937, CUL.
6. LG to Ernst Mayr, 5 November 1937, CUL.
7. James Chapin to LG, 28 August 1940, CUL.
8. LG to Ernst Mayr, 4 October 1944, CUL.
9. LG to Ernst Mayr, 9 October 1945, CUL.
10. Ernst Mayr to LG, 17 October 1945, CUL.
11. Josselyn Van Tyne to LG, 28 September 1948, CUL.
12. LG to Josselyn Van Tyne, 11 May 1951, CUL.
13. LG to Josselyn Van Tyne, 29 December 1952, CUL.
14. LG to Harold Mayfield, 15 April 1954, CUL.
15. LG to Kenneth C. Parks, 7 January 1955, CUL.
16. LG to Eugene Eisenmann, 12 December 1957, CUL.

8. Nuttall Ornithological Club

1. William E. Davis, Jr., *History of the Nuttall Ornthological Club, 1873–1986,* Memoir 11 (Cambridge: NOC, 1987).
2. NOC Council minutes, 5 December 1927, NOC archives, MCZ.
3. NOC minutes, 18 May 1931, NOC archives, MCZ.
4. NOC minutes, 6 November 1933, NOC archives, MCZ.
5. NOC minutes, 2 November 1936, NOC archives, MCZ.
6. NOC minutes, 1934–1943, NOC archives, MCZ.
7. NOC minutes, 3 February 1930, NOC archives, MCZ.
8. NOC minutes, 3 June 1935, NOC archives, MCZ.
9. NOC minutes, 2 June 1941, NOC archives, MCZ.
10. NOC minutes, 6 June 1955, NOC archives, MCZ.
11. NOC Council minutes, 21 December 1936, NOC archives, MCZ.
12. NOC minutes, 4 October 1937, NOC archives, MCZ.
13. NOC minutes, 17 November 1952, NOC archives, MCZ.
14. LG to Josselyn Van Tyne, 9 October 1952, CUL.
15. Wendell Taber, letter in Davis, *Nuttall Ornithological Club,* pp. 67–68.
16. Robert Walcott to LG, 2 December 1952, CUL.
17. Charles Blake, letter (3 June 1952) in Davis, *Nuttall Ornithological Club,* pp. 68–69.
18. LG to Charles H. Blake, 2 December 1953, CUL.

9. Museum of Science

1. LG to John K. Howard, 31 December 1937, CUL.
2. WED/Bradford Washburn, 22 January 1981.
3. LG to Bradford Washburn, 12 June 1939, CUL.
4. LG letter (first page missing), 1941. CUL.
5. LG to Bradford Washburn, 19 December 1941, CUL.
6. Irene McCulloch to Harold J. Coolidge, Jr., 8 March 1943, CUL.
7. Irene McCulloch to Harold J. Coolidge, Jr., 7 April 1943, CUL.
8. WED/Bradford Washburn, 22 January 1981.
9. Bradford Washburn to Trustees, 6 August 1946, CUL.
10. Terris Moore to LG, 11 May 1947, CUL.
11. WED/Bradford Washburn, 22 January 1981.

12. Ibid.
13. Ibid.
14. Ibid.
15. Bradford Washburn to LG, 15 October (no year given), CUL.
16. Bradford Washburn to author, 7 January 1993.

10. From Shotgun to Binoculars

1. LG, testmonial dinner speech, 28 November 1952.
2. Thomas Barbour, "Ornithologists alive! II Ludlow Griscom," *Bulletin of the Massachusetts Audubon Society* 28 (1944):194–196.
3. WED/Joseph A. Hagar, 7 August 1980.
4. Quoted in Bradford Washburn, "Griscom an Inspiration," *Newsletter* Museum of Science (Boston), 8, no. 6 (1959):1–2.
5. Roger Tory Peterson, "Introduction," in *The Birds of Cape Cod, Massachusetts* (New York: William Morrow, 1964).
6. Julian Huxley, *The Courtship Habits of the Great Crested Grebe* (1914; London: Jonathan Cape, 1968).
7. Witmer Stone, "The Ornithology of Today and Tomorrow," in *The Fiftieth Anniversary of the Nuttall Ornithological Club, December, 1923* (Cambridge: NOC, 1924).
8. Roger Tory Peterson, "The Era of Ludlow Griscom," *Audubon Magazine* 62 (1960):102–103, 131, 146.
9. Edwin Way Teale, "Ludlow Griscom, Virtuoso of Field Identification," *Audubon Magazine* 47 (1945):349–358.
10. LG to Olin Sewall Pettingill, Jr., 23 September 1949, CUL.
11. LG, 3 January 1914, Jour, PMS.
12. LG, 12 January 1923, Jour, PMS.
13. LG, 8 February 1925, Jour, PMS.
14. LG, 17 October 1935, Jour, PMS.
15. LG, 9 September 1944, Jour, PMS.
16. LG, 5 October 1946, Jour, PMS.
17. LG, 4 May 1950, Jour, PMS.
18. LG, 6 May 1950, Jour, PMS.
19. WED/Roger Tory Peterson, 21 December 1982.
20. Peterson, "Era of Ludlow Griscom," pp. 102–103, 131, 146.
21. Joseph J. Hickey to Roger Tory Peterson, 12 November 1927.
22. WED/Joseph J. Hickey, 28 October 1980.
23. Roger Tory Peterson, *A Field Guide to the Birds* (Boston: Houghton Mifflin, 1934).
24. Roger Tory Peterson, "Books of a Feather," *National Wildlife* 22, no. 1 (1984):22–28. Quoted with permission of the National Wildlife Federation.
25. Roger Tory Peterson, "Evolution of a Field Guide," *Defenders* 55 (1980):282–288.
26. Ibid.
27. Richard J. Eaton to Oliver L. Austin, Jr., 25 May 1973, NOC archives, MCZ.
28. Roger Tory Peterson to LG, 22 September 1933, CUL.
29. Fred M. Packard to Oliver L. Austin, Jr., 28 March 1973, NOC archives, MCZ.
30. Roger Tory Peterson to LG, 17 June 1937, CUL.
31. LG to Roger Tory Peterson, 3 April 1946, CUL.
32. LG to Guy Emerson, 5 September 1946, CUL.
33. Allen Morgan notes taken at NOC meeting, 1 June 1959.
34. Roger Tory Peterson, "In Memoriam: Ludlow Griscom," *Auk* 82 (1965):598–605.

11. Birdwatching with Griscom

1. LG to Guy Emerson, 4 August 1939, CUL.
2. LG to C. Russell Mason, 17 January 1942, CUL.
3. WED/Henry Parker, 12 April 1981.
4. Dorothy E. Snyder, "Ludlow Griscom" *Bulletin of the Massachusetts Audubon Society* 54 (1969):6–10.
5. WED/Roger Tory Peterson, 21 December 1982.
6. Roger Tory Peterson, "In Memoriam: Ludlow Griscom." *Auk* 82 (1965):598–605.
7. Annette Cottrell, manuscript, 1959.
8. WED/Juliet Richardson Kellogg French, 9 February 1981.
9. WED/Annette Cottrell, 28 December 1980.
10. WED/Andrew Griscom, 18 August 1981.
11. John H. Baker, "Ludlow Griscom—The Man," *Audubon Magazine* 61 (1959):200–201, 213, 238–239.
12. WED/Chandler S. Robbins, 27 September 1983.
13. Douglas Sands, undated letter to author.
14. Garrett Eddy to author, 1 August 1983.
15. LG, 11 November 1936, Jour, PMS.
16. WED/Ruth Emery, 15 February 1980.
17. WED/Wallace Bailey, 24 June 1981.
18. LG to Austin Riggs, II, 10 July 1945, CUL.
19. WED/Wallace Bailey, 24 June 1981.
20. WED/Allen Morgan, 8 July 1980.
21. David Garrison, journal, 29 December 1935.
22. WED/Ruth Emery, 15 February 1980.
23. WED/Sibley Higginbotham, 15 February 1980.
24. Tom Davis, "Robert W. Smart 1929–1979," *Birding* 11:106–107.
25. LG, 17 May 1931, Jour, PMS.
26. LG, 21 May 1933, Jour, PMS.
27. Roger Tory Peterson, *Birds over America* (New York: Dodd, Mead, 1948).
28. Florence Page Jaques, *Birds across the Sky* (New York: Harper & Brothers, 1942).
29. WED/Sibley Higginbotham, 15 February 1980.
30. James L. Whitehead,. A President goes birding. *Conservationist* (May–June 1977):20–23.
31. WED/Edith Griscom, 20 November 1980.
32. Andrew Griscom to author, 29 May 1989.
33. LG to Margaret L. Suckley, 4 June 1942, CUL.
34. Allen Morgan to Dorothy E. Snyder, 14 May 1969.

12. Sight Records and Collecting

1. LG to Harold Mayfield, 15 April 1954, CUL.
2. Richard Eaton to Oliver L. Austin, Jr., 25 March 1973, CUL.
3. LG to O. C. Bourne, 20 December 1941, CUL.
4. Headlines from a series of articles in the *Boston Herald* and *Boston Globe,* April 1941.
5. LG, handwritten note at the bottom of page 2 of a 1941 letter. The first page is missing, CUL.
6. LG, 9–23 December 1936, Jour, PMS.
7. LG, 24–27 January 1938, Jour, PMS.
8. LG, 21 October 1951, Jour, PMS.
9. LG, 6 March 1941, Jour, PMS.
10. LG, 20 August 1947, Jour, PMS.

11. LG, 20 October 1946, Jour, PMS.
12. G. L. Richardson to LG, 22 October 1938, CUL.
13. LG to G. L. Richardson, 28 October 1938, CUL.
14. LG to Clarence Cottam, 17 February 1940, CUL.
15. LG to O. C. Bourne, 15 December 1933, CUL.
16. LG to Walter P. Taylor, 27 October 1932, CUL.
17. LG to Ernst Mayr, 6 February 1946, CUL.
18. LG to Charles K. Nichols, 29 July 1952, CUL.
19. LG to Marston Bates, 28 March 1950, CUL.
20. Cora Wellman, "Birding with Ludlow Griscom," *Bulletin of the Massachusetts Audubon Society* 50 (1965):83–87.
21. C. Brooke Worth to LG, 29 August 1929, CUL.
22. LG to C. Brooke Worth, 30 August 1929, CUL.
23. LG to Chandler S. Robbins, 14 June 1935, CUL.
24. LG to W. H. Drury, Jr., 11 June 1937, CUL.
25. LG to Eleanor A. King, 18 February 1947, CUL.
26. LG to Witmer Stone, 18 May 1935, CUL.
27. LG to S. E. Eliot, 5 November 1937, CUL.
28. LG to C. Russell Mason, 6 February 1952, CUL.

13. National Audubon Society

1. The early history of bird conservation and the development of the conservation movement in general is presented in Mark V. Barrow, "Birds and Boundaries: Community, Practice, and Conservation in North American Ornithology, 1865–1935" (Ph.D. diss., Harvard University, 1992). See also Frank Graham, Jr., *The Audubon Ark: A History of the National Audubon Society* (New York: Alferd A. Knopf, 1990).
2. LG to John H. Baker, 28 July 1938, CUL.
3. LG to John H. Baker, 30 August 1935, CUL.
4. John H. Baker to LG, 10 Jun 1936, CUL.
5. LG to William Vogt, 27 January 1936, CUL.
6. LG to Clifford Pangburn, 12 May 1949, CUL.
7. Eleanor A. King to LG, 2 July 1943, CUL.
8. LG to Eleanor A. King, 31 October 1946, CUL.
9. John Baker to LG, 13 November 1941, CUL.
10. Eventually published as Harry C. Oberholser, *The Bird Life of Texas*, 2 vols. (Austin: University of Texas Press, 1974).
11. LG to Guy Emerson, 12 April 1943, CUL.
12. LG to F. H. Hamerstrom, Jr., 16 March 1943, CUL.
13. Guy Emerson to LG, 17 April 1942, CUL.
14. LG to Guy Emerson, 24 July 1946, CUL.
15. John Baker to LG, 23 October 1942, CUL.
16. LG to John H. Baker, 27 October 1942, CUL.
17. Guy Emerson to LG, 22 March 1944, CUL.
18. Carll Tucker to LG, 30 March 1944, CUL.
19. LG to Thomas Barbour, 21 March 1944, CUL.
20. LG to Guy Emerson, not dated, CUL.
21. LG to Carll Tucker, 5 April 1944, CUL.
22. LG to Roger N. Baldwin, 15 October 1946, CUL.
23. LG to Guy Emerson, 29 November 1944, CUL.
24. LG to Guy Emerson, 15 March 1945, CUL.

25. LG to Charles C. Adams, 28 May 1945, CUL.
26. WED/Roger Tory Peterson, 21 December 1982.
27. Carl Buchheister to author, 23 August 1986.
28. LG to Guy Emerson, 30 July 1942, CUL.
29. LG to David A. Aylward, 31 October 1945, CUL
30. LG, statement read at 24 March 1946 meeting of NAS Plan and Scope Committee, CUL.
31. LG, memorandum, undated, CUL.
32. LG to Hustace H. Poor, 6 February 1947, CUL.
33. LG to John Baker, 24 January 1945, CUL.
34. John H. Baker to Clarence Cottam, CUL
35. LG to Guy Emerson, 15 March 1945, CUL.
36. The citation accompanying the Audubon Medal, awarded to Griscom by the NAS, and his response to it, were published in John H. Baker, "Ludlow Griscom—The Man," *Audubon Magazine* 61 (1959):200–201, 213, 238–239.

14. Massachusetts Audubon Society

1. Richard K. Walton, "Massachusetts Audubon Society: The First 25 Years," manuscript, Massachusetts Audubon Society.
2. Henry Parker, manuscript given to author by Allen Morgan.
3. Carl Buchheister to LG, 7 January 1953, CUL.
4. LG to C. Russell Mason, 5 January 1940, CUL.
5. Robert Walcott to LG, 15 December 1945, CUL.
6. Parker manuscript.
7. Ibid.

15. Conservation

1. Ludlow Griscom, *Birds of the New York City Region*, AMNH Handbook Series no. 9 (New York: AMNH, 1923), p. 49.
2. LG to William C. Adams, 20 February 1923, CUL.
3. Scott V. Edwards, *Second Sightings: A History of Ornithology in Riverdale, New York.* (New York: Wave Hill, 1982).
4. For example, "Practically no really forest birds survive in this wrecked coastal plain." LG, 28 March 1937, Jour, PMS.
5. LG to Margaret M. Nice, 5 April 1944, CUL.
6. WED/Juliet Richardson Kellogg French, 2 September 1981.
7. Cora Welman, "Birding with Ludlow Griscom," *Bulletin of the Massachusetts Audubon Society* 50 (1965):83–87.
8. LG to Robert F. Griggs, 1945, pp. 1–2, CUL.
9. Ibid., p. 3, CUL.
10. LG to Fred Packard, 4 June 1947, CUL.
11. LG to Fred M. Packard, 3 January 1938, CUL.
12. Ludlow Griscom, "Fifty Years of Conservation," *Bulletin of the Massachusetts Audubon Society* 30 (1946):65–72.
13. LG, wire to unknown person, 25 October 1949, CUL.
14. LG to Judge Robert Walcott, 10 June 1938, CUL.
15. LG to J. Clark Salyer II, 28 October 1938, CUL.
16. LG to Clarence Cottam, 23 March 1940, CUL.
17. LG to Judge Robert Walcott, 16 March 1939, CUL.

18. LG to Ira N. Gabrielson, 24 March 1941, CUL.
19. Clarence Cottam to LG, 27 February 1940, CUL.
20. LG to Francis C. Smith, 30 November 1944, CUL.
21. Joseph A. Hagar, *Parker River National Wildlife Refuge: The Case for Revision of Plans.* Massachusetts Department of Conservation, 1945.
22. LG to Harold J. Ickes, 10 May 1945, CUL.
23. LG to Clarence Cottam, 27 February 1946, CUL.
24. LG to Fred Packard, 2 December 1953, CUL.
25. LG to James F. Mahoney, 4 March 1938, CUL.
26. LG to V. E. Shelford, 25 January 1944, CUL.
27. LG to S. Prescott Fay, 9 April 1947, CUL.
28. LG to Douglas McKay, 10 August 1953, CUL.
29. LG to Ira N. Gabrielson, 23 June 1953, CUL.
30. William Cottrell to Edith Griscom, 12 June 1959.

16. The Last Decade

1. LG to G. W. Cottrell, 23 December 1943, CUL.
2. LG letter, 10 September 1943, CUL.
3. LG to Guy Emerson, 11 March 1947, CUL.
4. LG to Mrs. J. J. Hickey, 30 April 1947, CUL.
5. LG to John H. Baker, 19 August 1949, CUL.
6. Thornton W. Burgess to LG, 30 July 1950, CUL.
7. Ira N. Gabrielson to LG, 14 September 1950, CUL.
8. WED/Edith Griscom, 18 September 1980, 1 June 1981.
9. WED/Roger Tory Peterson, 21 December 1982.
10. LG to Chandler S. Robbins, 7 September 1950, CUL.
11. WED/Sibley Higginbotham, 15 February 1980.
12. WED/Charles F. Walcott, 7 August 1983.
13. LG, OD, pp. 22–23.
14. LG to Francis M. Weston, 23 June 1953, CUL.
15. WED/Norman Hill, 1983.
16. LG to Alfred S. Romer, 13 October 1954, CUL.
17. WED/Sibley Higginbotham, 15 February 1980.
18. LG to M. Ellis, 7 December 1955, CUL.
19. E. Eisenmann, "The Birds of Massachusetts: An Annotated and Revised Check-list" (review), *Auk* 75 (1958):232–233.
20. Roger Tory Peterson, "The Birds of Massachusetts" (review), *Bulletin of the Massachusetts Audubon Society* 40 (1956):155.
21. Aaron M. Bagg, "The Birds of Massachusetts: An Annotated and Revised Check List" (review), *Wilson Bulletin* 68 (1956):85–86.
22. William H. Drury, Jr., "The Warblers of America" (review), *Bulletin of the Massachusetts Audubon Society* 42 (1958):49.
23. George Miksch Sutton, "The Warblers of America" (review), *Auk* 75 (1958):226–228.
24. R.H.M., "The Warblers of America—A Popular Account of the Wood Warblers as They Occur in the Western Hemisphere" (review), *Ibis* 100 (1958):288.
25. Phillips B. Street, "The Warblers of America" (review), *Wilson Bulletin* 70 (1958):99–101.
26. Olin Sewall Pettingill, Jr., "Birds of Martha's Vineyard with an Annotated Check List" (review), *Wilson Bulletin* 72 (1960):204–205.
27. Frances T. Elkins, "Birds of Martha's Vineyard" (review), *Bulletin of the Massachusetts Audubon Society* 44 (1959):44.

28. LG to George M. Sutton, 18 February 1955, CUL.
29. WED/Edith Griscom, 22 July 1980, 24 July 1980.
30. Ibid.
31. LG, 7 May 1956, Jour, PMS.
32. Josselyn Van Tyne to LG, 29 August 1956, CUL.
33. Edith Griscom to Josselyn Van Tyne, undated, CUL.
34. WED/Edith Griscom, 11 December 1980.
35. LG to Ernst Mayr, 14 September 1956, CUL.
36. LG to Richard J. Eaton, 24 August 1956, CUL.
37. LG to Dudly Ross, 19 December 1956, CUL.
38. John H. Baker, "Ludlow Griscom—The Man," *Audubon Magazine* 61 (1959):200–201, 213, 238–239.
39. G. R. McLachlan and R. Liversidge, revisors, *Roberts Birds of South Africa* (Cape Town: Cape Times Limited, 1940).
40. Peter Steyn to Edith Griscom, 6 December 1981.
41. WED/Edith Griscom, 22 February 1983.
42. WED/Edith Griscom, 20 May 1981.
43. LG, OD, p. 24.
44. WED/Edith Griscom, 22 July 1980, 24 July 1980.
45. WED/Joan Griscom, 20 February 1980.
46. WED/Annette Cottrell, 11 March 1982.
47. LG, 2 October 1958–12 May 1959, Jour, PMS.
48. LG, 13–14 May 1959, Jour, PMS.
49. WED/Edith Griscom, 16 October 1980.
50. Ibid.

Epilogue

1. Annette Cottrell to Dorothy Snyder, 29 December 1969.
2. Recent articles and book chapters that concern Ludlow Griscom include:
Walton, Richard K. 1984. "Ludlow Griscom." Chap. 7 in *Birds of the Sudbury River Valley—An Historical Perspective.* Lincoln: Massachusetts Audubon Society.
Peterson, Roger Tory. 1985. "Ludlow Griscom." *Birding* 17:105–110.
Kastner, Joseph. 1986. "Revolution in the Bronx: Chester Reed, Frank Chapman, Ludlow Griscom and the Bronx County Bird Club." Chap. 16 in *A World of Watchers.* New York: Alfred A. Knopf.
Hill, Norman P. 1988. "Ludlow Griscom and Mount Auburn Cemetery." *Newsletter of the Friends of Mount Auburn Cemetery.* Spring.
Parks, Kenneth C. 1989. "Ludlow Griscom." *Bird Watcher's Digest* 12(1):10. [This letter to the editor suggests that Griscom never mastered the art of preparing study skins.]
Davis, William E., Jr. 1993. "Ludlow Griscom: The Birdwatcher's Guru." *Bird Observer* (Massachusetts) 21:15–21.

Bibliography of Griscom's
Published Works

The published works of Ludlow Griscom cover a wide variety of topics and disciplines, with nearly twenty pertaining to botany, and the rest to some manifestation of ornithology. They include more than forty book and journal reviews, starting in 1919 with a series of reviews of the *Wilson Bulletin* in *Bird-Lore,* and a half dozen *In Memoriam* articles. The remainder are largely popular and scientific articles and books dealing with birds.

Griscom kept a list of his publications, upon which this appendix is based. It appears to be complete until after 1950, when he suffered his first major stroke. Griscom included thirty-seven Christmas counts in his list, which appeared in *Bird-Lore* from 1909 through 1929. I have not included these in this bibliography because after 1929 he did not include Christmas censuses, and he later apparently had some second thoughts about including earlier ones, as a note in his 1944 entries states, "Deduct 37 Xmas censuses."

His early publications largely concerned bird distribution, dealing with sight and collecting records, often of vagrants. He published more than sixty such notes in the *Auk,* starting in 1912, but gradually gave up the practice of publishing sight records of vagrants in this journal, the last appearing in 1941. After he moved to Massachusetts in 1927, he began publishing many of his sightings in the *Bulletins* of the Essex County Ornithological Club and Massachusetts Audubon Society. In addition to the *Auk,* he had published many records in the Abstracts of the *Proceedings* of the Linnaean Society of New York and in *Bird-Lore.* These distributional notes were important to him because they were one of the ways in which he was able to publicize his emphasis on rapid field identification of birds.

In 1936 he began to publish in *Bird-Lore* a series of regional distributional accounts under the title of "The Season: Boston Region." By the end of 1939, "The Season" reports were published in a supplement to *Bird-Lore,* and Griscom was writing a national summary of the regional reports in *Bird-Lore* called "The Changing Seasons." Two years later *Bird-Lore* became *Audubon Magazine,* and "The Season: Boston Region" appeared in a separately published Section II of the magazine. In 1945 "The Season: Boston Region" was renamed "Fall Migration," "Winter Season," and "Spring Migration" of the Boston region. By 1947 both "The Changing Seasons" and the Boston region report were published in *Audubon Field Notes,* and after yet another reshuffling, the Boston region was expanded to the "Northeastern Maritime Region," and a "Nesting Season" was added. He continued the regional reports until 1953 and "The Changing Seasons" summaries until 1956. In total he contributed seventy-seven regional reports and sixty-six national summaries. These reports are not included in the bibliography. Entries that are followed by an asterisk have not been examined by the author.

1908
"Central Park Notes." *Bird-Lore* 10:263–264.

1909
"More Central Park (New York City) Notes." *Bird-Lore* 11:130.

1910
Griscom, L., and S. V. LaDow. "1910 Bird Notes from Long Beach, L.I." *Bird-Lore*
    12:246–247.

1911
"Notes from Gardiner's Island." *Bird-Lore* 13:150–151.

1912
"1911 Bird Notes from Long Beach, L.I." *Bird-Lore* 14:167–168.
Johnson, J., and L. Griscom. "The Brown Pelican on Long Island." *Auk* 29:389.
"The Connecticut Warbler in Central Park, New York City." *Auk* 29:396.

1913
"The Orange-crowned Warbler at Englewood, N.J." *Auk* 30:585.

1914
"An Interesting Ornithological Winter Around New York City." *Abstracts, Proceedings Linnaean Society New York* 1912–1913 (1914), nos. 24–25:129–146. [Griscom published numerous sight records in the *Abstracts* from 1908–1926, the Secretary's Report in Nos. 24/25, and 26/27, and was one of the editors for the 1908–1911 issue, and nos. 24/25, and 32 (1920).]
"The Fox Sparrow in Central Park, New York City, in August." *Auk* 31:102.
"The Arkansas Kingbird (*Tyrannus verticalis*) in Rhode Island." *Auk* 31:248.
"The Short-billed Marsh Wren (*Cistothorus stellaris*) on Long Island in Winter." *Auk*
    31:253.
"The Acadian Chickadee (*Penthestes hudsonicus littoralis*) at Watch Hill, R.I." *Auk* 31:254.

1915
"The Little Black Rail on Long Island, N.Y." *Auk* 32:227–228.
"Prairie Horned Lark in Rhode Island in Summer." *Auk* 32:229.

Griscom, L., and F. Harper. "The Bohemian Waxwing *(Bombycilla garrula)* at Ithaca, N.Y." *Auk* 32:369.

1916

[Four articles reporting on the progress of the spring migration, *Ithaca Daily Star.*]*

Nichols, J. T., and L. Griscom. "Orange-crowned Warbler *(Vermivora celata celata)* in North Carolina." *Auk* 33:78.

Griscom, L., and J. T. Nichols. "Recent Occurence of Iceland Gulls Near New York." *Auk* 33:318–319.

"The Arctic Tern in Central New York." *Auk* 33:319.

"The European Widgeon in Central New York." *Auk* 33:320.

"Notes From Leon Co., Florida." *Auk* 33:329–330.

1917

Nichols, J. T., and L. Griscom. "Fresh-water Fishes of the Congo Basin Obtained by the American Museum Congo Expedition, 1909–1915." *Bulletin American Museum of Natural History* 37:653–756.

Metcalf, F. P., and L. Griscom. "Notes on Rare New York State Plants." *Rhodora* 19:28–37.

———. "Notes on Rare New York State Plants." *Rhodora* 19:48–55.

Johnson, J. M., J. T. Nichols, and L. Griscom. "Notes from North Carolina." *Auk* 34:219–220.

Nichols, J. T., R. C. Murphy, and L. Griscom. "Notes on Long Island Birds." *Auk* 34:434–444.

1918

"The Starling at Plattsburg, N.Y." *Auk* 35:481.

1919

"War Impressions of French Bird Life." *Natural History* 19:411–415.

Review of "The Wilson Bulletin." *Bird-Lore* 21:254–255.

"European Widgeon on Long Island in Winter." *Auk* 36:560.

"Further Notes From Leon Co., Florida." *Auk* 36:587–589.

1920

Griscom, L., and J. T. Nichols. "A Revision of the Seaside Sparrows." *Abstracts, Proceedings Linnaean Society New York* 1919–1920:18–30.

Review of "Wilson Bulletin." *Bird-Lore* 22:175.

"Notes on the Winter Birds of San Antonio, Texas." *Auk* 37:49–55.

Griscom, L., and E. R. P. Janvrin. "The Black Skimmer on Long Island, N.Y." *Auk* 37:126.

Miller, W. DeW., and L. Griscom. "Breeding of the Mourning Dove in Maine." *Auk* 37:130.

———. "Breeding of the Canadian Warbler and Northern Water-Thrush in New Jersey." *Auk* 37:137–138.

———. "The Bluebird in Cuba." *Auk* 37:140.

1921

"Some Notes on the Winter Avifauna of the Camargue." *Ibis* 11th series, vol. 3, no. 4:595–609.

Review of "Supplement to the Birds of Essex County, Massachusetts," by Charles Wendell Townsend. *Bird-Lore* 23:99.

Review of "Bulletin of the Essex County Ornithological Club, vol. 2, no. 1, December, 1920." *Bird-Lore* 23:99.
Review of "The Wilson Bulletin." *Bird-Lore* 23:100.
Review of "The Wilson Bulletin." *Bird-Lore* 23:212–213.
Miller, W. DeW., and L. Griscom. "Notes on *Ortalis vetula* and Its Allies." *Auk* 38:44–50.
———. "The Type Locality of *Ortalis v. vetula*—A Correction." *Auk* 38:455.
"The Mockingbird of St. Thomas, West Indies." *Auk* 38:461.
Dwight, J., and L. Griscom. "A Revision of *Atlapetes gutturalis* with Descriptions of Three New Races." *American Museum Novitates*, no. 16. 4 pp.
Miller, W. DeW., and L. Griscom. "Descriptions of Proposed New Birds from Central America, with Notes on Other Little-Known Forms." *American Museum Novitates*, no. 25. 13 pp.
[List of birds] in *Palisades Interstate Park* [a descriptive pamphlet issued by American Geographical Society], pp. 14–16.*

1922
Review of "The Wilson Bulletin." *Bird-Lore* 24:229–230.
"Problems of Field Identification." *Auk* 39:31–41.
Griscom, L., and E. R. P. Janvrin. "Shoveller in Bergen Co., New Jersey, in Spring." *Auk* 39:100.
Griscom, L., and J. M. Johnson. "Black Tern on Long Island in Spring." *Auk* 39:101.
Griscom, L., and E. R. P. Janvrin. "Cory's Shearwater off Newfoundland, with Remarks on Its Identification." *Auk* 39:103–104.
"What Is *Buteo rufescentior* Salvin and Codman?" *Auk* 39:107.
Griscom, L., M. S. Crosby, and E. R. P. Janvrin. "Notes on Crossing the Mexican Gulf from Key West to Galveston." *Auk* 39:117–119.
"Field Studies of the Anatidae of the Atlantic Coast, Part I." *Auk* 39:517–530.

1923
Fifty Common Birds of the New York City Region. Nature Garden Guide [leaflet published by the Scholl Garden Association of New York], vol. 3, no. 2.*
Birds of the New York City Region. American Museum of Natural History, handbook series no. 9. New York, 400 pp.
"Descriptions of Apparently New Birds from North America and the West Indies." *American Museum Novitates*, no. 71. 8 pp.
Review of "The Wilson Bulletin." *Bird-Lore* 25:56–57.
"Field Studies of the Anatidae of the Atlantic Coast, Part II." *Auk* 40:69–80.
"Notes on *Donacobius.*" *Auk* 40:214–217.
"Baird's Sandpiper in Dutchess County, N. Y. with Remarks on its Identification in Life." *Auk* 40:529–530.
"Dickcissel in Central Park, New York City." *Auk* 40:541–542.
Crosby, M. S., A. Frost, and L. Griscom. "Blue-gray Gnatcatcher in Dutchess County, N.Y." *Auk* 40:544.

1924
Chapman, F. M., and L. Griscom. "The House Wrens of the Genus *Troglodytes.*" *Bulletin American Museum of Natural History* 50:279–304.
"Descriptions of New Birds from Panama and Costa Rica." *American Museum Novitates*, no. 141. 12 pp.

Dwight, J., and L. Griscom. "Descriptions of New Birds from Costa Rica." *American Museum Novitates,* no. 142. 5 pp.

In "The Waterfowl of Back Bay, Virginia." (Long quote from an L. Griscom letter, unsigned.) *Natural History* 24:209–210.

"Bird Hunting Among the Wild Indians of Western Panama." *Natural History* 24:509–519.

"The Arctic Three-toed Woodpecker in New Jersey." *Bird-Lore* 26:65.

Review of "The Wilson Bulletin." *Bird-Lore* 26:66.

Review of "The Wilson Bulletin." *Bird-Lore* 26:133.

"A Review of the West Indian Black Swift." *Auk* 41:68–71.

"Black Tern Near New York City in Spring." *Auk* 41:337.

Griscom, L., and J. M. Johnson. "Ring-necked Duck in Northern New Jersey." *Auk* 41:339.

"Arctic Three-toed Woodpecker in New Jersey." *Auk* 41:343–344.

"Seaside Sparrow in Central Park, New York City." *Auk* 41:346.

"Philadelphia Vireo in the New York City Region." *Auk* 41:347–348.

"Bicknell's Thrush in Northern New Jersey." *Auk* 41:349.

Crosby, M. S., A. Frost, and L. Griscom. "Junco Nesting in Dutchess County, N.Y." *Auk* 41:613.

1925

[Article on birds in New York City parks]. *New York Times Magazine,* February 12.*

Miller, W. DeW., and L. Griscom. "Descriptions of New Birds from Nicaragua." *American Museum Novitates,* no. 159. 9 pp.

———. "Notes on Central American Birds, with Descriptions of New Forms." *American Museum Novitates,* no. 183. 14 pp.

———. "Further Notes on Central American Birds, with Descriptions of New Forms." *American Museum Novitates,* no. 184. 16 pp.

"The Coastal Prairies of Southern Texas." *Natural History* 25:70–75.

"Bird-hunting in Central Park." *Natural History* 25:470–479.

"The Linnaean Society of New York" (unsigned). *Natural History* 25:490.

"Benson in Panama" (unsigned). *Natural History* 25:493.

Review of "A Monograph of the Birds of Prey *(Order Accipitres),*" by H. Kirke Swann. *Natural History* 25:510–511.

"The Vanishing Heath Hen." *Natural History* 25:503–504.

"The Dwight Collection of Central American Birds" (unsigned). *Natural History* 25:504–505.

Review of "The Wilson Bulletin." *Bird-Lore* 27:275.

"Early Arrival of the Evening Grosbeak in the Hudson River Valley." *Bird-Lore* 27:394.

"King Eider in North Carolina." *Auk* 42:264.

Griscom, L., and M. S. Crosby. "Birds of the Brownsville Region, Southern Texas, Part I." *Auk* 42:432–440.

———. "Birds of the Brownsville Region, Southern Texas, Part II." *Auk* 42:519–537.

1926

"Notes on the Summer Birds of the West Coast of Newfoundland." *Ibis* 12th series, vol. 2, no. 4:656–684.

"The Ornithological Results of the Mason-Spinden Expedition to Yucatan, Part I: Introduction; Birds of the Mainland of Eastern Yucatan." *American Museum Novitates,* no. 235. 19 pp.

"The Ornithological Results of the Mason-Spinden Expedition to Yucatan, Part II: Chinchorro Bank and Cozumel Island." *American Museum Novitates,* no. 236. 13 pp.

A Bird Study Calendar. Nature Garden Guide [leaflet published by the School Garden association of New York], vol. 6, no. 2.*

Griscom, L. and M. S. Crosby. "Birds of the Brownsville Region, Southern Texas, Part III." *Auk* 43:18–36.

Review of "The Wilson Bulletin." *Bird-Lore* 28:291.

1927

[Review of William Beebe's *Pheasants: Their Lives and Homes*] *New York Evening Post Literary Review,* February 12.*

Review of "The Migration of Birds," by Alexander Wetmore. *New York Evening Post Literary Review,* February 19.*

Dwight, J., and L. Griscom. "A New and Remarkable Flycatcher from Guatemala." *American Museum Novitates,* no. 254. 2 pp.

———. "A Revision of the Geographical Races of the Blue Grosbeak *(Guiraca caerulea)."* *American Museum Novitates,* no. 257. 5 pp.

"Undescribed or Little-known Birds from Panama." *American Museum Novitates,* no. 280. 19 pp.

"An Ornithological Reconnaissance in Eastern Panama in 1927." *American Museum Novitates,* no. 282. 10 pp.

Review of "The Wilson Bulletin." *Bird-Lore* 29:288.

Review of "The Wilson Bulletin." *Bird-Lore* 29:441.

"Rare Alcidae in Barnegat Bay, New Jersey." *Auk* 44:555.

"The White-fronted Goose *(Anser albifrons gambeli)* in South Carolina." *Auk* 44:559.

"The White-fronted Goose *(Anser albifrons gambeli)* in New Jersey." *Auk* 44:560.

"The Observations of the Late Eugene P. Bicknell at Riverdale, New York City, Fifty Years Ago." *Abstracts, Proceedings Linnaean Society New York* 1925–1926:73–87.

1928

Griscom, L., and H. K. Svenson. "Carex Mitchelliana and Other Rare Plants Near Cohasset, Massachusetts." *Rhodora* 30:198–199.

"Four Days in May, 1928, in Essex County." *Bulletin Essex County Ornithological Club,* 8–15.

Griscom, L., and C. W. Townsend. "A Wilson's Phalarope at Ipswich, Massachusetts" *Bulletin Essex County Ornithological Club:*52– 53.

"*Spizella taverneri* on Migration in Montana." *Auk* 45:509–510.

[In *Biological Abstracts:* vol. 1: nos. 1828, 1830, 14314, 14318, 14336, 14345, 14372, 14386, 14409; vol. 2: nos. 4267, 4273, 4274, 4286, 4290, 4296, 4297, 4298, 4299, 4300, 4303, 4304, 4305, 4306, 4312, 4313, 4315, 4316, 4318, 4319, 4320, 4322, 4324, 4329, 4330, 4332, 4333, 4339, 4340, 4341, 4342, 4346, 4353, 4362, 4365, 4366, 8449, 8532.]*

"New Birds from Mexico and Panama." *American Museum Novitates,* no. 293. 6 pp.

Peters, J. L., and L. Griscom. "A New Rail and New Dove from Micronesia." *Proceedings New England Zoological Club* 10:99.

1929

"Field Identification of Massachusetts Gulls." *Bulletin Essex County Ornithological Club*:13–26.
"The Role of the Amateur." *Northeastern Bird-banding Association Bulletin* 5:16–20.
"A Collection of Birds from Cana, Darien." *Bulletin Museum of Comparative Zoology* 69:149–190.
"Studies from the Dwight Collection of Guatemala Birds, I." *American Museum Novitates*, no. 379. 13 pp.
"Changes in the Status of Certain Birds in the New York City Region." *Auk* 46:45–57.
Peters, J. L., and L. Griscom. "The Central American Races of *Rupornis magnirostris.*" *Proceedings New England Zoological Club* 11:43–48.
"A Review of *Eumomota superciliosa.*" *Proceedings New England Zoological Club* 11:51–56.
"Notes on the Rough-winged Swallow (*Stelgidopteryx serripennis* (Aud.)) and Its Allies." *Proceedings New England Zoological Club* 11:67–72.

1930

"Revisions of Two Central American Birds." *Occasional Papers Boston Society Natural History* 5:287–292.
"Critical Notes on Central American Birds." *Proceedings New England Zoological Club* 12:1–8.
"The Ornithological Year 1926 in the New York City Region." *Abstract, Linnaean Society New York*, no. 39. 20 pp.
Griscom, L., and Warren F. Eaton. "The Ornithological Year 1927 in the New York City Region." *Abstracts, Linnaean Society New York.* 18 pp.
"The Interesting May of 1930." *Bulletin Essex County Ornithological Club*, 5–13.
"Studies from the Dwight Collection of Guatemala Birds, II." *American Museum Novitates*, no. 414. 8 pp.
"Studies from the Dwight Collection of Guatemala Birds, III." *American Museum Novitates*, no. 438. 18 pp.
"The Marbled Godwit (Limosa fedoa) in Essex Co., Massachusetts" *Auk* 47:77–78.
"New Name for *Caprimulgus ridgwayi minor.*" *Auk* 47:85.
Emilo, S. G., and L. Griscom. "The European Black-headed Gull (*Larus ridibundus*) in North America." *Auk* 47:243.

1931

"Notes on Rare and Little Known Neotropical Pigmy Owls." *Proceedings New England Zoological Club* 12:37–43.
"Maunsell Schieffelin Crosby" (in memoriam). *Auk* 48:320–322.
"Dwarf Mistletoe and Other Plants New to New Jersey." *Rhodora* 33:101.
"Another Station for *Panicum calliphyllum* Ashe." *Rhodora* 33:131–132.

1932

Griscom, L., and R. J. Eaton. "The Variations of *Aster foliaceus* in New England." *Rhodora* 34:13–16.
Eaton, R. J., and L. Griscom. "A Few Noteworthy Plants From Southern Vermont." *Rhodora* 34:31–34.
"Notes on Essex County Birds in the Jeffries Collection." *Bulletin Essex County Ornithological Club*, 4–9.

"The Ornithology of the Caribbean Coast of Extreme Eastern Panama." *Bulletin Museum of Comparative Zoology* 72:303–372.
"The Distribution of Bird-life in Guatemala." *Bulletin American Museum of Natural History* 64:1–439.
Bangs, O., and L. Griscom. "New or Little Known Birds from Costa Rica." *Proceedings New England Zoological Club* 13:47–53.
"New Birds from Honduras and Mexico." *Proceedings New England Zoological Club* 13:55–62.
"European Teal (*Nettion crecca*) in Essex Co., Massachusetts." *Auk* 49:79.
Allen, F. H., and L. Griscom. "The Gray Kingbird in Massachusetts." *Auk* 49:87–88.
"Notes on Imaginary Species of *Ramphocelus*." *Auk* 49:199–203.
Emilio, S. G., and L. Griscom. "The Migration and Winter Range of the Labrador Savannah Sparrow (*Passerculus sandwichensis labradorius*)." *Auk* 49:229–230.

1933

"Southern New Hampshire, a Neglected Botanical Field." *Bulletin Boston Society of Natural History*, no. 67:3–7.
"The Remarkable May of 1933 in Eastern Massachusetts." *Bulletin Essex County Ornithological Club*, 4–13.
"Notes on the Collecting Trip of M. Abbott Frazar in Sonora and Chihuahua for William Brewster." *Auk* 50:54–58.
"Notes on the Havemeyer Collection of Central American Birds." *Auk* 50:297–308.
"The Birds of Dutchess County New York from records compiled by Maunsell S. Crosby." *Transactions Linnaean Society of New York* 3:1–184.

1934

Weatherby, C. A., and L. Griscom. "Notes on the Spring Flora of the Coastal Plain of South Carolina North of Georgetown." *Rhodora* 36:28–55.
Eaton, R. J., and L. Griscom. "*Potomogeton panormitanus* in the Sudbury River." *Rhodora* 36:312–313.
"*Plantago altissima* in Massachusetts." *Rhodora* 36:389–390.
"The Ornithology of Guerrero, Mexico." *Bulletin Museum of Comparative Zoology* 75:367–422.
"The Pine Grosbeaks of Eastern North America." *Proceedings New England Zoological Club* 14:5–12.

1935

"Critical Notes on Rare Panama Birds." *Occasional Papers Boston Society Natural History* 8:119–204.
"Observations on the Behavior of Animals During the Total Solar Eclipse of August 31, 1932: Birds." *Proceedings American Academy Arts and Sciences* 70, no. 2:51–61.
Svenson, H. K., and L. Griscom. "*Isoetes macrospora* in the Shenandoah Valley." *American Fern Journal* 25, no. 2:70–71.
Griscom, L., and S. A. Eliot, Jr. "The Coast of Essex County and the Connecticut Valley." *Bulletin Massachusetts Audubon Society* 19, no. 2:11–14.
"Critical Notes on Central American Birds in the British Museum." *Ibis* 5:541–554.
"A New *Carex* Hybrid." *Rhodora* 37:128.
Fernald, M. L., and L. Griscom. "Three Days of Botanizing in Southeastern Virginia."

Contributions from the Gray Herbarium of Harvard University 107:129–157, 167–189.
"The Birds of the Sierra de las Minas, Eastern Guatemala." *Ibis* 5:807–817.
"Wilson's Phalarope in Essex County, Massachusetts in Spring." *Auk* 52:82.
Conkey, J. H., and L. Griscom. "Probable Occurrence of Little Gull in Massachusetts." *Auk* 52:85–86.
"The Rediscovery of *Chlorospingus flavovirens* (Lawrence)." *Auk* 52:94–95.
"The Ruff (*Ohilomachus pugnax*) near Boston, Massachusetts, with Remarks on Its Recognition in Winter Plumage." *Auk* 52:184–185.
"The Ornithology of the Republic of Panama." *Bulletin Museum of Comparative Zoology* 78:261–382.

1936
"Notes on New England Hairy Woodpeckers." *Bulletin, Essex County Ornithological Club*, 4–6.
"September Nineteenth at Nahant." *Bulletin, Essex County Ornithological Club*, 11–12.
"Notes From Northwestern Florida." *Rhodora* 38:48–50.
"Modern Problems in Field Identification." *Bird-Lore* 38:12–18.
"The Decrease of Wildlife." In *Handbook of Conservation for Essex County, Massachusetts*, pp. 30–33. Salem: Peabody Museum and the Society for Preservation of Landscape Features, Essex County, Mass.*
"Wild Life in the Public Reservations." In *Handbook of Conservation for Essex County, Massachusetts*, pp. 76–78. Salem: Peabody Museum and the Society for Preservation of Landscape Features, Essex Co., Mass.*
Eliot, S. A., Jr., and L. Griscom. "Seacoast and Valley." *Bulletin Massachusetts Audubon Society* 20, no. 7:3–8.
"Another Black-headed Gull at Newburyport." *Bulletin Massachusetts Audubon Society* 20, no. 8:5–6.

1937
Fernald, M. L., and L. Griscom. "Notes on Diodia." *Rhodora* 39:306–308.
———. [Description of new variety: *Trichostema dichotomum* L., var. *puberulum*.] In Fernald, "Local Plants of the Inner Coastal Plain of Southeastern Virginia." *Rhodora* 39:379–415, 433–459, 466–491 (445).
———. "The Identity of *Lobelia glandulosa* Walt." *Rhodora* 39:497.
"Observation on Bird Migration." *Bulletin Massachusetts Fish and Game Association* 1, no. 1:7–8.
"Observations on Bird Migration." *Bulletin Massachusetts Fish and Game Association* 1, no. 2:10–11.*
"High Lights of the May Migration." *Bulletin Massachusetts Audubon Society* 21, no. 5:5–6.
In "The Birds of Lake Umbagog Region of Maine" by William Brewster. *Bulletin Museum of Comparative Zoology* 66, part 3:405 (editorial foreword); 503–508 (account of Canada Jay *Perisoreus canadensis canadensis*); 518–521 (account of Bronzed Grackle *Quiscalus quiscula aeneus*).
"A Monographic Study of the Red Crossbill." *Proceedings Boston Society of Natural History* 11:77–210.
Griscom, L., and J. C. Greenway. "Critical Notes on New Neotropical Birds." *Bulletin Museum of Comparative Zoology* 81:417–437.

"European Dunlins in North America." *Auk* 54:70–72.
"A Collection of Birds from Omilteme, Guerrero." *Auk* 54:192–199.
"Royal Tern in Massachusetts." *Auk* 54:206.
"Black Skimmers in New England." *Auk* 54:206–207.
Tousey, R. H., and L. Griscom. "Sycamore Warbler in Massachusetts." *Auk* 54:210–211.
"Yellow-headed Blackbird at Monomoy, Massachusetts." *Auk* 54:211.
"New Name for *Otus flammeolus guatemalae* preoccupied." *Auk* 54:391.
Review of "Bartlett's 'Birds of Eastern New York.'" *Auk* 54:404.
"Leach's Petrel off Coast of Venezuela." *Auk* 54:530.
"Herring Gull at Barbados." *Auk* 54:539.
"Palm Warbler in Bermuda." *Auk* 54:543–544.

1938
"Decrease and Increase of Massachusetts Birds." *Bulletin Massachusetts Audubon Society* 22, no. 3:10–14.
"A Phenomenal Spring Migration." *Bulletin Massachusetts Audubon Society* 22, no. 5:1–3.
Peters, J. L., and L. Griscom. "Geographical Variation in the Savannah Sparrow." *Bulletin Museum of Comparative Zoology* 80:445–478.
"The Birds of the Lake Umbagog Region of Maine." *Bulletin Museum of Comparative Zoology* 66, part 4:525–620.
"In Memoriam: John Charles Phillips, 1876–1938." *New England Naturalist* no. 1:20.
"Dickey and Van Rossem's 'Birds of El Salvador.'" *Auk* 55:557–559.

1939
Review of "Bicknell's Thrush, Its Taxonomy, Distribution and Life History," by G. J. Wallace. *Bird-Lore* 41:179– 180.
"A Bird New to New England." *New England Naturalist* no. 3:27.
"Peculiarities of Cape Cod Bird-life." *Bulletin Massachusetts Audubon Society* 22, no. 9:2–4.
Review of "The California Woodpecker and I," by W. M. Ritter. *Bulletin Massachusetts Audubon Society* 22, no. 9:12–13.
"Eleven Years' Birding in Massachusetts." *Bulletin Massachusetts Audubon Society* 23, no. 4:2–6.
"The Ring-necked Duck as a Transient in the Northeastern States." *Auk* 56:134–137.
"Migration of the Red Phalarope off Massachusetts." *Auk* 56:185.
"Gull-billed Tern in Massachusetts." *Auk* 56:186.
"Long-billed Curlew in Massachusetts." *Auk* 56:332–333.

1940
"New England Migration Flyways, Part I." *Bird-Lore* 2:161–168.
Fernald, M. L., and L. Griscom. [Descriptions of: new species *Boltonia ravenelii,* pp. 488–489; new varieties: *B.diffusa interior,* pp. 490–491, *B. latisquama recognita, decurrens, and microcephala,* pp. 491–492]. In Fernald, "A Century of Additions to the Flora of Virginia." *Rhodora* 42:355–521.
"New England Migration Flyways, Part II." *Bird-Lore* 42:259–264.
"Black Gyrfalcon at Newburyport." *Bulletin Massachusetts Audubon Society* 24, no. 1:11.
"The Year 1939 in Eastern Massachusetts." *Bulletin Massachusetts Audubon Society* 24:26–27.
Review of "Hyde's 'Life History of Henslow's Sparrow.'" *Auk* 57:120–121.

1941

"The Recovery of Birds from Disaster." *Audubon Magazine* 43:191–196.

Review of "A Field Guide to Western Birds," by R. T. Peterson. *Audubon Magazine* 43:378–379.

"Eastern Massachusetts Birds in 1941." *Bulletin Massachusetts Audubon Society* 25:40–41.

"Migration Routes of New England Birds." *Bulletin Massachusetts Audubon Society* 25:53–62.

Review of "A Field Guide to Western Birds," by R. T. Peterson. *Bulletin Massachusetts Audubon Society* 25:147–148.

Griscom, L., and J. C. Greenway, Jr. "Birds of Lower Amazonia." *Bulletin Museum of Comparative Zoology* 88:81–344.

"Curlew Sandpiper in New England." *Auk* 58.95.

"Two Yellow Warblers New to Massachusetts." *Auk* 58:100.

"Kentucky Warbler in Massachusetts." *Auk* 58:100–101.

"Hoyt's Horned Lark in Massachusetts." *Auk* 58:409.

"Second Flight of the Sitka Crossbill to Massachusetts." *Auk* 58:411–413.

Review of "A Field Guide to Our Common Birds," by Irene T. Rorimer. *Wilson Bulletin* 53:54–55.

1942

"Report on Federal Hunting Regulations." *Audubon Magazine* 44:248–251.

Review of "Birds Around New York City," by A. D. Cruickshank. *Audubon Magazine* 44:313–314.

"The Barn Owls of Martha's Vineyard." *Bulletin Massachusetts Audubon Society* 25:191–196.

"A Review of 1941." *Bulletin Massachusetts Audubon Society* 26:46.

"A Year's Birding by Automobile." *Bulletin Massachusetts Audubon Society* 26:97–101.

Review of "Birds Around New York City," by Allan Cruickshank. *Bulletin Massachusetts Audubon Society* 26:198–199.

"Origin and Relationships of the Faunal Areas of Central America." *Proceedings Eighth American Scientific Congress* 3:425–430.

1943

"Oceanic Birds." In *Science from Shipboard,* chap. 10, pp. 207–227. Washington, D.C.: Science Services. [Other editions were published by the American National Red Cross, and as a supplement to the Infantry Journal by the U. S. Army.]

"Resume of the Year in Eastern Massachusetts." *Bulletin Massachusetts Audubon Society* 27:42–43.

"Notes on the Pacific Loon." *Bulletin Massachusetts Audubon Society* 27:106–109.

"Notes on the Jaegers." *Bulletin Massachusetts Audubon Society* 27:198–200.

Review of "Systematics and the Origin of Species from the Viewpoint of a Zoologist," by Ernst Mayr. *Wilson Bulletin* 55:136–137.

1944

"The Year in Eastern Massachusetts." *Bulletin Massachusetts Audubon Society* 28:46–47.

"Massachusetts Rails." *Bulletin Massachusetts Audubon Society* 28:73–84.

Review of "A Guide to Bird Watching," by J. J. Hickey. *Bulletin Massachusetts Audubon Society* 28:140–141.

"Difficulties with Massachusetts Gulls." *Bulletin Massachusetts Audubon Society* 28:181–191.
"A Second Revision of the Seaside Sparrows." *Occasional Papers Museum Zoology, Louisiana State University* no. 19:313–328.

1945

"Observations of Rare Northern Gulls in Virginia." *Raven* 16, nos. 1 & 2:1.
"An Ornithologist Looks at Progress in Conservation." *Audubon Magazine* 47:369–371.
"Night Flight of Thrushes and Warblers." *Bulletin Massachusetts Audubon Society* 29:43.
"A Record New England List." *Bulletin Massachusetts Audubon Society* 29:171–173.
Modern Bird Study. Cambridge: Harvard University Press. 190 pp. [Several additional printings.]
Review of "A Field Guide for Birds of the Southwest Pacific," by Ernst Mayr. *Auk* 62:319–321.
"Barrow's Golden-eye in Massachusetts." *Auk* 62:401–405.
Review of "The Distribution of the Birds of California," by Joseph Grinnell and Alden H. Miller. *Wilson Bulletin* 57:207–209.

1946

"The Passing of the Passenger Pigeon." *American Scholar* 15, no. 2:212–216. Reprinted in *Writing Techniques: With Illustrative Readings,* by Norbert and John Engles.
"Frank Michler Chapman 1864–1945, a Tribute and a Valedictory" (in memoriam). *Audubon Magazine* 48:49–52.
"A Tribute to Frank M. Chapman" (unsigned). *Audubon Magazine* 48:50.
"The Black Duck—A Tribute and a Plea." *Bulletin Massachusetts Audubon Society* 29:305–307.
"Fifty Years of Conservation." *Bulletin Massachusetts Audubon Society* 30:65–72.
Review of "The Lost Woods," by E. W. Teale. *Bulletin Massachusetts Audubon Society* 30:99–100.
"Thomas Barbour: Ornithologist and Naturalist 1884–1946" (in memoriam). *Bulletin Massachusetts Audubon Society* 30:141–142.
"An Ornithologist Looks at the Waterfowl Problem." *Bulletin Massachusetts Audubon Society* 30:277–285.
Review of "Audubon Bird Guide: Eastern Land Birds," by R. H. Pough. *Bulletin Massachusetts Audubon Society* 30:304–305.

1947

"An Ornithologist Looks at the Waterfowl Problem." *New York State Conservation Council Bulletin* no. 85:1–3.*
"An Ornithologist Looks at Waterfowl." *Audubon Magazine* 49:37–46.
Review of "Spring in Washington," by L. J. Halle, Jr. *Bulletin Massachusetts Audubon Society* 31:295.
Review of "Footnotes on Nature," by J. Kieran. *Bulletin Massachusetts Audubon Society* 31:298–299.
"Waterfowl." In *Duck Shooting Along the Atlantic Tidewater,* edited by E. V. Connett, pp. 288–299. New York: William Morrow.
"Common Sense in Common Names." *Wilson Bulletin* 59:131–138.
[Species accounts]: Pacific Loon, pp. 1–2; Eskimo Curlew, p. 92; Ruff, p. 104; Black-

headed Gull, p. 104; Little Gull, pp. 113–114. In R. T. Peterson, *A Field Guide to the Birds*. Boston: Houghton Mifflin.

"Possible Developments in New Hampshire Ornithology." *Bulletin Audubon Society of New Hampshire* 18(2):43–48.

Review of "A Field Guide to the Birds, Eastern Land and Water Birds," by R. T. Peterson. *Audubon Magazine* 49:371– 372.

1948

Griscom, L., and E. V. Folger. *The Birds of Nantucket*. New England Bird Studies I. Cambridge: Harvard University Press. 156 pp.

"Duck Shooting Can be Saved." *Field and Stream* 52(9):22–23, 83–85.

"The Present Status of New England Waterfowl." In *Proc. 1948 Northeastern Game Conference, pp. 79–85*. Boston: Massachusetts Fish and Game Association.*

"The Year 1947 in Massachusetts." *Bulletin Massachusetts Audubon Society* 32:93–94.

Review of "Field Guide to Birds of the West Indies," by J. Bond. *Bulletin Massachusetts Audubon Society* 32:156–157.

"Notes on Texas Seaside Sparrows." *Wilson Bulletin* 60:103–108.

"The Western Lark Sparrow in the Eastern United States." *Auk* 65:310–311.

"A Note on the Western Swamp Sparrow (*Melospiza georgiana ericrypta* Oberholser)." *Auk* 65:413.

"Allen Frost" (in memoriam). *Auk* 65:649–650.

1949

"An Ornithologist Looks at the Atlantic Flyway." In *Transactions 14th North American Wildlife Conference*, pp. 75–86.

The Birds of Concord. New England Bird Studies II. Cambridge: Harvard University Press. 340 pp.

1950

"The Natural History Values of the Concord River Meadows." In *Report of the Sudbury Valley Commission, p. 1*. State of Massachusetts.*

"John James Audubon, Artist and Ornithologist, Part I." *Audubon Magazine* 52:110–115.

"John James Audubon, Artist and Ornithologist, Part II." *Audubon Magazine* 52:184–189.

"Distribution and Origin of the Birds of Mexico." *Bulletin Museum of Comparative Zoology* 103:341–382.

Audubon's Birds of America, Popular Edition. Introduction and text for 288 plates. New York: Macmillan. 320 pp.

Friedmann, H., L. Griscom, and R. T. Moore. "Distributional Check-list of the Birds of Mexico, Part I." *Pacific Coast Avifauna* 29. Berkeley: Cooper Ornithological Club. 202 pp.

1951

"Birds of the Proctor Sanctuary." *Bulletin Massachusetts Audubon Society* 35:181–186.

"Fernald in the Field." *Rhodora* 53:61–65.

1952

Review of "A Fish and Wildlife Survey of Guatemala," by George B. Saunders. *Auk* 69:332.

Review of "Mexican Birds: First Impressions Based on an Ornithological Expedition to Tamaulipas," by G. M. Sutton. *Bulletin Massachusetts Audubon Society* 36:79.
Review of "A Field Guide to the Mammals," by W. H. Burt. *Bulletin Massachusetts Audubon Society* 36:362, 364.
"In Memoriam—Richard Cary Curtis." *Bulletin Massachusetts Audubon Society* 36:381–382.
Review of "Stalking Birds with Color Camera," by Arthur A. Allen. *Bulletin Massachusetts Audubon Society* 36:79–80.

1953
"Ornithologists Alive! XII Guy Emerson." *Bulletin Massachusetts Audubon Society* 37:17–18.
In "Testimonial to Ludlow Griscom a Happy Occasion." *Bulletin Massachusetts Audubon Society* 37:28–30. [With long remarks by L. Griscom]

1954
"Early History of Cambridge Ornithology." *Proceedings Cambridge Historical Society* 35 (1954?):11-16.
"Thumbnail Sketches of Our Vice-Presidents: S. Gilbert Emilo." *Bulletin Massachusetts Audubon Society* 38:270–271.
"The Future of Our Waterfowl." *Audubon Magazine* 56:64–65, 82–83.
"Historical Development of Sight Recognition." *Proceedings Linnaean Society New York,* nos. 63–65:16–20. Reprinted in *Chat* 18:58–61.
Review of "A Field Guide to the Birds of Britain and Europe," by R. T. Peterson, G. Mountfort, and P. A. D. Hollom. *Bulletin Massachusetts Audubon Society* 38:274.
Gabrielson, I. N., L. Griscom, and H. Lloyd. "Special Report and Proposals Regarding Conservation Activities of the American Ornithologists' Union." *Auk* 71:108–110.
———. "Report of the American Ornithologists' Union Advisory Committee on Bird Protection." *Auk* 71:186–190.
"Philosophy of Waterfowl Abundance." In *Transactions Nineteenth North American Wildlife Conference* 19:110–113.

1955
Plum Island and Its Bird Life. Massachusetts Audubon Society Special Pamphlet. 24 pp.
Review of "Life Histories of Central American Birds (Families Fringillidae, Thraupidae, Icteridae, Parulidae, and Coerebidae)," by A. F. Skutch. *Bulletin Massachusetts Audubon Society* 39:141, 143.
"The Yellow-billed Cuckoo Flight of 1954." *Bulletin Massachusetts Audubon Society* 39:151–156.
Griscom, L., and D. L. Snyder. *The Birds of Massachusetts: An Annotated and Revised Check List.* Salem: Peabody Museum. 295 pp.
Gabrielson, I. N., L. Griscom, and H. Lloyd. "Report of the Bird Protection Committee." *Auk* 72:110–112.

1956
Gabrielson, I. N., J. Delacour, L. Griscom, H. Lloyd, and R. T. Peterson. "Report of the Committee on Bird Protection to the American Ornithologists' Union." *Auk* 73:119-123.

Review of "The Wren," by E. A. Armstrong. *Bulletin Massachusetts Audubon Society* 40:281-282.
Griscom, L., and A. Sprunt, Jr., eds. *The Warblers of America*. New York: Devon-Adair. 356 pp.

1957
Gabrielson, I. N., J. Delacour, L. Griscom, H. Lloyd, and R. T. Peterson. "Report of the Committee on Bird Protection to the American Ornithologists' Union." *Auk* 74:90-93.
Miller, A. H., H. Friedmann, L. Griscom, and R. T. Moore. "Distributional Check-list of the Birds of Mexico, Part II." *Pacific Coast Avifauna* 33. Berkeley: Cooper Ornithological Club. 436 pp.

1959
Griscom, L., G. Emerson. *Birds of Martha's Vineyard with an Annotated Check List*. Martha's Vineyard: privately printed. 164 pp.

Index

—birdwatching: ornithological diaries, 4–5, 6–7, 10–11, 28–29, 67, 69, 194; sixteen volumes of ledgers, 103. *See also* Birdwatching and listing; Birdwatching with Griscom
—education: early, 6; at Columbia University, 10–12; at Cornell University, 10–12; lack of doctorate, 13–14; thesis on duck identification, 13
—health problems: early onset, 181–82; heavy smoking and, 182, 183–84; strokes, 53, 86, 95, 156, 177, 181–82, 189; trips despite poor health, 184–85, 188–89, 191–93
—major ornithological expeditions: British Honduras, 60–63; Caribbean, 67–68; Guatemala, 66; Jamaica, 66–67; Latin America, 56–58; marriage's effect on trips, 63–64; Nicaragua, 57–58; Panama, 59–60, 64–65
—ornithological career. *See* American Museum of Natural History; American Ornithologists' Union (AOU); Museum of Comparative Zoology (MCZ)
—published works of: *Birds of Concord,* 50; *The Birds of Dutchess County . . .,* 49; *Birds of Lower Amazonia* (and Greenway), 50; *Birds of Martha's Vineyard* (and Emerson), 188; *Birds of Massachusetts* (and Snyder), 114, 186; *The Birds of Nantucket,* 50, 51; *Birds of the New York City Region,* 11, 29–30, 107–8, 141, 165; *Distributional Checklist of the Birds of Mexico* (et al.), 48; *The Distribution of Bird-Life in Guatamala,* 48; "Fifty Years of Conservation," 169; *Modern Bird Study,* 50, 51; *Monographic of the Red Crossbill,* 49; *The Ornithology of the Republic of Panama,* 49; "Problems of Field Identification," 141
Griscomisms, 115–16

Hagar, Connie, 69, 140
Hagar, Joseph A., 23, 84–85, 100, 133–34, 173–75
Halberg, Edith, 118
Halberg, Henry, 118
Hall, Minna B., 160
Harper, Francis, 79
Harris, Stuart K., 84
Harrison, Benjamin, 4
Harvard Defence Group, 176
Harvard Ornithological Club ("H.O.C. Boys"), 45, 120
Harvard Traveler's Club, 89

Harvard University Press, 39, 45–46
Heffron, Josephine, 192–93
Hemenway, Harriet, 160
Henshaw, Samuel, 39
Hickey, Joseph J., 44, 107–8
Higginbotham, Sibley, 118, 124, 183–84, 186
Hill, Norman, 23, 101, 185
Hinchman, Richard, 83, 84, 123
"H.O.C. Boys," 45, 120
Hornblower, Ralph, 89
Houghton Mifflin, 109–11
Howard, John K., 88–89
Hunnewell, Frank, 67
Hunnewell, Louisa, 67
Huxley, Julian, 101, 193

Ibis, 30, 31, 49–50
Ickes, Harold J., 174
Institute of Geographical Exploration (Harvard), 89
International Ornithological Congress(es), 66, 79
Ithaca Daily Star, 13
Izaak Walton League, 168

Jaques, Florence, 127–28
Jaques, Francis Lee, 127
Jones, Lombard Carter, 146
Junior League Magazine, 64

Kiernan, John, 23
King, Eleanor A., 148–49
King, Ralph, 166
Kirkland House, 45
Kuerzi, Jack, 107

Lack, David, 76
Latham, Mrs. F. E. B., 9
Lawson, Ralph, 163
Leopold, Aldo, 170
Lethal Tour, 126
Lincoln, Frederick C., 50
Linnaean Society: founding and history, 9; Griscom's early involvement with, 8–9, 11, 30; Griscom's presidency of, 30
Liversidge, Richard, 192
Lloyd, Thomas, 3
Locke, S. B., 172

bership for women, 83; joins, 79; appointments and offices, 79, 85; feud with Taber, 83–86; influence, 78–87; presidency, 85–87

Oberholser, H. C., 28, 42, 150
Old Colony Bird Club, 118
Ornithological golf, 10
Ornithologische Monatsberichte, 43
Ornithology: avian systematics, 48, 55–56; binoculars and, 10, 31, 80; changes in, summary of, 101–2; field guide concept, 81; gamegetter, 61; Griscom's two specialties, 29; lumper versus splitter, 48; military ornithology, 28–29; shotgun school versus binocular school, 9–10, 31, 70, 80, 99–112; status in early century, 9–10; subspecies concept, 55–56; trinomial nomenclature, 55–56
The Ornithology of the Republic of Panama (Griscom), 49
Osborn, Henry Fairfield, 33
Our Common Birds and How To Know Them (Grant), 5
Outer Circle Bird Club, 118

Packard, Frank M., 110
Packard, Winthrop, 163
Parker, Henry M., 85, 114, 161, 163–64, 195
Parker River National Wildlife Refuge, 172–76
Parker River National Wildlife Refuge (Hagar), 174
Parkes, Kenneth C., 76
Parkhurst's "Bird Calendar," 8
Peabody Museum, 103
Pearson, T. Gilbert, 146
Pease, Arthur, 16
Peters, James Lee, 23, 42, 79, 140–41; as Griscom's antithesis, 46; Checklist(s), 31, 50, 58, 60, 63; death's effect on NOC, 84; Griscom on, 74; "ornithological golf," 10
Peterson, Roger Tory, 46, 83, 120, 150, 187; field guide concept, pioneer in, 81; *Field Guide to Birds,* 108–110, 134; *Field Guide to Eastern Birds,* 110–12; on Griscom after stroke, 183; on Griscom as administrator, 155–56; on Griscomisms, 115; on Griscom-led Big Days, 125–27; on Griscom's birding, 100–101; on Griscom's influence on field

study, 107, 108, 111–12; Ludlow Griscom Award recipient, 198; on Peters, 46
Philadelphia Book Company, 37–39
Phillips, John, 163
Pitelka, Frank, 50
Plough's field guide, 134
Poor, Hustace, 83, 158
"Problems of Field Identification" (Griscom), 141
Proceedings of New England Zoological Club, 32
Pusey, Nathan, 186

Rapallo, Antonio, 15
Rare birds: committees on, 142; Griscom's study of, 106–7
Reed Bird Guide, 8, 109
Research Committee on Faunistics of North American Birds, 74
Rhodora, 30
Richards, Tudor, 83
Richardson, Juliet French, 116–18, 162, 167
Richardson, Mr. (correspondent), 135–36
Richardson, William B., 34, 57
Ridgway, Robert, 55
Rivers School, 109
Robbins, Chandler S., 120, 183
Roberts Birds of South Africa (Liversidge and McLachlan), 192
Romer, Alfred S., 53, 185–86
Roosevelt, Franklin Delano: birding with Griscom, 128–30
"Ruffed Grouse Management" (King), 166

Salyer, Clark II, 170
Sand County Almanac (Leopold), 170
Sands, Douglas, 120
Schmitts, Edward A., 38
Seebeck, Newton, 106
Shelford, Victor E., 176
Sibley and Monroe taxonomy, 60
Sight records, 131–42; censoring of, 137; Griscom on, 131–32; Griscom on amateur records, 99, 138–40; Griscom on philosophy of, 136–37; Griscom on proliferation of, 137; paradox of, 138
Silver Cities of Yucatan (Mason), 61
Sloan, Samuel, 15
Small, Arnold, 184

ACR 9585

QL
31
G737
D38
1994